ULTIMATE

Bar Book

ULTIMATE

--- BAR BOOK ---

The Comprehensive Guide

TO OVER 1,000 COCKTAILS

BY MITTIE HELLMICH

ILLUSTRATIONS BY ARTHUR MOUNT

CHRONICLE BOOKS
SAN FRANCISCO

Library of Congress Cataloging-in-Publication Data available.

ISBN-13: 978-0-8118-4351-5

Manufactured in China.

Designed by Warmbo Design.

40 39 38 37 36 35 34 33 32 31

Chronicle Books LLC, 680 Second Street, San Francisco, California 94107

www.chroniclebooks.com

Introduction

AH, THE COCKTAIL! Epitomized by the languorous promise of a shimmering Martini, surrounded by glamour and ritual, cocktails are back in style, riding a wave of nostalgia. Savvy establishments offer their own signature concoctions and creatively infused spirits, and swank, retro-style bar equipment and glassware are now hip accessories for home entertaining.

However, many of us know little about the finer points of mixing and serving drinks—skills that often seem to belong to a bygone era. For our parents' and grandparents' generations, a savvy finesse behind the home bar was de rigueur, but many of us have not seen the need for those skills—until now. This book is meant to assist a new generation of mixologists and bring the cocktail into the new century.

Over the course of the twentieth century, the cocktail evolved into an art form. From the speakeasies of the 1920s to the toasting when Prohibition was repealed, and from the celebrations at the end of World War II through the Martini-chilling atomic cocktail age of the 1950s, the first half of the century saw the creation of many of the cocktails that are now considered classics. Martini innovation ensued in the 1960s and early '70s, with vodka eclipsing gin and high-octane drinks such as the Long Island Iced Tea, novelties like the Harvey Wallbanger, and the sexily named shot drinks were finding a wide audience. Over the next twenty years, a renewed interest in retro cocktails took hold and a few "new classics" such as the Cosmopolitan and the Lemon Drop were added to the established bar repertoire.

With the new millennium, the cocktail, and the art of the cocktail party, have become especially hot. However, today's cocktail party libations reflect the contemporary preference for high-quality ingredients. The liqueur-heavy, oversweet cocktails made with cheap bottled mixes, which we suffered through in the 1970s and '80s, are being edged out by well-balanced elixirs made with fresh ingredients and quality spirits, resulting in superior variations of old favorites, as well as new combinations.

Not surprisingly, all this creative mixology has fueled an enormous interest in mastering basic cocktail techniques, along with the desire to be knowledgeable about spirits, liqueurs, and wine.

Ultimate Bar Book is written specifically to help you learn the basic but essential techniques involved in the alchemy of mixing and serving cocktails. Informative and easy to use, it offers a wide spectrum of mixological know-how, to help answer your queries and fill in the gaps in your knowledge. So whether your interests lie in setting up a great home bar, mastering one of the classic cocktails, concocting a newer contemporary hybrid or your own innovative cocktails, or gleaning tips for entertaining and serving up festive, crowd-pleasing pitchers of Sangria, this tome will give you the confidence to shake and pour with style and ease. And whatever your tastes, you'll find cocktails here to match, from the sophisticated Latin Caipirinha and Mojito to the classic Martini and Old-Fashioned to elegant pousse-cafés and fun and lively shooters and gelatin shots.

Salut! and enjoy,

Mittie Hellmich

CHAMPAGNE COUPE

Liquid Mobility:

NAVIGATING THIS GUIDE

rkling wine / beer & sake / brandy

THE COMPREHENSIVE GUIDE

ULTIMATE
Bar Book

TO OVER 1,000 COCKTAILS

gin / rum / tequila / vodka / whis

This comprehensive bar guide is an invaluable reference, not only for home entertaining, but also for bartenders, who will appreciate the A-to-Z drink index for quickly looking up specific drinks.

To make navigation easy, this book is divided into two distinct parts. The first section is dedicated to the many basic elements involved in composing, structuring, and enjoying mixed drinks; the second is dedicated to the spirits and the drink recipes. Measurements are given in ounces as well as other common units, such as teaspoons and cups. Dashes are the smallest bar measurement given.

The drinks are organized according to the main alcoholic ingredient, to help you quickly find a particular drink. For example, if you're looking for a specific drink made with brandy, or suggestions for drinks that use brandy, you can simply turn to the brandy section, where the drinks are listed alphabetically.

The section on wine includes drinks based on fortified wine, such as port or sherry. However, champagne, although a type of wine, has its own section. Champagne cocktails, popular for many celebratory occasions, are in a festive class all their own and deserve a separate section.

A few drink genres hold a uniquely popular niche, namely punches, shooters, hot drinks, and hangover remedies. These are placed in their own sections, allowing for quick access when the appropriate occasion arises.

CROSS-REFERENCED INDEX

At the back of the book is a two-part index to assist you in searching for a subject, specific drink, or drink made with a specific ingredient. This is a key organizational tool. Although the drink recipes are conveniently organized into sections according to their major liquor ingredients, you can use the cross-referenced drinks by liquor type index to find drinks that include a particular liqueur or spirit, or you can use the subject index to quickly find a drink by name as well as basic topics.

A FEW DETAILS CONCERNING THE RECIPES

The glass icon that appears with each drink recipe indicates the recommended glassware. Use these icons not only to determine the appropriate glassware, but also as a reminder to get the glasses into the refrigerator or freezer before you begin making drinks.

All drink recipes make one cocktail, to serve one person, unless otherwise stated. When the drink recipe tells you to "Shake the ingredients vigorously with ice," use a standard cocktail shaker to do so.

❧ **JUICES** The recipes in this book almost always call for freshly squeezed citrus juices, but you may certainly substitute bottled juices or juices made from concentrate if fresh juice is unavailable, or if that is your preference.

❧ **RAW EGGS** You will find eggs used frequently in many of the classic cocktails, harking back to a time before salmonella poisoning became a concern. Although raw eggs are included in the classic recipes for authenticity, you have the option of using pasteurized eggs or egg white powder or of omitting the egg altogether. Use raw eggs at your own discretion.

❧ **SIDEBARS** To highlight classic drinks like the Margarita or famous signature drinks such as the Hemingway Daiquiri, these popular drink recipes are in sidebars for quick recognition.

MARGARITA GLASS

.02

The Essential Bar

sparkling wine / beer & sake / brandy

THE COMPREHENSIVE GUIDE

ULTIMATE
Bar Book

TO OVER 1,000 COCKTAILS

gin / rum / tequila / vodka / whis

Basic Equipment

------- ・ -------

WHAT APPEALS TO US MOST IN BAR EQUIPMENT, besides the high-tech stainless steel gleam, is how easy a well-designed bar tool makes the preparation of cocktails.

Given the wide variety of cocktail gadgets and gizmos available, choosing the most essential tools for a well-functioning home bar can be somewhat daunting. Although some may insist on having a glamorous retro glass martini pitcher or chrome ice bucket, a few crucial bar tools are all you really need to concoct even the most elaborate of drinks.

You'll want a good cocktail shaker with a built-in strainer, a double-headed jigger/pony, a sharp paring knife for cutting fruit and garnishes, a good corkscrew and bottle opener, a hand-held citrus juicer (indispensable when you need more than a quick squeeze of fresh citrus juice), and a high-caliber blender that pulverizes ice. Besides a few additional handy bar tools (such as a cutting board for cutting fruit, an easy-peel citrus stripper, a bar spoon, a bar towel, and a few stylish cocktail picks), it's best to acquire bar equipment slowly over time, as your repertoire of cocktails expands.

GLOSSARY OF BAR EQUIPMENT

The following is an extensive list of bar tools, from the most essential and functional bottle opener to the flashy electric juicers, with descriptions to assist you in smoothly concocting all varieties of drinks.

ABSINTHE SPOON

Antique decorative spoons used as part of the absinthe cocktail ritual. Typically trowel shaped and perforated with holes, they were designed to hold a sugar cube over a glass of absinthe. Water dribbled onto the sugar cube drips through the spoon into the absinthe.

BAR SPOON

For stirring and mixing tall, noncarbonated drinks, muddling ingredients, and measuring teaspoons of sugar. Look for a skinny, long-handled one (some have a twirled shaft in the middle) with a small spoon on the end. Stainless steel is preferable.

BLENDER

A must-have for fruity frappés and Daiquiris. The ideal cocktail blender has a powerful motor, is able to crush ice and purée fruit, and has a stainless steel container for the quick-chill factor.

BOSTON SHAKER

The classic industrial unit preferred by bartenders. It comes with a large steel, cone-shaped cup and a slightly smaller mixing glass that fits snugly upside down into the top to create a sealed container for shaking. It requires a separate cocktail strainer, either a hawthorn or a julep strainer, which fits over the top when ready to pour.

BOTTLE OPENER

A small metal tool, also called a "church key," typically with a rounded cutout at one end to pop the tops off bottles, and sometimes a can opener, with a pointed triangular end, at the other end.

CHAMPAGNE STOPPER

A spring-loaded stopper designed to clamp tightly around the neck of a champagne bottle, to help conserve the carbonation in champagne or other sparkling bottled beverages once opened. Most devices have a rubber washer on the rounded end that helps seal the bottle, with two metal wings that fold down around the neck.

CITRUS JUICER

When you need small amounts of fresh citrus juice, this simple but effective gadget will save you from the tiresome hand-squeezing method. A variety of styles and sizes are available, depending on the volume of juice needed, from plastic, ceramic, and glass bowl styles with a pouring spout to handheld wooden reamers. High-tech electric juicers, made for high-volume juicing, are especially helpful when entertaining.

CITRUS SPOUT

A spout-shaped tool that screws into the stem end of a lemon, lime, or orange, with a built-in strainer, for extracting small amounts of juice. Also known as a lemon spout.

CITRUS SQUEEZER/EXTRACTOR

A hand-held metal press that extracts the juice from a halved citrus fruit. This device is quick and very handy, and comes in a variety of sizes that accommodate lemons, limes, or oranges.

CITRUS STRIPPER

A stainless steel tool that is essential for cutting lemon, lime, and orange twists and spiral peels. A channeled edge peels off 1/4-inch strips of citrus rind. This tool is also handy for making ginger, cucumber, or chocolate shavings. A vegetable peeler will do in a pinch, but it's clumsier and less precise.

COCKTAIL SHAKER

Also known as a standard shaker. The beauty of this essential bar tool is in the simplicity of its built-in strainer design. Styles range from a classic stainless steel version with a built-in strainer and a tightly fitted top (in my opinion, the best device for chilling, shaking, and pouring a drink) to elegant glass ones with a silver top (frequently with a built-in strainer and pour spout), novelty shapes, and high-tech brands with metal mesh casings. The choice between the standard shaker and the Boston shaker is largely an aesthetic one for the home bartender, whereas the Boston shaker's ease of use and quick cleanup appeal to professional bartenders.

- -

CORKSCREWS

Devices for removing corks come in many styles, but the best are simple ones with a thick, sturdy metal coil (called the spiral screw or worm), such as the winged corkscrew or sommelier's corkscrew.

~ *BUTLER'S FRIEND (CORK PULLER OR CORK FORK)* A perfect gadget for older, crumbling, or spongy corks that would fall apart if removed with a conventional corkscrew. It consists of two prongs, which are inserted into the neck of the bottle on opposite sides of the cork. The cork is removed by gently pulling the handle while rocking and turning it.

~ *CLASSIC CORKSCREW* The most basic, conventional design—a coil attached to a wooden or metal handle. Once the coil is screwed into the cork, pulling on the handle removes the cork.

~ *LEVER PULL (OR DOUBLE-ACTION CORKSCREW)* A high-tech gadget that fits snugly around the top of the bottle, with a lever that extracts the cork with one pull of the handle.

~ *SCREWPULL* A wing-nut-shaped handle attached to a coil and two pronged supports that fit over the neck and supply the leverage as the handle is turned to pierce, embed, and extract the cork.

~ *SOMMELIER'S CORKSCREW (WAITER'S FRIEND OR WAITER'S CORKSCREW)*
Most commonly used by waiters, this design is small and port-able, holding a corkscrew coil, a bottle opener, and a knife to remove the foil and wax on the top of the bottle.

~ *WINGED CORKSCREW (WING OPENER OR GOURMET CORKSCREW)*
One of the easiest corkscrews to use, this device uses twin lever arms attached to a gearlike mechanism to extract the cork. As the centered coil is screwed down into the cork, the

arms rise up as the coil is embedded. Pressing the arms back down extracts the cork.

CUTTING BOARD

A good, sturdy wooden cutting board is a handy surface for preparing fruit, herbs, and garnishes.

DECANTER

Glass decanters are best, as they are a neutral-tasting vessel that shows off the color of your wine or spirit. The ideal decanter will have a stopper top, helping to avoid exposing delicate wines to excessive oxygen. The larger magnum decanters or an openmouthed glass carafe or pitcher are perfect for aerating wines, especially young ones, which need to be opened up to release their bouquet.

FOIL CUTTER

A handy little gadget used to easily cut and remove the foil (seal) around the top of wine bottles.

HAWTHORN STRAINER

A stainless steel handheld strainer with a spring coil designed to fit snugly over the opening of a 16-ounce mixing glass or shaker, for straining cocktails and mixed drinks.

ICE BUCKET

Another completely functional accessory to add to your bar equipment. Ice buckets come in a range of styles, from glass, silver, or stainless steel to colored plastic. Some are insulated, with a lid to keep the ice colder longer. A pair of metal or plastic ice tongs is frequently included to handle your cubes when serving cocktails.

The ultimate is a high-tech vacuum ice bucket, typically in silver or chrome, that comes with a glass liner for insulation and has an automatic snug lid that keeps the ice from melting too quickly.

JIGGER

A standard liquid measure equaling 1¹/₂ ounces, used when making mixed drinks. Also the name of a metal or glass cup, measuring a jigger. This cup is frequently incorporated into a classic hourglass-shaped measuring device called a double-ended jigger, which has a 1¹/₂-ounce jigger on one end and a 1-ounce pony on the other end. Not all jiggers hold exactly 1¹/₂ fluid ounces, so be sure to measure the true capacity of yours before the mixing starts.

JULEP COCKTAIL STRAINER

An alternative to the hawthorn strainer, this oval-shaped metal strainer perforated with holes works equally well with a mixing glass or shaker.

MARTINI PITCHER AND STIRRER

These tall, elegant glass pitchers are used for stirring and chilling crystal-clear cocktails such as Martinis or Manhattans, and are ideal when mixing more than two drinks at a time. The best pitchers will have a pinched, molded spout that holds back the ice when you pour and come with a glass stirring rod, useful in stirring cocktails made with champagne or other carbonated liquid (see page 142).

MEASURING SPOONS

The nesting metal kitchen variety, ¹/₄ teaspoon up to 1 tablespoon. These come in handy when you need to measure less than ¹/₂ ounce of a liquid or for recipes that call for small measurements of a dry ingredient.

MIXING GLASS

A tall 16- to 20-ounce mixing glass used to stir, not shake drinks. Some are designed with a pouring spout, but any large glass will work, including the Boston shaker's mixing glass.

MUDDLER

A very handy device for crushing or mixing ingredients together in the bottom of a glass to release their essence. Typically made of rounded hardwood, the muddler (or pestle) is useful in mashing limes and sugar for a Caipirinha, smashing herbs such as mint for juleps, or cracking ice. A wooden spoon or ceramic mortar and pestle can also be used.

PARING KNIFE

A small knife for detail cutting, from garnish preparation to slicing ingredients like ginger and small fruit. A serrated knife is great for slicing citrus and other fruit.

SWIZZLE STICKS

Individual drink stirrers, great for fishing out garnishes and stirring things up. Have an assortment of kitschy vintage plastic ones from Trader Vic's or more elegant handblown glass shapes and other ornamental varieties.

WINE COOLER

A widemouthed bucket with handles, usually metal, that, when filled with ice, will keep your champagne, white wine, or sweet dessert wines chilled.

Other alternatives for chilling bottles include the following:

~ *COOLING JACKET OR SLEEVE* A thermal sleeve filled with coolant that is kept in the freezer until placed around the bottle. It's as effective as a wine cooler, and more portable.

~ *VACUUM BOTTLE COOLER* Keeps bottles at a consistent temperature (whether cooled whites or warmer temperatures for reds) no matter what the ambient temperature.

Glassware Guide

A TRANSPICUOUS CLARIFICATION

GLASSES COME IN AN ENDLESS VARIETY OF DESIGNS, styles, and colors and serve a multitude of functions. To help you navigate through all the choices out there, this section clarifies which glass is appropriate for which drink, from the most commonly used glassware to the specialty glasses designed specifically for a particular cocktail or alcoholic beverage. Included are a few intriguing throwbacks to the cocktail's halcyon days, and if you can find them, they will add that certain mystique to your favorite classic drink.

Presentation plays an important role in the much-ritualized cocktail experience, visually enticing our palates with the promise of refreshment. There is no denying that the right glass will add a touch of elegance to even the simplest drink, but a particular cocktail can also be served in a particular glass for purely functional reasons. Each style of glassware is designed to serve a purpose besides simply holding the correct amount of liquid for its intended drink or keeping the drink cold. It really helps to know which glassware is best suited for muddling ingredients, enhancing the bouquet of a sherry, Cognac, or wine; or preserving the carbonation of a fine champagne, and therefore this information has been included in the descriptions.

The illustrations of glassware that accompany the descriptions in this section are represented in the most basic iconic design and shape. You will find the same illustrations accompanying the drink recipes throughout the book, as a quick reference to the appropriate glass.

It is also important to note that the capacities given in the description for each glass are approximations based on the typical size of that glass, and match the yield of the drink recipes in this book. Contemporary cocktail glassware, especially the martini glass, has become progressively larger and oversized compared to the more traditional classic styles, so be sure to proportion your drinks accordingly if your glassware is on the gargantuan side.

When it comes to setting up your home bar, don't let this glassware section intimidate; your repertoire of glassware doesn't have to be extensive to be stylishly appropriate and proficiently functional. Here are a few basic styles that will see you beautifully through a multitude of drinks:

- Cocktail glasses

- Highball glasses

- Old-fashioned glasses

- Double old-fashioned glasses

- Champagne flutes

- Wineglasses—wineglasses used for red wine are more versatile than the white, but for wine enthusiasts I would suggest having both types of wineglasses on hand

GLASSWARE DESCRIPTIONS

BEER MUG
Especially great for tap beer, these are typically 10 to 16 ounces, made of glass, large, heavy handled, and pint-sized. Put them in the freezer for a frosty glass of beer.

BRANDY SNIFTER
The short-stemmed, distinctly round, globe-shaped bowl is perfectly designed for swirling and capturing the aromatic bouquet of brandy, fine Cognac, or liqueurs. Sizes range from 5 to 25 ounces and even up to 48 ounces.

CHAMPAGNE COUPE (OR SAUCER)
We've all heard the legend of the champagne glass modeled after Marie Antoinette's breast, that saucer-shaped glass called the coupe. This traditionally shallow champagne glass holds 3 to 6 ounces and is used for many a wedding toast. Although glamorous and iconic in shape, it is ineffective in preserving the bubbles and thus is better suited for serving Daiquiris and sours.

CHAMPAGNE FLUTE
The preferred glass for champagne and sparkling wines, this glass is tall with a narrow opening to prevent the bubbles from dissipating, helping preserve the effervescence in champagne and capturing the wine's bouquet. Holding 6 to 9 ounces, this elegant long, thin-stemmed glass is also called a tulip glass and is perfect for serving multi-ingredient champagne cocktails.

COCKTAIL GLASS
The traditional cocktail glass is similar to the martini glass, with a slightly more rounded bowl. Ranging anywhere from 3 to 6 ounces, and up to 10 ounces, it is the quintessential glass for serving shaken or stirred cocktails. The terms "cocktail glass" and "martini glass" are used interchangeably.

COLLINS GLASS
Frequently interchangeable with the highball glass, but slightly more narrow, this tall 10- to 14-ounce glass is perfect not only for collinses, but for many mixed drinks served with ice, such as the Mojito, Iced Tea, Sea Breeze, and fizzy summer coolers. A taller collins glass, known as a chimney, holds 16 ounces and is used for specialty drinks such as the Singapore Sling, Mai Tai, or Zombie.

CORDIAL GLASS

Available in a variety of shapes, this little stemmed glass holds 1 or 2 ounces, and up to 4 ounces. It is used for sipping sweet liqueurs, fruit brandies, and pousse-cafés. The smaller 1-ounce cordial glass is also known as a pony.

HIGHBALL GLASS

This versatile bar glass is tall, straight sided, and slim, meant to be filled with ice and a fizzy highball, cooler, frosty julep, Cape Codder, Bloody Mary, or other long drink. It comes in both an 8- to 10-ounce size and a taller 12- to 14-ounce version called the chimney, and is frequently interchangeable with a collins glass.

HURRICANE GLASS

Short stemmed, with a tall, curved bowl that resembles a hurricane lamp, and named for the New Orleans cocktail, this glass is able to hold 16 to 20 ounces of your favorite frozen or tropical drink.

IRISH COFFEE GLASS

This heat-proof 8- to 10-ounce glass is usually made of clear, thick glass and either is short stemmed with a handle or has a stainless steel base and handle. It serves also as a hot toddy or buttered rum glass.

MARGARITA GLASS

Beside the Margarita, for which it was specifically designed, these 6- to 8-ounce (and even up to 10 to 14 ounces) festive dessert bowls on stems are great for any frozen, blended concoction. You can also substitute a large wine goblet for the same purpose.

MARTINI GLASS

A 4- to 6-ounce glass with the familiar conical, flared cup and a thin, elegant stem. It is the perfect glass for those clear or jewel-colored shaken or stirred cocktails.

OLD-FASHIONED GLASS

A 4- to 8-ounce short, stocky, straight-sided glass with a heavy glass bottom to stand up to muddling. This sturdy glass is best suited for drinks served over ice, such as Scotch and Soda. Also referred to as a whiskey glass, rocks glass, or tumbler.

DOUBLE OLD-FASHIONED GLASS
Also known as a double-rocks glass, this 12- to 16-ounce tumbler is used for larger lowballs and double-shot drinks with mixers on the rocks.

PARFAIT GLASS
Slightly curved and elegant, holding 8 to 10 ounces, this glass is meant for frozen and fruity sweet liqueur drinks. Also known as a frappé glass.

PILSNER GLASS
This tall, elongated glass, named after and designed for a Czech lager, is V shaped with a rounded base and holds 10 to 16 ounces. It is used to serve beer and ale, either bottled or from the tap.

PONY GLASS
Holding 1 to 2 ounces, this stemmed glass for liqueurs and brandies is also known as a cordial glass.

POUSSE-CAFÉ GLASS
Designed specifically for pousse-café drinks, this 2- to 4-ounce straight-sided glass with a short stem is perfect for layering liqueurs by floating one on top of the other.

PUNCH CUP
A rounded crystal cup with a handle, similar to a teacup. It holds 6 to 8 ounces and is typically found as part of a punch bowl set.

SHERRY OR PORT GLASS
A short-stemmed glass holding 1 to 3 ounces. It can also be used for cordials, liqueurs, and aperitifs. The more traditional Spanish *copita* is a small, flower-shaped sherry glass. An exaggerated version of a wineglass, at 4 ounces, it better enables the drinker to enjoy the aroma of the sherry.

SHOT GLASS

A sturdy little glass that typically holds 1½ ounces when full. A narrow, taller version, 2 to 4 ounces, is also known as a vodka, schnapps, or aperitif glass. Occasionally used as a jigger for measuring, the shot glass is more frequently used for shots or shooters.

SOUR GLASS

Otherwise known as the whiskey sour or Delmonico glass, this short-stemmed, 5- to 6-ounce tulip-shaped glass is traditionally used for sours of all kinds, but is also frequently used to serve crustas.

WINEGLASSES

Taller in the stem and wider in the bowl than the usual bar wineglass, a good wine glass is designed to keep the wine in the bowl to allow swirling.

WINEGLASS, RED

The typical all-purpose wineglass used for red wine holds 10 to 14 ounces (but is available up to 24 ounces), and is larger than the one used for white wine, with a wider mouth designed to let the bouquet of the wine open up and release its aroma. The larger, rounder goblets known as balloon wineglasses hold 16 ounces and are great for Burgundy and other full-bodied reds. They are also frequently used to add elegance to highball drinks, large tropical drinks, spritzers, Sangria, and sangarees.

WINEGLASS, WHITE

Holding from 6 to 12 ounces, the wineglass used for white wine is typically narrower in the bowl and slightly smaller than the one used for red wine, which helps to keep the wine chilled. They are also frequently used to serve mixed drinks over ice.

Stocking the Home Bar

THE ESSENTIAL LIQUID PORTFOLIO

WHETHER YOU HAVE A SWANK BAR SETUP in your favorite entertaining room or an area set aside in the kitchen, having all the necessary supplies on hand will ensure that you're ready for any party or occasion. The minimal bar approach, with all the essentials needed to make many of the classic and standard drinks, is a fine place to start, but if you're a mixological overachiever, you'll also find suggestions for a full-on fully stocked bar. Of course, at that point you might as well get a liquor license and go into business. This section will help with the basics you'll need to set up a well-functioning home bar. Treat it as a template of options, adjusting the list according to your personal preferences and entertaining needs. Your home bar will eventually expand as you widen your cocktail repertoire. When it comes to choosing brands, strive to stock the best spirits that your pocketbook will allow—you and your guests will appreciate it in the long run.

THE BASIC "MINI" BAR

------- GARNISHES AND COCKTAIL FLAVORINGS -------

1 BOTTLE EACH:
- Angostura bitters
- Grenadine
- Sweetened lime juice, such as Rose's
- Tabasco sauce
- Worcestershire sauce

1 JAR EACH:
- Green cocktail olives
- Cocktail onions
- Horseradish
- Maraschino cherries

- Lemons (for garnishes and freshly squeezed juice)
- Limes (for garnishes and freshly squeezed juice)
- Oranges (for garnishes and freshly squeezed juice)
- Kosher salt and freshly cracked pepper
- Sugar (superfine granulated and powdered)
- Nutmeg (whole or ground)
- Simple syrup (page 72)
- Sugar cubes

------- EQUIPMENT -------

- Bar spoon
- Measuring spoons
- Measuring cup
- Bar towel
- Bottle opener/church key
- Corkscrew
- Cocktail napkins
- Jigger
- Paring knife
- Cutting board

- Cocktail shaker (or Boston shaker and cocktail strainer)
- Blender (one that grinds ice)
- Ice bucket and tongs (or ice scoop)
- Swizzle sticks and straws
- Bowls/glasses to hold garnishes and straws
- Ice cooler or large container filled with ice to keep carbonated beverages, beers, and wine chilled

The basic liquid components needed for entertaining.

∾ LIQUORS

ONE 750-ML BOTTLE EACH:
- Bourbon (ideally small-batch bourbon)
- Brandy (ideally French brandy)
- Blended whiskey
  (such as Canadian whisky)
- Blended scotch (unless you prefer
  sipping single-malt)
- Gin (London dry)
- Light rum
- Tequila (ideally 100 percent agave)
- Vodka

∾ LIQUEURS

- Apricot brandy
- Cointreau (or other orange liqueur)
- Crème de cacao (white and dark)
- Crème de menthe
- Kahlúa (or other coffee liqueur)
- Pernod (or other anise-flavored
  liqueur)
- Other liqueurs, according to your
  cocktail preferences, such as
  amaretto, crème de cassis,
  Chambord, Frangelico, sambuca

∾ WINES

- Fino sherry
- Ruby or tawny port
- Dry vermouth
- Sweet vermouth
- Dry red wine
- Dry white wine
- Brut champagne or sparkling wine

∾ BEERS

- 24 bottles of beer, lager, or ale

- A variety of nonalcoholic mixers,
  such as juices, soda, and
  sparkling water

------- FULLY STOCKED BAR -------

If you're ready to go above and beyond the essentials, choose from this list,
according to your personal preferences.

∾ LIQUORS

- Añejo tequila
- Cachaça
- Dark rum

- Flavored vodkas
  (lemon, currant,or other flavors)
- Grappa

- Jamaican rum
- Pear brandy
- French V.S.O.P. Cognac
- Single-malt scotch
- Irish whiskey

❧ APERITIFS

- Campari
- Dubonnet Rouge
- Fernet Branca
- Lillet Blanc
- Pimm's No. 1

❧ LIQUEURS

- Bénédictine
- Blackberry brandy
- Blue curaçao
- Calvados or other apple brandy
- Chambord
- Chartreuse (green or yellow)
- Crème de banane
- Drambuie
- Frangelico
- Galliano
- Grand Marnier
- Irish cream liqueur
- Jägermeister
- Maraschino liqueur
- Midori melon liqueur
- Ouzo
- Peach schnapps
- Sambuca
- Sloe gin
- Southern Comfort
- Strawberry liqueur
- Tuaca

❧ NONALCOHOLIC BEVERAGES AND MIXERS

1 LITER EACH:

- Club soda
- Lemon-lime soda
- Ginger ale
- Cola
- Still mineral water
- Tonic water

1 QUART EACH:

- Orange juice
  (freshly squeezed or pasteurized)
- Cranberry juice
- Grapefruit juice
- Tomato juice
- Cream or half-and-half
- Milk

- 20 to 30 pounds crushed ice

❧ ABOVE AND BEYOND

- Ginger beer
- Fruit-flavored sparkling beverages
  such as Orangina
- Pineapple juice
- Cream of coconut
- Tropical fruit juices and nectars,
  such as guava, mango, papaya,
  passion fruit, peach, and lychee

THE ESSENTIAL BAR

Measurements

AND INGREDIENT EQUIVALENTS

COMMON LIQUID MEASUREMENTS

Dash = $1/3$ bar spoon = $1/8$ teaspoon = 0.6 ml

Bar spoon = $1/2$ teaspoon = $1/6$ tablespoon = 2.5 ml

1 teaspoon = 8 dashes = 5 ml

1 tablespoon = 3 teaspoons = $1/2$ fl oz = 15 ml

2 tablespoons = 1 pony = 1 fl oz = 30 ml

3 tablespoons = 1 jigger = 1 $1/2$ fl oz = 45 ml

$1/8$ cup = 1 fl oz = 30 ml

$1/4$ cup = 2 fl oz = 60 ml

$1/3$ cup = $2 2/3$ fl oz = 83 ml

$1/2$ cup = 4 fl oz = 120 ml

$2/3$ cup = 5 fl oz = 165 ml

$3/4$ cup = 6 fl oz = 180 ml

1 cup = $1/2$ pint = 8 fl oz = 8 ponies = $5 1/3$ jiggers = 250 ml

2 cups = 1 pint = 16 fl oz = 500 ml

4 cups = 2 pints = 1 quart = 1/4 gallon = 32 fl oz = 1 liter

8 cups = 4 pints = 2 quarts = 1/2 gallon = 64 fl oz = 2 liters

16 cups = 8 pints = 4 quarts = 1 gallon = 4 liters

Classic/common bar wine glass = 4 ozs = 1/2 cup

1 liter bottle = 33.8 ounces

OTHER MEASUREMENTS

Pinch—the amount of a powdered ingredient that can be held between the thumb and forefinger

Splash—typically more than a dash but less than 1/2 ounce, depending on the mixologist

---

INGREDIENT EQUIVALENTS

1 medium lime = 2 tablespoons or 1 ounce juice = 2 teaspoons grated zest

1 medium lemon = 3 tablespoons or 1 1/2 ounces juice = 1 tablespoon grated zest

1 medium orange = 1/3 cup or 2 2/3 ounces juice = 2 tablespoons grated zest

1 cup heavy cream when whipped will yield 2 cups

4 to 6 whole eggs yield 1 cup

8 to 11 egg whites yield 1 cup

12 to 14 egg yolks yield 1 cup

1 pound granulated sugar = 2 cups

1 pound unsifted confectioner's (powdered) sugar = 4 1/2 cups

1 pound brown sugar = 2 1/2 cups

LIQUOR BOTTLES

NAME	OLD BOTTLE SIZE	NEW METRIC MEASURE	NUMBER OF 1½-OUNCE SHOTS PER BOTTLE
Miniature	1.6 oz	50 ml = 1.7 oz	1
Half pint	8 oz	200 ml = 6.8 oz	4½
Pint	16 oz	500 ml = 16.9 oz	11¼
Fifth	25.6 oz	750 ml = 25.4 oz	17
Quart	32 oz	1 l = 33.8 oz	22
Half gallon	64 oz	1.76 l = 59.2 oz	39½

WINE BOTTLES

NAME	METRIC MEASURE	U.S. MEASURE	NUMBER OF 4½-OUNCE SERVINGS PER BOTTLE
Split	187 ml	6.3 oz	1½
Tenth	375 ml	12.7 oz	3
Fifth	750 ml	25.4 oz	6
Quart	1,000 ml	33.8 oz	8
Magnum	1.5 l	50.7 oz	12
Double magnum	3 l	101.4 oz	24

COCKTAIL TERMINOLOGY

ABV

Alcohol by volume, the percentage of alcohol in a given beverage. For example, if the ABV is 40 percent, it indicates that the spirit is 40 percent alcohol, 60 percent water. The ABV is frequently specified on the label along with the proof.

APERITIF

A light alcoholic cocktail or other drink taken before a meal to stimulate the appetite. The term is from the Latin verb meaning "to open" and refers to the opening of your palate. Aperitifs that are frequently enjoyed are anise-flavored or wine-based spirits, including bitters and aromatized and fortified wines. Popular American aperitifs tend toward cocktails such as the Martini, Sidecar, white wine spritzer, Manhattan, or Old-Fashioned. Europeans enjoy their vermouth, Amer Picon, Cynar, Campari, Dubonnet, kir, Lillet, or sherry, preferably served neat or over ice, as well as cocktails such as champagne cocktails, Americano, Negroni, and anise-flavored Pernod, pastis, or ouzo mixed with soda or water. Germans prefer a beer as an aperitif.

AQUA VITAE

Meaning "water of life," this is the original Latin term for spirits. It has been translated into the Danish *akvavit*, French *eau-de-vie,* Irish Gaelic usquebaugh, and the Scottish Gaelic uisce beatha.

AROMATIZED WINES

Fortified wines that have been "aromatized" with the addition of various herbal flavorings. Bottled aperitifs such as Lillet, Cynar, Dubonnet, and vermouths fall into this category.

BITTERS

A highly concentrated alcoholic elixir made from a distilled combination of liquor and various herbal and fruit ingredients, originally developed for medicinal purposes. Angostura and Peychaud's bitters are so concentrated that they are measured out in drops, whereas other bitters such as Campari can be enjoyed over ice.

CHASER

The beverage you drink immediately after you have downed anything alcoholic, usually a shot. A typical chaser can be either beer, club soda, or juice.

CORDIAL

A term often used interchangeably with "liqueur."

DASH

Either a shake from a bitters bottle or the equivalent of $1/8$ teaspoon (some say only $1/16$ teaspoon).

DIGESTIF

Spirits imbibed to aid the digestion after a meal, from bitters served neat such as a Fernet Branca, to an after-dinner drink or nightcap, such as B&B, Brandy Alexander, or White or Black Russian.

DISTILLATION

The process of extracting alcohol from a fermented liquid by using heat through either a pot still or continuous still. The resulting vapor is collected, and as it cools condensation occurs, to revert back to a liquid that is more purified, with a higher alcohol concentration.

DRAM

A term used in many countries, including Ireland, Scotland, and the Caribbean, for a small glass of spirit.

DRY

A term meaning "not sweet," used either in reference to a dry wine or to describe nonsweet spirits or cocktails, such as the dry Martini, which uses dry vermouth rather than sweet vermouth. Dryness results during fermentation when the yeast consumes almost all of the sugar and converts it to alcohol.

EAU-DE-VIE

Meaning "water of life" in French, this term describes a wide group of colorless spirits distilled from fermented fruit, typically not aged, and potent. Technically, a French brandy is an eau-de-vie made from grapes, kirsch is made from cherries, and Poire Williams is made from pears.

FLOAT

A cocktail term describing the technique of slowly pouring a small amount of spirit (usually a liqueur or cream) over the top of the surface of a drink so that it floats, or sits atop another liquid without being mixed. The customary technique involves slowly pouring the liquid over the back of a spoon. (See the description of floating techniques and layering pousse-café techniques on page 44.)

FORTIFIED WINES

Wines that are enhanced and sweetened with brandy or other spirits. Sherry, port, and Madeira are all fortified wines. These are frequently also categorized as dessert wines.

GRENADINE

A sweet, deep crimson syrup originally made from pomegranates from the Caribbean island of Grenada, but most brands today are made with other fruit juice. With a low to no alcohol content, depending on the brand, it is used mainly for sweetening and for adding color to mixed drinks.

MIXER

Any nonalcoholic beverage, such as fruit juice, soda, cream, or club soda, that is added to a drink containing liquor.

MODIFIER

A cocktail ingredient that is integral to the flavor of the drink. Bitters, syrups, and other sweeteners such as Rose's lime juice or coconut cream are all modifiers, adding flavor or texture.

MOUTHFEEL

A term used when tasting wine or spirits to describe the impact of the shape and texture of a spirit or wine on the palate.

MUDDLE

A technique that involves mashing fruits or herbs (usually together with bitters and/or sugar) in the bottom of the glass with a small wooden muddler or spoon to release their aromatic flavors.

NEAT

Describes a single spirit or liqueur served in a glass "straight up," enjoyed on its own, unchilled, and without ice, water, or any other ingredients.

NEUTRAL SPIRIT

A spirit distilled from grain to produce a virtually tasteless, colorless alcohol that is 95.5 percent ABV. It is used as a base for spirits such as vodka or gin or for blending with straight whiskeys or other spirits and liqueurs.

NOSE

The scent or aroma of a spirit.

ON THE ROCKS

A term used to describe any liquor or mixed drink served over ice (the rocks being the ice cubes), as opposed to a drink served "up" (without ice).

PERFECT

A term used to describe specific cocktails that contain equal parts dry and sweet vermouth, as in a Perfect Manhattan or Perfect Martini.

PROOF

A legal measurement of a liquor's alcoholic strength. In the United States, it is calculated thusly: 1 degree of proof equals 0.05 percent alcohol by volume, or ABV. Therefore, a spirit labeled "80 proof" is 40 percent ABV. A 100-proof spirit is 50 percent ABV, and so on.

SPLASH

A small amount that can fall anywhere between a dash and about an ounce, depending on who's doing the splashing.

STRAIGHT

Describes a spirit served without any other liquor or mixers, either poured into a chilled glass or over ice, occasionally with the addition of a splash of club soda or water.

SWIZZLE STICK

The original swizzle stick was a twig used to agitate tall rum drinks in the Caribbean. Used for stirring drinks, swizzle sticks now come in various styles and lengths, from glass rods to plastic or wood.

TO TOP OR TOP OFF

A term used by bartenders to describe the act of pouring the last ingredient into a drink, usually club soda or ginger ale, filling to the top of the glass. Also used to describe filling a beer mug from a tap.

UP

Describes a drink served without ice in a cocktail glass. Usually the drink is shaken in a cocktail shaker and strained "up" into a chilled cocktail glass, as opposed to "on the rocks" and served over ice.

TYPES OF DRINKS

BUCK

This drink, which originated in the 1890s, is made with a base liquor, traditionally gin, the juice squeezed from a wedge of lemon or lime, and ginger ale. It is also traditional to drop the citrus wedge, once it's been squeezed, into the glass, and to serve the drink in a highball glass. Other buck drinks besides the Gin Buck include the Apple Buck, Brandy Buck, New Orleans Buck, and Peach Buck.

COBBLER

Dating back to the early 1800s, cobblers traditionally were made of wine or sherry combined with a simple (or fruit) syrup, served over crushed ice in a wine goblet, and classically garnished with fresh fruit and mint sprigs. The more recent versions of the cobbler use any combination of liquors and liqueurs, powdered sugar for sweetener, and even a splash of club soda.

COLLINS

Invented and named after barman John Collins of Limmer's Hotel in London around the early 1800s, the collins was originally made with genever (a pungent Holland gin), sugar, lemon juice, and soda water. A later variation that became more popular used Old Tom gin, sweeter than the Holland gin, which inspired the name change to Tom Collins. Brought to the United States by World War I vets who were fans of the London cocktail, it eventually evolved into the favorite drink of the 1950s suburban set, made with London dry gin, sugar, and the juice of one lemon, in a tall glass filled with ice, and topped with club soda. Although a John Collins is made with Holland gin in London, if you order a John Collins in America, it will frequently be made with bourbon or whiskey.

Tom Collins is the most famous of these drinks, but there are other collinses made with other liquors: a Pedro Collins is made with rum, a Rum Collins is made with dark rum, a Captain Collins is made with Canadian whisky, a Sandy Collins is made with scotch whisky, a Colonel Collins is made with bourbon, a Mike Collins is made with Irish whiskey, a Pierre Collins is made with Cognac, a Jack Collins is made with apple brandy, a Vodka or Joe Collins is made with vodka, a Ruben or Pepito Collins is made with tequila, and a Pisco Collins is made with pisco brandy.

COOLER

A drink combining a base of spirits or wine with any carbonated beverage, served over ice in a tall glass and typically garnished with a long citrus peel spiral.

CRUSTA

Characterized by a sugared rim and a lemon peel spiral, the crusta was invented in New Orleans at Santina's Saloon in the mid-1800s. Traditionally made with brandy, lemon juice, maraschino liqueur, and Cointreau, variations substitute bourbon, gin, or rum for the brandy—but all must have the signature sugar-coated glass rim and long citrus peel spiral.

DAISY

An American drink dating from the 1850s, consisting of a base spirit (bourbon, brandy, gin, or rum), a fruit syrup or grenadine, and a small splash of club soda, served over crushed ice. Early versions were served in an iced metal mug, but today they are frequently served over ice in a highball glass.

FIZZ

Like the collins drinks, a fizz contains a spirit, citrus juices, sugar, and club soda. The difference is in the method—fizzes are always shaken while collinses are mixed once the ingredients are in the glass. The classic is the Gin Fizz, but variations abound, using different base spirits and fruit juices, adding liqueurs, or adding egg white to give the drink more froth, as in the Silver Fizz. The technique is the same—the ingredients are shaken vigorously, poured into an ice-filled old-fashioned glass, and topped with a carbonated beverage. Other fizzes include the Golden Fizz, made with egg yolk; the Royal Gin Fizz, made with a whole egg; and the Sloe Gin Fizz, made with sloe gin in place of the gin.

FLIP

A cocktail characterized by the use of whole raw egg in combination with a wine, spirit, liqueur, or beer, together with sugar and sometimes cream. Served straight up in a wine goblet, hot or cold, with fruit garnish. The original flips were named after concoctions heated by a hot iron called a "flip iron." The flip iron was heated in the fire until red hot, and then plunged into a mug of spiced wine, rum, or beer, sometimes together with an egg, to heat the beverage. If you prefer to avoid raw eggs, substitute pasteurized eggs.

HIGHBALL

The main characteristics of a highball drink are that it has two ingredients— one spirit and one mixer (usually carbonated) poured into an ice-filled tall, narrow glass (which helps to contain the carbonation)—and that it can be mixed very quickly. The original highball was created in the 1890s by New York bartender Patrick Gavin Duffy, who purportedly got the name from a railroad signal in which a raised ball on a pole signaled the engineer to speed up. Typically, the proportions are 1 1/2 ounces of spirit to 5 or 6 ounces of mixer. Ice is an American option, as the British prefer to go without. Traditionally, highballs are made with whiskey and club soda. Other classic highballs include Gin and Ginger, Gin and Tonic, Horse's Neck, Rum and Coke, Scotch and Soda, and Seven and Seven.

JULEP

Derived from the Arabic term *julāb* ("rose water"), the word "julep" was used by pharmacists in the 15th century to denote sweetened liquid medicines—in effect, the sweetening of bitter herbs with sugar or syrup. Early versions of the julep combined mint with brandy, peach brandy, or Cognac. Later, the drink used mint to mask harsh, low-quality whiskey, then bourbon as it became more refined, leading to the popular Mint Julep of today.

LOWBALL

As opposed to a highball in a tall glass, a lowball is any drink served with ice in a short glass, such as an old-fashioned glass.

MIST

Any straight spirit served by being poured over crushed ice in a short glass, which causes a "mist" to occur. One made with scotch would be called a Scotch Mist, one using Cointreau would be called a Cointreau Mist.

POUSSE-CAFÉ

Literally translated as the "coffee-pusher," this after-dinner drink layers colorful strata of liqueurs, syrups, spirits, and creams in a stemmed glass. The multiple layers—as many as seven—are artfully floated one on top of another so that each stratum remains separate. The heaviest liquid goes in first; the lightest is added last.

PUFF

A combination of equal parts liquor and milk, topped with club soda and typically served over ice in an old-fashioned glass.

RICKEY

Similar to a collins or fizz, the Rickey's defining characteristic is the refreshingly tart omission of sugar. As legend has it, the Rickey originated at Shoemakers Restaurant in Washington, D.C., in 1893, where the bartender created and named the drink after a frequent patron, American lobbyist Joe Rickey. It is traditionally prepared with gin, the juice and squeezed shell of half a lime, and club soda, and is served on the rocks in an old-fashioned glass. Variations include muddling the half lime with sugar, adding grenadine, and substituting other spirits such as rum or bourbon, apricot liqueur, or Amer Picon for the gin.

SANGAREE

Influenced by the Spanish Sangria, this early American cocktail originally consisted of fortified wines sweetened with sugar and served over ice, with a signature dusting of nutmeg. Versions have evolved to include two or more spirits, such as the Brandy Sangaree with port and chilled club soda. It is sometimes even served as a hot drink.

SLING

Evocative of tall tropical coolers, slings characteristically use a fruit brandy to sweeten a drink that is otherwise basically a collins. Many variations stem from the popularity of the famous classic Singapore Sling, originating at Raffles Hotel, Singapore, in 1915. It is traditionally made with gin, cherry brandy, Bénédictine, and lemon juice, and served over ice in a tall glass, topped with club soda and garnished with the classic lime peel spiral.

SMASH

Similar to a julep, a smash is made by muddling mint together with the liquor of choice and simple syrup. It is usually served in an iced old-fashioned glass with sprigs of mint and fruit.

SOUR

Appropriately named for its use of fresh lemon juice, the sour is one of America's oldest cocktails, dating back to the mid-1800s. The original sour was made with brandy and egg white, but American whiskey gradually replaced brandy as the French imports became scarce, and by the 1900s whiskey had replaced brandy as the spirit of choice. Basically a collins without the carbonation, the sour is a combination of lemon juice, whiskey, and sugar, always shaken, and traditionally served up in a sour glass (but it can also be served over ice in a highball or old-fashioned glass) and garnished with an orange slice and maraschino cherry. Brandy eventually made a comeback in the form of the Pisco Sour, made with Chilean pisco brandy. Other variations include the Gin Sour, Rum Sour, and Applejack Sour.

SWIZZLE

This drink is named for the action of "swizzling" the ingredients with a long stick—rubbing a long swizzle stick vigorously between one's palms to twirl it and mix the drink. The first swizzles date as far back as the early 1800s in the Caribbean, where they were traditionally tall drinks made of rum poured over crushed ice and mixed with long twigs to blend and chill the drink. These days, bar spoons are more commonly used to stir a swizzle, and they can be made with a variety of liquors, such as Rum Swizzle, Scotch Swizzle, or Gin Swizzle.

TALL DRINK

Also known as a long drink, a tall drink is served in either a collins or high-ball glass and typically contains 6 or more ounces. Tall drinks are requested when one wants a slightly more diluted variation of a short-glass cocktail.

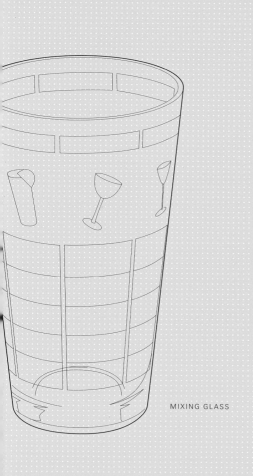

MIXING GLASS

.03 ~

Mixology 101

arkling wine / beer & sake / brandy

THE COMPREHENSIVE GUIDE

ULTIMATE
Bar Book

TO OVER 1,000 COCKTAILS

gin / rum / tequila / vodka / whis

ARTFUL DRINKOLOGY

The key to mixing the perfect drink lies in the attention to detail—the drinks being poured should be balanced proportionately and perfectly executed. Making a drink can be an artistic exercise, an orchestration of ingredients and technique, and a mixologist is viewed as a knowledgeable maestro. Building perfection in a glass takes but a few basic bar skills, such as shaking cocktails like a pro, having ready the perfect frosted glass, being familiar with the essential tools and techniques for garnishing drinks, and knowing the distinguishing characteristics of various spirits, wines, and liqueurs.

A FEW WORDS ON INGREDIENTS

From the liquor all the way down to the juice, a drink is only as good as its ingredients.

A premium-quality spirit is discernible and appreciated anytime one spirit is at least 90 percent of the drink, such as when served on the rocks or in a Martini, but it will get lost if mixed in a cocktail, becoming more of a foolish extravagance. Be selective; for example, you may want to save that expensive five-year-old añejo tequila for sipping, but drinks such as the Gin and Tonic are greatly improved by a premium gin such as Bombay Sapphire, as is a Mint Julep made with a single-barrel bourbon such as Knob Creek or Woodford Reserve. As a rule, when it comes to most mixed drinks, an inexpensive to moderately priced spirit is perfectly suitable. And sometimes it comes down to a matter of quality versus quantity. If you are mixing Margaritas for a small group of friends, go ahead and use your best tequila, but if you are making huge blender batches of Piña Coladas, Daiquiris, or Margaritas, it's more prudent to use a moderately priced rum or tequila. Fruity ingredients become the dominant flavor in such drinks, and that goes for most mixed drinks with lots of flavored liqueurs and fruit juices as well.

While we are on the subject, it is imperative that you use fresh juices and fruits whenever possible, to uphold the level of quality. Fresh juices make all the difference between an okay drink and a fabulous cocktail. You cannot beat a Sidecar made with freshly squeezed lemon juice or a Screwdriver made with fresh orange juice.

A Daiquiri made with good-quality rum deserves fresh lime juice and fresh fruit; otherwise, the quality level falls. You can also find juices in bottled, canned, and frozen form, including grapefruit juice, cranberry juice cocktail, unsweetened pineapple juice, and tomato juice.

------- **MIXERS** -------

The most frequently used mixers are tonic water, seltzer, ginger ale, cola, and lemon-lime soda. Mixers usually make up two-thirds of the drink, and are used to either dilute a spirit or add flavor. Be sure to keep them chilled in the refrigerator, as room-temperature mixers tend to melt ice faster and will dilute your drink.

------- **ORANGE FLOWER WATER** -------

This fragrant distillation of bitter-orange blossoms imparts a perfumy orange flavor to a drink, and is the key ingredient in the classic Ramos Gin Fizz. It is typically found in supermarkets and liquor stores.

------- **SYRUPS** -------

❧ **ORGEAT SYRUP**   This intensely almond-flavored syrup made from almonds, sugar, and rose water or orange flower water is an ingredient in many drinks. If it is not available, substitute almond syrup or sirop d'amandes.

❧ **GRENADINE**   A sweet, deep crimson syrup originally made from pomegranates from the Caribbean island of Grenada. Most brands today are made with other fruit juice. With a low to no alcohol content, depending on the brand, it is used mainly for sweetening and for adding color to mixed drinks.

Other syrup mixers frequently used in mixed drinks:

- Monin: passion fruit syrup

- Sirop de cassis: black currant syrup

- Sirop de citron: a sweet, zesty lemon syrup

- Sirop de groseilles: red currant syrup

------- **CREAM** -------

Cream lends a rich, thick texture to the body of many drinks. When a recipe calls for cream, use heavy cream; although half-and-half can be used in its place, the body will be thinner.

------- **A NOTE ABOUT POWDERED SUGAR** -------

Many of the classic recipes from the golden age of cocktails call for quickly dissolving powdered sugar, which is made with cornstarch—not the most appealing ingredient for cocktails. In the spirit of good taste, replace it whenever possible with granulated or superfine sugar, or with simple syrup.

------- **THE RAW EGG QUESTION** -------

Egg whites or yolks have traditionally been used in cocktails to give them body and froth, harking back to a time before concerns about salmonella poisoning. If you prefer, you can use pasteurized eggs or egg white powder, or you can omit the egg altogether. Use raw eggs at your own discretion.

ANATOMY OF A COCKTAIL

A cocktail is made up of three principal components: the base alcohol (or basis), the body (or modifier), and the perfume (or flavoring agent).

------- **THE BASE** -------

This is the main liquor ingredient that the cocktail is built upon. It is the largest component of a drink, and thus not only determines the type of drink but also dictates the other elements that are appropriate in the drink. For example, in a Sidecar, the base is brandy, and so it is considered a brandy cocktail, whereas in a Daiquiri, the rum is the base. In the classically proportioned cocktail, mixing bases, such as gin with tequila, is a mixological faux pas, but this rule is frequently broken, such as in the Long Island Iced Tea.

------- **THE BODY** -------

The technical term is "modifier," meaning an ingredient that modifies but does not completely dominate the base spirit. Without it, the drink is no longer a cocktail. The body is the component that holds the drink together, adding a consistency, weight, or texture, whether it be a light juice, a champagne, a clear vermouth, or heavy cream.

------- **THE PERFUME** -------

The perfume accentuates and enhances the base alcohol and is typically the smallest element proportionately. It could be a fruit, nut, coffee, or herbal liqueur or even a syrup or bitter, which sometimes brings a new dynamic to the drink with aromatic notes, such as hazelnut, orange, strawberry, vanilla, or cherry. The flavor agent can bring sweetness, bitterness, or color to the drink and, even in minute amounts, completes the fine balance of the cocktail.

- Base: gin
- Body: sweet vermouth
- Perfume: Campari

MEASURING UP

Leave the eyeballing to the professionals. I have a sneaking suspicion that their drinks taste different each time anyway. The best way to arrive at the result intended by the perfected recipe is to use a jigger in a precise manner—this is like chemistry, after all. If you do, you will be spared the cocktail that doesn't quite hit the right note. This book uses fluid ounces, but many older cocktail books use old-school bar-speak, talking about jiggers, ponies, and dashes, or they give ratios, such as 2 parts spirit to 1 part liqueur, or percentages. Once you become familiar with the classically balanced cocktails, you will notice that most of them have the same basic formula, and the ratios will make perfect sense.

PREPARING GLASSWARE

Whether you're serving a spirit neat or shaken, such as a Martini, a sparkling clean, clear glass is an important detail. To enjoy the flavor of the premium spirits, glassware should be hand-washed with unscented dish soap and thoroughly rinsed with hot water, or your drink will taste of dish soap. Glassware stored in the cupboard will pick up a particular "cupboard" flavor, and should be polished with a dry, soft, lint-free cloth before using.

Presentation is all, and a prechilled frosty glass straight from the freezer is the ideal way to serve your guests a cocktail, not to mention the best way to keep your drinks cold. Rinsing a glass in cold water and then chilling it in the freezer for an hour or so will give it that frosty patina. If you need a chilled glass pronto, the quickest way to get it is to fill the glass with cracked ice and club soda or cold water and let the glass chill while you're mixing the drinks. Toss out the ice, wipe out any excess water, and pour in the drink. If you have fine crystal, chill it in the refrigerator or with the ice cube chilling method, to avoid cracking the glass.

THE ICE

Ice can affect the flavor of your drinks, and the best way to guarantee neutral and tasteless ice is to make it fresh from filtered spring or bottled water. If possible, avoid making ice with tap water. The most essential element to chilling cocktails, ice comes in many functional forms, from cubes for stirring, shaking, and serving drinks "on the rocks" to cracked ice, which is great for blender drinks and single-spirit drinks, such as a mist. Cracked ice can be purchased in bags or cracked by hand. Simply place ice cubes in a plastic bag, cover with a towel, and crack them with a wooden mallet or other heavy, blunt tool.

TO SHAKE OR TO STIR

That is the question. The classic rule of thumb is that any drink made with clear spirits (such as the Martini, Manhattan, Gimlet, or Stinger) is to be stirred. Stirring chills with minimum dilution while not disturbing the spirit's characteristic clarity and texture. Shaking would render the drink too cloudy and frothy. If you are mixing spirits with juices, creams, and liqueurs, or you have many ingredients, the shaken method is ideal, as these drinks are meant to be characteristically frothy and light. The vigorous shaking action also does a much more thorough job of mixing ingredients of various weights and textures.

Where Gin Martini drinkers may prefer theirs stirred (so as not to bruise the gin), Vodka Martini drinkers tend to agree with James Bond, preferring them shaken. It all comes down to personal preference—a shaken drink may be cloudier, but with the frosty advantage of fine slivers of ice, and a proper Martini must be somewhat diluted by the ice.

------- **SHAKING** -------

Most drinks that call for shaking can be made in either a standard shaker or a Boston shaker (see page 17). The drinks that ask for a shakerful of liquid ingredients exceeding 4 ounces in total volume are best shaken in the standard three-piece stainless steel cocktail shaker; with its reliably snug top and larger capacity, it will prevent spillage.

The quickest way to look like a mixology master is to shake those cocktails in a shimmering blur of chrome. Vigorous shaking will leave refreshing shimmery shards of ice floating on the surface of the drink. As a rule, drinks using cloudier ingredients such as sugar, cream, fruit juices, and liqueurs are best shaken, since they need vigorous movement to blend well.

Once the cocktail glass is chilling in the freezer and the drink's garnish has been cut, it is time to shake your cocktail.

To shake a drink in a standard shaker, put a glassful of cracked ice (or ice cubes) in the base, add the ingredients, and cap with the top. Grasp the shaker with both hands, one holding the lid on, and shake until the shaker becomes frosty. Don't be shy—shake up and down with vigorous intent. Take the top off, and quickly strain the mixture through the built-in strainer into a chilled glass.

To shake a drink with a Boston shaker, fill the glass mixing tumbler two-thirds full with ice, pour in the ingredients, cap snugly with the steel tumbler, and, with a hand holding each end, shake vigorously up and down. Push or tap gently but firmly on one side to break the seal. With the shaker still to-gether, turn it over so the glass tumbler is on top. Remove the glass tumbler from the steel tumbler. Fit a coil-spring hawthorn strainer over the mouth of the steel tumbler, and strain the mixture into a serving glass.

------- **SULTRY STIRRING** -------

There is something evocatively classic in the ritual of stirring a cocktail with ice, and in that tinkling sound of the cubes as they circle around in a vortex, chilling the crystal-clear liquid and frosting the pitcher or glass. Drinks that are ideal for stirring are those made of clear ingredients, like the Gin Martini or Manhattan, and those containing champagne or other carbonated bever-age. Shaking anything with bubbles will flatten the effervescence as well as cloud clear, pure liquors. To stir a drink, put a handful of ice cubes (about 5 or 6) in a martini pitcher, pour the liquor over the ice, and stir firmly, from the bottom up, to chill. Pour into a chilled glass. Ice cubes are preferable over cracked ice, as the pinched lip on the pitcher won't always hold cracked ice back. The mixing glass that comes as the bottom half of a Boston shaker can also be used to stir drinks; you will need to fit a hawthorn strainer (page 20) snugly over the mouth of the glass to restrain the ice. When stirring a drink made with champagne or other carbonated beverage, always use a glass stirring rod or long-handled wooden spoon, and never a metal bar spoon, as metal will cause a reaction that dissipates carbonation.

BLENDER DRINKS

Preparing cocktails in a blender is a quick, easy way to combine a multitude of ingredients, and larger quantities, with ice. The blender is pressed into service when you need to purée solid fruit ingredients, pulverize ice for a frozen drink or smoothie, or blend large quantities all at once to serve more than two people. Great for tropical drinks, a blender really comes in handy for large batches of Margaritas and Piña Coladas. When it comes to frozen drinks, with all the ice, it's always a good rule of thumb to increase all the ingredients slightly, as the slushy ice tends to dilute the drink more than in other methods of chilling. Crushed ice is best for the blender, since it is easier on the motor and blades, especially if the blender is not an industrial model. The ice should go in first, then the ingredients. Blend at a low speed initially, then increase it to high after a few seconds.

FLAMING DRINKS

This technique is frequently used for hot drinks and for a few cold cocktails that call for spirits with high alcohol levels. Extreme caution is required due to the flammable nature of alcohol, and these drinks are really best left to the professionals. Most types of alcohol must first be heated, at which point they begin to vaporize and become extremely flammable; otherwise, they will not ignite. To be ignited cold, the alcohol level must be very high, at least 100 to 151 proof. Professionals always use a very small amount, about ¾ ounce, which controls the flame size, and they stand as far from the flaming as possible, igniting the alcohol with a very long fireplace-style wooden match.

A few cautionary tips: Never pour alcohol from a bottle into a mixture that is already flaming (whether in a flaming cup or chafing dish), or the flames could back blow, igniting the entire bottle. Never bend or hover over a flaming drink or dish. Never leave open bottles near an open flame.

FLOATING

The technique of floating one liquid on top of another is easy to master with a touch of patience and a spoon. It is usually called for in drinks using cream or a liqueur and involves slowly pouring a small amount of spirit (usually a liqueur or cream) over the surface of a drink so that it floats, or sits, atop another liquid without being mixed. The customary technique is to slowly pour the liquid over the rounded back of a bar spoon, keeping the spoon as close to the layer below without touching it.

A pousse-café usually layers equal amounts of 3 to 6 liqueurs, with the heaviest on the bottom and the lightest on top. Many find that the multiple layers of liqueurs are sometimes more visually pleasing than the resulting flavor. The point is to be able to enjoy each one separately as you sip through the layers. Pousse-cafés can be made ahead of time and refrigerated.

CHILLING WINE

Champagne and most white wines and sweet wines need to be sufficiently chilled to be properly enjoyed. One very important point to remember— never freeze champagne, or any beverage with carbonation, or it will explode. There are two easy ways to go about chilling your bottles of wine.

------- THE SLOW CHILL -------

This method takes a few hours, so place your bottle of champagne, white wine, or dessert wine in the refrigerator at least two to three hours before serving.

------- FAST COOLING -------

Fill an ice bucket with a combination of ice cubes and water, and leave the bottle in the bucket. This method takes 15 to 30 minutes. To help accelerate the chilling, smoothly turn the bottle back and forth, agitating it in the ice water mixture.

You can also purchase special cooling jackets and vacuum bottle coolers (see "wine cooler" in the Glossary of Bar Equipment, page 22).

EXTRACTING CITRUS JUICE

A multitude of drinks are made with citrus juice. Here are a few techniques that are handy in extracting juice from limes, lemons, oranges, tangerines, or grapefruit. Rolling citrus fruit before juicing helps loosen and separate the juice from the firm pith inside the fruit. Just roll the fruit on a hard surface, pressing firmly with your palm.

Another way to extract more juice is to set the citrus fruit in hot water for about half an hour. Then cut it in half with a fruit or paring knife and squeeze with your hand or use a citrus reamer or citrus press.

Garnishes & Rims

COCKTAIL AESTHETICS AND DRINK DECOR

WHETHER YOU ARE SERVING AN ELEGANT MARTINI, an amber-hued Manhattan, a jewel-toned elixir, or a tropical cooler, a drink seems positively naked without some visual accompaniment. Even the smallest of citrus peels will add a lovely fragrant dynamic to the drink. The garnish is where you can really get creative, and it's the perfect visual cue to help set the tone of your cocktail. Even the most stoic of drinkers can appreciate artfully done garnishes, so don't always settle for the standard and pedestrian orange slice and maraschino cherry.

A garnish can be as simple as a fresh sprig of mint or a refreshing and elegant thin slice of citrus floating on top. Equally elegant and sculptural are long, spiral peels, and for the more elaborate flora and fauna traditional of tropical cocktails, edible flowers give an exotic touch—and can be found in the produce section of many grocery stores. For a delicate aromatic experience, place a few sprigs of a fresh herb, like rosemary, basil, or sage, into your next Vodka Martini or Tequila and Tonic. Or take a more esoteric and extreme route with your Martini, replacing the pedestrian olive with an octopus tentacle, anchovy, Hershey's Kiss, mini pickled corn, or jalepeño pepper.

When it comes to the classic cocktails, typically any drinks with brown goods (such as whiskey) and sweet vermouth will have a maraschino cherry garnish; a drink made with a dry vermouth will usually have a citrus (lemon or orange) twist. The contemporary cocktail garnish may need to be elegantly minimal, such as a thin slice of lime floating on the surface, but others, such as the tropical cocktail genre, call for more elaborate posturing. Whichever aesthetic path you choose, be it a single floating rose petal or a full-on shish kebob of flora and plastic fauna on a Honolulu Lulu, your garnish should complement your drink with style. It should always be the last step, after the drink has been prepared and poured, and should be attended to with style and ceremony, whether you're running a lemon peel around the rim and twisting it over the top of the drink or delicately balancing a skewer on the side.

Cocktails give you an open invitation to embellish, to be creative and whimsical, artistic and elegantly romantic. A frosty chilled glass rimmed with a dusting of sweet cocoa, sea salt with citrus zest, or jewel-like turbinado sugar adds a fabulous flavor dimension to the cocktail, as well as visual intrigue. A perfectly placed orchid on the rim or fresh fruit beautifully arranged on a skewer creates sophisticated elegance with the utmost simplicity. A single citrus spiral winding through a crystal clear Martini fans the desire to sip blissfully away. This hands-on guide to cocktail styling covers all the essentials, from preparing a simple lemon twist to spirals, wheels, and slices, to more elaborate cocktail garnishing and frosted rims.

GARNISHES

------- THE CITRUS GARNISH -------

Considering that many drinks are citrus based (lemon, lime, or orange), it's not surprising that a citrus garnish is frequently used as a natural complement. Choose unblemished citrus fruit, and wash before preparing. When cutting citrus peel for twists, spirals, or zest, avoid as much of the bitter white pith as possible.

❧ **ZEST**   Grate the shiny outer peel of the citrus fruit into zest by using a fine grater or a zester (a sharp metal tool with a row of tiny holes at the end) to scrape the outer peel. You can infuse syrups and teas, rim glasses, or sprinkle zest over hot, cream-topped drinks.

❧ **TWISTS**   With a sharp paring knife or vegetable peeler, remove 2-inch-long strips of peel lengthwise from the citrus fruit. Twist the peel, with the rind side down, holding it just above the drink to release the aromatic oil over the surface. Then run it around the rim and drop it into the drink.

❧ **SPIRALS**   Citrus peel spirals add a delicate elegance to any cocktail. The easiest way to remove a long, thin peel is with a vegetable peeler or sharp paring knife. Starting at one end of the fruit, pare off a continuous peel, slowly working your way around the fruit, to make one long spiral. Twist it around your finger, and then slowly drop it, letting it spiral down into the drink.

------- **FRUIT SLICES AND WHEELS** -------

From the traditional citrus wheels to the more exotic slice of star fruit, kiwi, blood orange, or kumquat, fruit wheels can be decoratively appealing, adding color and texture. The basic method for preparing slices or wheels of fruit is with a sharp paring knife. Cut off both ends of the fruit. Placing the fruit on its side, cut crosswise segments approximately ¼ inch wide. To use as a garnish, cut a slice in the wheel so you can position it on the edge of the glass.

❧ **BANANA SLICES**   Prepare the slices just before serving. You may choose to leave the yellow, unblemished peel on for color, slicing the banana crosswise at a slight angle. To prevent discoloration, dip the slices in lemon juice.

------- **KUMQUAT "FLOWERS"** -------

This flowerlike garnish made from a tiny member of the citrus family adds an aromatic ornament to fizzy citrus-based drinks. To prepare a festive kumquat flower, using a sharp paring knife, start at one end of the kumquat and cut 3 or 4 sections of the peel away from the fruit, leaving the peels attached at the bottom end. Peel the sections back like petals, making an elegant and exotic garnish. Skewer a few with a cocktail pick, and balance the pick on the rim of the glass.

------- **MELON** -------

Melon garnishes can add a sculptural element to the rim of that Midori-green cocktail. Cut watermelon, with its dark green rind, or the cool green of a honeydew, into wedges or slices 1 inch wide and 2 to 3 inches long, and place on the edge of a glass. To make a colorful assemblage of melon balls, use a melon scoop to remove spheres from cantaloupe, honeydew, and watermelon, and spear onto wooden skewers or cocktail picks.

------- **COCONUT** -------

Grate the flesh of the coconut, brown skin and all, and sprinkle on top of drinks, or cut the coconut into ¼-inch segments with a sharp paring knife, making a partial cut in the slice so you can position it on the rim. Or add a wedge of coconut to a cocktail pick of fruits, for the perfect garnish to accent those potent tropical concoctions.

❧ **COCONUT CUPS** Sometimes you just have to go all out, island-style, and give that Tobago Coconut Flip the cup it deserves. Look for the "easy crack" coconuts that have been scored around the center to obtain the best, hollowed-out coconut half. With a pointed, sharp instrument and a hammer, pierce the eyes, making holes so the coconut water can drain out into a glass. Tap the coconut shell with a hammer at the scored line to open. For easy-prep "coconut cups," place the drained coconut into an oven preheated to 350°F for 10 minutes. The flesh will shrink from the shell, making it easier to extract.

------- **PINEAPPLE** -------

In the realm of garnishes, the pineapple is a very versatile fruit and can be used from top to bottom. Incorporate the spiny leaves as a green accent with other colorful fruit garnishes. Lay the pineapple on its side and cut ½-inch slices crosswise to create pineapple wheels with the rind left on for texture. Or quarter the slices for smaller pineapple wedges.

ෆ **PINEAPPLE SHELL** A festive way to enjoy a rum punch. Cut off the spiny top of a pineapple and, using a sharp knife and spoon, scoop out the flesh, leaving the shell intact. Refrigerate until ready to use the shell as a cup. Save the fruit and juice as a base for future drinks.

------- **FLOWERS** -------

Edible flowers, such as nasturtiums, orchids, violets, borage, rose petals, orange blossoms, and hibiscus, add an exotic island touch to any tropical drink. Gently rinse the flower or petals, and float them on top of the cocktail, or skewer them with a cocktail pick and set it on the rim, or attach them to the stem of a glass with a bit of florist's wire.

You can also decorate a drink with larger orchids or hibiscus by attaching them to the stem of a glass with a bit of florist's wire.

------- **FRUIT SKEWERS** -------

Place three different kinds of fruits, vegetables, or flowers in a pleasing combination on a cocktail toothpick or sword. Balance on the rim of the drink or drop the spear into the drink. Be inspired by the flavors and colors in the drink, such as a lemon and orange slice skewered with a few violets for a Parfait Amour–based drink, or a wedge of pineapple, a wheel of lime, and a segment of tangerine to garnish a tropical drink.

------- **SUGARED SLICES** -------

Popular with the more contemporary, sweet cocktails, these are an easy way to add elegance to a sugar-rimmed cocktail. Simply roll a peeled slice of citrus (such as a lemon, lime, tangerine, or blood orange) or perhaps a strawberry in a few tablespoons of granulated sugar. Cut a slit in the middle and slide it onto the rim to garnish.

------- **COCKTAIL ACCESSORIES** -------

Cocktails are by definition festive, and there are endless possibilities to set the mood, from the ornamental paper umbrella to a glass with hanging plastic monkeys. A wide variety of kitschy drink accessories are available to add visual fun, such as plastic swordfish, monkeys, mermaids, or lizards that you can slip into a classic Gin and Tonic, float in a Martini, or poise on the edge of a green elixir. Anything unexpected will liven up even the most serious of cocktails.

FROSTING RIMS

Rim a frosty, chilled glass with a dusting of something sweet or tart, textural and colorful, and you bring visual appeal and instant elegance to a drink. The added accent not only embellishes your favorite cocktail but gives it an exciting multidimensional flavor.

The basic method of rimming a glass can be applied to a variety of ingredients. Ideally the glass should be chilled, but an unchilled glass will work in a pinch.

------- **BASIC METHOD** -------

1) Rub a lemon or lime wedge once around the rim of the glass to moisten it.

2) Pour 5 to 6 tablespoons of an ingredient (such as salt or sugar) onto a small plate or a small, wide bowl, and shake gently to distribute evenly.

3) Turn the glass upside down and set the rim in the ingredient of choice. Gently turn the glass back and forth, to coat the rim completely, and shake off any excess.

4) Carefully pour in your cocktail, so as not to disturb the rim.

------- **SALT RIM** -------

Moisten the rim with lime or lemon juice, using sea salt for flavor and texture, and proceed according to the basic method.

------- **SUGAR RIM** -------

A touch of sweetness is a great addition to a tart cocktail such as a Sidecar or Lemon Drop. Moisten the rim with a citrus wedge, and use superfine sugar for your rim, proceeding according to the basic method. Powdered sugar gives a delicate, elegant touch, while turbinado sugar can give a bejeweled texture, a perfect accompaniment when you are serving chocolate- or coffee-based cocktails.

------- **SALT AND SUGAR RIM** -------

For those who prefer a sweet-and-sour combination, this is a super rim for Margaritas or Daiquiris. Moisten the rim with a lime and combine 3 tablespoons of sea salt and 3 tablespoons of granulated sugar in a small, wide bowl. Prepare according to the basic method.

------- **CITRUS ZEST RIMS** -------

A rim of salt and lime zest enhances the usual salt-only Margarita rim, and mixing orange, lemon, or lime zest with sugar for rimming gives a flavor boost to your favorite citrus-based cocktail. Moisten the rim of the glass with a complementary juice or liqueur. Mix 4 tablespoons of granulated sugar or salt with 3 tablespoons of finely grated orange, lemon, or lime zest. Proceed according to the basic method. Depending on the size of the glass, the mixture will cover 3 or 4 rims.

------- COCONUT RIM -------

A festively tropical rim of finely grated fresh coconut or dried, unsweetened coconut adds a textural touch to coconut-based drinks. Dip the rim into a wide, shallow bowl filled with ¼ cup of a complementary flavored liqueur such as Cointreau or Chambord. Prepare according to the basic method. Note that ½ cup of coconut flakes will coat 3 or 4 glass rims.

------- GRATED CHOCOLATE OR COCOA RIMS -------

You may want to rim your drink with a few tablespoons of finely grated semisweet chocolate. The perfect complement to a drink with lemon or orange flavors, the chocolate adds sweetness to those slightly more bitter espresso- or coffee-liqueur-based drinks. A cocoa rim is a fine addition to cream or ice cream drinks. Just a few tablespoons of unsweetened cocoa powder in a small, wide bowl will coat several glasses. You also might want to try adding half a teaspoon of nutmeg to your cocoa powder.

Infusions & Syrups

FOR THE DREAMER AND THE DRIVEN, when someone else's over-the-counter concoctions will not suffice, it's time to get innovative and adventurous. This section contains recipes for homemade spirits and syrups infused with fruits and herbs, as well as the essential simple syrup and sweet-and-sour recipes.

INFUSIONS

Infused liquors may seem like the new creative expression in the realm of cocktail mixology, what with all the various commercially flavored vodkas, rums, and even gins on the market. But this method of infusing neutral spirits with flavoring agents such as herbs, spices, and fruits has been around for centuries. The chilly Northern Hemisphere, from the Netherlands to Russia, is steeped in a long history of home-prepared infusions made not only to mask subpar spirits, but also as herbal medicinal remedies.

Vodka is the ideal blank canvas for infusing a neutral-tasting spirit that can easily take on the flavors of an ingredient. But you can also infuse rum with complementary flavors such as vanilla or tropical fruits such as banana or pineapple. Give tequila an additional fiery bite with hot peppers, or use strawberries for a fruity flavor. Always start with good-quality spirits and fresh herbs, fruits, and spices. The spirit is interchangeable in any of these versatile recipes. Infusions are surprisingly easy to make, and the end result adds an exceptionally wonderful depth of flavor to any spirit.

Here are a few basic guidelines:

Use a clean, large (at least 1.5 liter) glass container with an airtight lid for your infusion. Save your original liquor bottle; you will need it to strain the infused mixture into.

Infusion times vary, depending on the ingredient. Strong flavors like lemon take less time to steep (24 to 48 hours), while milder flavors such as raspberries or pineapple may take 1 to 3 weeks to fully infuse. When the infusion is ready, place a funnel in the bottle, and pour the infused spirit through a fine-mesh wire strainer. Some ingredients may turn bitter if left too long, or may break down to the point that you'll need to line the strainer with a coffee filter or cheesecloth. Infusions are best stored in the refrigerator; chilling helps preserve the flavors longer than if kept at room temperature.

------- **RUM INFUSIONS** -------

These infusions have a tropical bent. Enjoy sipping them straight to enjoy the fine nuance of flavor, or use them to add a new dimension to your favorite Daiquiri or punch.

Pineapple-Infused Rum

1 whole fresh pineapple
One 750-ml bottle good-quality light rum

With a sharp knife, peel off the rind and core the pineapple. Cut the pineapple into small cubes. Place the cubed pineapple in a large glass container, add the rum, and cap tightly.

Let stand at room temperature for 1 week, shaking gently every couple of days.

Refrigerate the mixture for another week, shaking it gently every couple of days. Taste for the preferred flavor intensity, steeping for another week if it needs more time. Strain the mixture into the original bottle. Cap tightly, label, and refrigerate until ready to serve.

Coconut-Infused Rum

3 cups freshly grated coconut
One 750-ml bottle good-quality light rum

Place the coconut in a large glass container, add the rum, and cap tightly. Let stand at room temperature for 3 weeks, shaking gently every couple of days. Taste for the preferred flavor intensity, infusing for another week if it needs more time. Strain the mixture into the original bottle. Cap tightly, label, and refrigerate until ready to serve.

Vanilla-Infused Rum

4 vanilla beans, broken into small pieces
One 750-ml bottle silver or gold rum

Add the vanilla bean pieces to the bottle of rum and cap tightly. Let stand for at least a week, shaking gently every couple of days. Leave the vanilla in the bottle to infuse indefinitely, and refrigerate. When ready to use, slowly strain the vanilla-infused rum with a fine-mesh wire strainer into the jigger or glass.

These infusions make for very aromatic Vodka Martinis. Infuse your liter of vodka with 2 cups of fresh mint or ½ cup of fresh rosemary or 2 vanilla beans. For a citrus version, add the peel from a large lemon, orange, tangerine, or lime. For spicy clove vodka, infuse with 25 whole cloves. For a coffee bean vodka, infuse with 20 coffee beans. Steep for 24 to 48 hours, as needed. For berry-flavored vodka, add 2 cups of fresh strawberries, raspberries, or blackberries, and steep for at least 1 week and up to 2 weeks, as needed.

Ginger Vodka   *The spicy ginger flavor adds a Pan-Asian elegance to any cocktail.*

1 cup thinly sliced ginger
One 750-ml bottle good-quality vodka

Place the ginger in a large glass container, add the vodka, and cap tightly. Let stand at room temperature for 48 hours, shaking gently occasionally. Taste for the preferred flavor intensity, infusing for up to 4 days if needed. Strain the mixture back into the original vodka bottle, cap, and refrigerate until needed.

Floral-Herbal Infusion   *This vodka-infused bouquet has a delicate, fragrant flavor, perfect for a Martini. Gin is also a great choice for this infusion. Fresh petals are preferable, but you can use dried flower petals, available at health food stores. If using dried flowers, you need only ¼ cup of each type of flower.*

1 cup fresh hibiscus petals
1 cup fresh orange blossom petals
1 cup fresh violet petals
¼ cup fresh lavender
1 small piece vanilla bean
One 750-ml bottle good-quality vodka

Place the flower petals and the vanilla bean into a large glass container, add the vodka, and cap tightly. Let stand at room temperature for 2 weeks, shaking gently every 3 to 4 days. Taste for the preferred flavor intensity, infusing for up to 4 weeks if needed. Strain the mixture through a coffee filter back into the original bottle. Cap, label, and refrigerate until needed.

For a fabulous flavor treat, substitute tequila in the Vanilla-Infused Rum recipe in this section.

Pepper Tequila *The hottest thing to hit tequila since the worm—a spicy addition perfect for a Bloody Maria.*

1 serrano chile pepper, stemmed, quartered lengthwise, and seeded
1 jalepeño chile pepper, stemmed, quartered lengthwise, and seeded
1 red chile pepper, stemmed, quartered lengthwise, and seeded
1 liter good-quality silver tequila

Place the peppers into a large glass container, add the tequila, and cap tightly. Let stand at room temperature for 2 days, shaking gently occasionally. Strain the tequila back into the original bottle. Cap tightly, label, and refrigerate until needed.

Strawberry Tequila *This infusion adds a sweet strawberry flavor to the basic Margarita.*

3 cups fresh strawberries, hulled and sliced
One 750-ml bottle good-quality tequila

Place the strawberries in a large glass container, add the tequila, and cap tightly. Let stand at room temperature for 1 week. Taste for the preferred flavor intensity, allowing it to infuse for another week if needed. Do not allow it to infuse any longer than 3 weeks, or a bitter flavor will result. Strain the infused mixture back into the original bottle. Cap tightly, label, and refrigerate until needed.

SYRUPS

When it comes to mixing a superb drink, fresh, quality ingredients are essential. Some flavored syrups and infused spirits are readily available in stores, but when you make your own, the flavor you gain is worth the effort.

Infusing syrups and spirits with the essence of a fruit, spice, or herb is surprisingly easy and opens up a multitude of possibilities for drink creativity.

Homemade syrups are a convenient and quick way to add the essence of a fruit or a spice to a drink. Dissolving faster than granulated sugar, syrups blend with ease in mixed drinks. They can be made ahead of time and stored in the refrigerator, where they will keep for up to 2 weeks.

Sweet-and-Sour *This is one of those "cut-to-the-chase" ingredients used by professional bartenders. It is an integral part of many drinks, including the Margarita. Covering both the sweet and citrus factors at the same time, it is very handy to have on hand. There is no comparison between the store-bought mix and the marvelous quality provided by this freshly made sweet-and-sour. For the best flavor, use spring or filtered water instead of tap water. This recipe makes enough for approximately 10 drinks.*

MAKES 2 CUPS

½ cup cooled simple syrup (recipe follows)

¾ cup fresh lime juice

¾ cup fresh lemon juice

¼ cup water

Pour all the ingredients into a clean glass jar with a tight-fitting lid. Close the lid tightly, and shake the contents together until well mixed. Refrigerate until needed. It will keep for a week to 10 days.

Basic Simple Syrup *Also known as sugar syrup, this is an essential ingredient in many drinks, as it requires no dissolving or excessive stirring to incorporate, unlike granulated sugar. You can multiply the formula given here or cut it in half. When stored in a clean, covered jar and refrigerated, the syrup will keep for up to 1 month.*

MAKES 2 CUPS

1 cup water

2 cups sugar

In a small saucepan, bring the water to a boil. Remove the pan from the heat and add the sugar. Stir until the sugar is completely dissolved. Cool completely before using or refrigerating. Pour into a clean glass jar, cap tightly, and store in the refrigerator until needed.

The following flavor variations can be used with the Basic Simple Syrup recipe. Add the flavor ingredients when the sugar has completely dissolved and the mixture is still hot. Once the syrup has cooled, strain it through a fine-mesh metal strainer into a clean glass jar. Cap and refrigerate for up to two weeks.

- Ginger syrup: Add 2 tablespoons fresh, finely grated ginger to the hot syrup mixture.

- Kumquat syrup: Add 10 small kumquats, sliced in half, to the hot simple syrup mixture. Allow them to infuse the syrup for 45 minutes, until cool. Save the poached kumquats in another container and put in the freezer to use as flavored "ice cubes" in your favorite exotic drink.

- Orange syrup: Add 1/2 cup grated orange zest to the hot syrup.

- Mint or basil syrup: Add 1/2 cup fresh mint or basil leaves to the hot syrup.

- Vanilla syrup: Add 1 vanilla bean to the hot syrup.

- Lemon or lime syrup: Add 1/2 cup grated lemon or lime zest to the hot syrup.

- Cinnamon syrup: Add 1 tablespoon ground cinnamon to the hot syrup.

- Clove syrup: Add 1 tablespoon ground cloves to the hot syrup.

- Tea syrup: Replace the water with strongly steeped tea (from black to green, Earl Grey to Red Zinger).

- Lemongrass syrup: Add 2 stalks fresh lemongrass, cut into 1/2-inch pieces, to the hot syrup.

- Hibiscus syrup: Replace the water with strongly steeped hibiscus tea.

BRANDY SNIFTER

.04 ~

Smooth Entertaining

Seemingly effortless entertaining takes planning. So for those who love to entertain but are a bit overwhelmed by the prospect of having a crowd clamoring in a large conga-sized line for drinks, here are some party-throwing tips and suggestions that can assist you through any event. From shaking and pouring multiple cocktails for a small group to mixing pitchers of Sangria and large-scale bowls of punch with floating ice sculpture, these organizational preparation tips are geared to free the host or hostess up to schmooze the night away. Of course, you may decide that the scale of the party has gotten too large to handle alone and seek the assistance of a caterer as well as a bartender.

Whatever it takes to allow you more quality time to socialize, relax, and enjoy your guests is what it's really all about anyway.

CHOOSING A THEME

The cocktail is the liquid asset to any event, looked forward to with anticipation by thirsty guests. What better way to wow them than to entice them to your party with the promise of a few fabulous cocktails built around a personal celebration or special occasion? Or perhaps you are simply looking for a reason to have a party, even if it hangs on the mere premise of a theme.

Choosing a theme not only serves as a festive excuse to throw a party, but also will help the drink ideas to flow forth and fall into place. Typically, the weather outside and time of year are strong incentives for certain themes, inspiring everything from hot and sultry tropical soirees and patio parties to festive winter hot toddy holiday parties or rainy-day cocktail hour perk-ups. Perhaps a favorite travel locale or classic movie will conjure a theme that might just add the right evocative ambience and tone to the party.

Regardless of your theme, every party requires a little planning and panache to ensure a successful event. Get started by sending out invitations about two weeks in advance so guests have time to get it on their schedule. You don't necessarily have to get elaborate or go all out—it can simply be a matter of an evocative and fun invitation, enticing your friends with the lure of sublimely refreshing cocktails.

MOOD MUSIC

Music can make or break the mood, as it sets the ambience and tone of the party. Choose sounds that fit your theme or the mood you are after. Whether you are going for a sophisticated urban affair with Frankie, or the sultry Brazilian sounds of Bebel Gilberto, or perhaps a classic cocktail party sound of jazz piano, or funky and fun with retro Mancini, or tropical lounge from the fifties. Whatever you choose to play, be sure to have it all queued up and ready to go.

CHOOSING A DRINK MENU

As much as I take pride in my cocktails, I hate missing out on all the fun that might be happening while I'm shaking away. The motivating factor for me when choosing which cocktails to serve is the need to comfortably accommodate everyone with ease—and that means offering your guests just a few tantalizing cocktail options to help narrow down the mixing and shaking time.

Serving relatively quick and easy cocktails, such as the Sidecar, Cosmo, Daiquiri, and Margarita, even if you add a few exciting variations, can be done without too much extra fuss, and most new cocktails are variations on these classics anyway. For smaller groups of two to four people, you may even want to attempt a few of the more elaborate cocktails, such as the Mai Tai or layered pousse-café drinks. A large cocktail shaker will easily handle two cocktails at a time without losing the balance of the proportions.

One libation inherently geared for entertaining is Sangria. One of my personal favorites, it is easy to make, and you can quickly whip up a fruity pitcher or two a few hours ahead of time and have them chilling in the refrigerator until guests arrive. Pitchers of champagne-based Mimosas and Bellinis are also great candidates for entertaining with ease. The oranges can be juiced or the white peach purée prepared in advance. When the guests arrive, all you need to do is combine them in a pitcher with chilled champagne.

Blender drinks are another relatively quick and easy option when there are more than three or four guests. They can be made in larger volumes to accommodate more guests, especially if the idea of shaking drinks all night doesn't appeal. To accelerate the proceedings, and to add more chill to your frozen, fruity drinks, simply precut the chosen fruit and store it in the freezer until ready to use.

If you are expecting a crowd larger than six to eight people, you might want to consider a punch. Punches are the ideal libation for relaxed entertaining when larger groups require larger quantities of refreshment. Chill the ingredients before you start mixing to help retain the chill factor once poured. Some punches can be conveniently mixed ahead of time and refrigerated. Punches can be an elegant centerpiece to an occasion when presented in an attractive vessel, such as a beautiful large glass bowl, to show off the colorful liquid and floating fruit. A colorful glazed pottery bowl is also a good choice.

------- **OTHER BEVERAGES** -------

A variety of refreshments should be on hand for those who prefer beverages with lower alcohol levels. Have a selection of beer and dry white wine chilling in the refrigerator, as well as a few bottles of red on hand. Guests who would like a cocktail but wish to drink in moderation could be offered low-proof cocktails. Campari and Soda or other tall, refreshing coolers, made with a low amount of alcohol and lots of fresh juice, a bit of sugar or sweetness, and a fizzy topper such as champagne or ginger ale, are fine options.

While many of your guests may be enjoying more spirited concoctions, some will choose not to indulge. Keep everyone's thirst quenched by stocking up on plenty of nonalcoholic beverages such as bottled and sparkling water, sparkling soda, or a variety of juices.

A selection of sparkling beverages such as Orangina, Jamaican ginger beer, or Martinelli's sparkling cider will add a celebratory touch for those who prefer to abstain from champagne. Or better yet, shake a few elegant "mocktails" made with fresh juices, a dash of Italian syrup, orgeat, or fresh mint, and serve up in a chilled cocktail glass.

∾ *IF YOU DRINK , DON'T DRIVE, DON'T EVEN PUTT.* —DEAN MARTIN

RESPONSIBLE REVELRY

Thoughtful hosts will not only have nonalcoholic and low-alcoholic beverages, but will practice the fine art of etiquette and hospitality, helping guests avoid becoming inebriated by serving lighter drinks as the night progresses. That way, everyone can have an enjoyable time.

Of course, your party will be considered the event of the season, but remember that some of your guests' decidedly cheerful dispositions at the end of the evening may be more a result of their enjoying spirited concoctions than of their festive surroundings. Keep an eye out for guests who don't look as though they can drive, and arrange a ride or call a cab for them if needed.

SERVING FOOD

Always offer food with cocktails. Food not only can be the perfect accompaniment to a cocktail but also plays a fundamental role in absorbing the alcohol, which keeps everyone nourished as well as upright. A cocktail party needs only a few choice hors d'oeuvres, tapas, mixed nuts, pretzels, and other finger foods to balance and complement the cocktails. Ideally, they should be bite-size or small enough to fit on a cocktail napkin or small plate.

PARTY PREPRODUCTION

Party preparation is crucial for everything to go smoothly, and that means gathering all the ingredients ahead of time and prepping what you can in advance, before your first guest arrives. You can have all the garnishes cut, the juice squeezed, the rims of cocktail glasses sugared, the glassware chilled, and batches of drinks mixed and chilled in pitchers in advance, so you can relax and be happy you did so once the party hits full swing.

------- **FRESH JUICES** -------

Fresh juices will make all the difference in your cocktails; they are worth the effort required, and your guests will be so appreciative as they sip their sublime drinks. Have lots of fresh juice presqueezed and ready to go, to avoid a scenario of desperately juicing citrus while a growing line of guests impatiently wait for that fabulous Margarita or Daiquiri you've promised. A citrus reamer comes in handy, but an electric juicer is even better for large volumes. If you prefer shortcuts to the fresh-squeezed scenario, these days you can buy freshly squeezed juice, a fine substitute and good to have as a backup if you run out of fruit. Frozen fruit concentrate is also perfectly suitable in a pinch; great for blender drinks, it can conveniently be stored in the freezer.

If you are planning to serve muddled citrus drinks, such as Caipirinhas, preslice all the wedges of fruit an hour ahead of time, to help speed up the cocktail-making process.

------- **SERVING WINE** -------

Be sure to have the white wine and champagne chilling in the refrigerator a few hours before the party. Depending on the occasion, you can reasonably assume you'll need about half a bottle of wine per person as the night progresses, usually served before and during a meal. Be sure to accompany the wine with glasses of water, frequently refreshed. Also have on hand at least two different wine glasses to accommodate both white and red wine and, of course, if you'll be serving champagne, chilled champagne flutes.

------- **PREPARING GLASSWARE** -------

Glassware showcases your cocktails and should be sparkling clean. Avoid using plastic; it sets the wrong tone, and glass makes your drinks look much more refreshing and will keep the drinks chilled longer. To be sure those glasses are nice and frosty for your event, save room in your refrigerator or freezer (if it's not your fine crystal), and have the glassware chilling in advance. If you've run out refrigerator room or the prechilled glasses have been used, the quick-chill method (see page 53) will suitably chill them.

Be sure to gauge the amount of glassware needed—you'll typically need two styles per person—to avoid having to resort to other, possibly unattractive options. For large parties, a restaurant supply store will have an extensive selection of various styles, a large quantity, and affordable prices. Another option is to rent your glassware from a party supply store.

------- **STOCKING ICE** -------

Always stock the freezer with plenty of ice. Ice is probably the least expensive and most essential item you will need for your celebration. To keep from running out midparty, stock your freezer with premade ice cubes and a few bags of crushed ice to help keep those fabulous drinks chilled. For larger events, fill a cooler with ice, and have it conveniently handy near your bar setup for quick, easy access.

If you are serving a punch, big blocks of ice are best. These are easily made by filling a small metal pan, bowl, plastic container, or, more festively, a Bundt pan with filtered water and then freezing it. Blocks and rings are a great showcase for fruit or edible flowers frozen in the ice.

------- **GARNISHES** -------

Depending on the drinks you choose for your event, whether elegant Martinis, tropical blender drinks, or tall, fizzy coolers, the garnish may be a small detail, but it can set the tone of your cocktail party. People love to be visually wowed, so take the garnish as an opportunity to evocatively exude the theme of your event, having fun with the creative options. Edible flowers give an exotic touch, adding that illusion of equatorial romance. Elegant and sculptural long spiral peels give clear, shimmery Martinis a refreshingly urbane effect, or go for the more elaborate flora and fruit to set a tropical theme. The garnish can be as simple as an aromatic fresh sprig of mint or a refreshing and elegant thin slice of citrus floating on top.

Plan to cut the garnish, and assemble if needed on cocktail picks, an hour or so in advance, and store them in the refrigerator. Any earlier, and the cut fruit may start to wilt, dry out, or brown.

------- **SETTING UP FOR COCKTAILS** -------

Whether you have a bar set up in the kitchen or in the main event room, your "home bar" will be ready for action. You may wish your bar had all the bells and whistles—a retro glass martini pitcher and stir rod, chrome vacuum-topped ice bucket, and an easy-peel zester—but in my experience, you really need only a few crucial bar tools to have a functional bar setup.

A cocktail shaker, a jigger, a sharp paring knife, a handheld citrus juice extractor, and a good blender, and other bar basics such as a cutting board for garnishes, a bar spoon, and a fun bar towel, will see you through even the most elaborate of drinks.

An ice bucket with tongs is not only a nice touch as a sleek icon of the cocktail presentation, but functional and convenient for serving drinks at smaller gatherings, and it allows your guests to help themselves without having to grab a handful of freezing, wet cubes.

Creative decor, inventive invitations, the proper menu, mood music, and, of course, the perfect cocktail—your own personal flair can take it from there. Most importantly, your gala is best enjoyed with plenty of laid-back attitude.

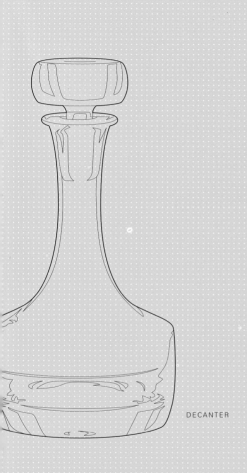

DECANTER

.05 ~

Spirits & Drinks

rkling wine / beer & sake / brandy

THE COMPREHENSIVE GUIDE

ULTIMATE
Bar Book

TO OVER 1,000 COCKTAILS

gin / rum / tequila / vodka / whis

Beer & Sake

BEER

∼ *IN THE BOWLING ALLEY OF TOMORROW, THERE WILL EVEN BE MACHINES THAT WEAR RENTAL SHOES AND THROW THE BALL FOR YOU. YOUR SOLE FUNCTION WILL BE TO DRINK BEER.* —DAVE BARRY, *American humorist*

THIS HOP-HAPPY BREW MADE FROM GRAINS is one of the most ancient forms of fermented beverage. First enjoyed by the Egyptians, who were brewing beer 6,000 years ago, it was eventually brewed by ancient cultures throughout the rest of the world. These early beers were only a vague facsimile of the beer we are familiar with today. The crucial inclusion of hops in the brew wasn't introduced until the 15th century, by the Dutch, not only as a flavoring agent but also as a preservative, giving beer its characteristically assertive, bitter taste. The ancestral origins of Scottish whisky are deeply rooted in beer. Also made from malted barley, mashed, and fermented, it could be considered, at its most basic, a distillate of beer.

The beginning of modern beer goes back to 1295 in Bavaria and Bohemia, where King Wenceslas granted all the burghers of Pilsen the right to brew beer at home, using prized Bohemian hops. By 1516 the Germans were producing quality beers, by regulations decreed by the Elector of Bavaria that are still followed today. With their rich brewing history, they continue to make premium lagers and ales, and drink them—only the Czechs drink more beer than the Germans. Ireland and Britain are known for their robust porters and stouts, while the Germans are prolific at making fine wheat beer, and many sing the praises of Belgian lagers. In America, quality beers can be found from larger producers of premium beer, such as Samuel Adams, which makes a fine Boston lager, to the popular microbrewed beers, called "craft beers," producing high-quality brews with perfection and complex subtleties.

To make beer or ale, one must start with malted barley, which is roasted at varying temperatures to impart color and taste. Low heat produces a pale, light malt, and the longer the malt is roasted, the darker and more robust it is (and the darker the beer). The roasted barley is ground and blended to make a mash and then cooked with hops to produce a liquid called wort. The hops help to balance the sweet malt with their bitter flavor, as well as acting as a preservative. The wort is fermented with the addition of a particular type of yeast, which defines whether it becomes an ale or a beer. Lager is made by yeast working at lower temperatures, which ferments at the bottom of the vat, whereas ales are made by yeast that ferment best at the warmer temperatures at the top of the vats. After fermentation and a cooling and storing period of at least two to four weeks, the beer is filtered, bottled, frequently pasteurized (especially for canned beer), and capped.

The differences between lager and ale lie not only in the fermentation process but also in the flavor and texture. Ales are brewed at higher temperatures, are typically more robust and bitter, and are slightly less carbonated than lagers, with a higher alcohol content. Lagers are aged longer in refrigerated containers to gently ferment, ergo the name, which means "store" in German. Americans love their lagers, which are pale, light-bodied beers.

Lagers are cooled bottom-fermented beers that are aged (or lagered) longer than ales, a method producing a style that is light in flavor and body. Although the American-style lagers tend to be pale and weak flavored, there are many tawny-hued lagers with rich flavor. These come in several types:

Pilsner: The only true pilsner is brewed in Pilsen, in the Czech Republic, and is a light-colored, dry lager. Other beers called pilsner that are brewed elsewhere have simply been made in the pilsner style. American light lagers are an example of the pilsner style—pale with a slight flavor.

Bock: These beers are strong, dark amber in color, full-bodied, malty, and sometimes sweet, such as the stronger, darker version called double bock, or *dopplebock*. Sweet and malty, the *eisbock,* or ice bock, is made by freezing the brew. Once the ice is removed, the resulting beer has a higher alcohol content. A slightly sweet and malty bock called the *maibock* (May bock) is made in the spring, and *märzen,* which is made in March, is aged through the summer, for a slightly darker bock made in anticipation of the Oktoberfest.

Rauchbier: Similar to scotch in its smoky spiciness, this "smoked beer" gets its distinct flavor from the malted barley, which is dried over wood or peat fires.

Malt liquor: Any malt beverage that is deemed by state law to be too high in alcohol content to be defined as a beer. Barley wine, for example, is a sweet British-style beer, dark and strong, thick in texture, and usually too high in alcohol (typically 14 percent) to be designated an ale, and so it is considered a malt liquor.

Light beer: This term is used differently, depending on the country. In Europe it is used to distinguish between pale and dark lagers, while in the United States it is a brew with reduced calories and usually less alcohol.

Ice beer: Beer that has been lagered (or aged) at cold temperatures to the point of freezing. Once the ice is extracted, the remaining beer has a higher alcohol concentration, reaching 13 percent alcohol.

Under lagers: American microbrew-style lagers, which are more complex than standard American beer. Amber-colored, with a typically dark, rich, sweeter flavor, they are closer to a bock than to a pilsner.

------- STYLES OF ALE -------

Ales are produced by top fermentation brewing and are usually full-bodied, with a heavy hop flavor. From the famous English "bitter" beers and amber ales to the German and Belgian wheat beers, there are several types:

Amber ale: Made in various styles, usually heavier than lager, with medium to heavy hop flavor and a pale to deep amber color.

Bitter: Also known as amber ale. Made bitter with hops, it has an assertive, bitter hop flavor.

Brown ale: Sweet and dark in color.

Cream ale: A light-bodied ale, sometimes blended with a lager; low in alcohol.

Mild ale: Lightly hopped; a dark-colored sweeter ale.

Old ale: As the name suggests, this dark, sweet, sherrylike ale has had a longer aging period in the casks, or has aged in the bottle with the help of additional yeast.

Pale ale (or India pale ale, known as IPA): Light gold-colored ale with a "hoppy" flavor.

Porter: A light-bodied ale with a dark, rich color, this is basically a stout with a lower alcohol content. A distinctly British-style ale known for its rich, coffee-like flavor.

Scotch ale: A dark brown ale, slightly sweet, lightly hopped, and heavily flavored with malt, brewed in Scotland.

Stout: Originating in Great Britain, stout is made with dark-roasted grain for a full-bodied, dark black ale. It is very malty, hoppy, and high in alcohol content, with roasted barley added for color and flavor. It comes in three styles: Imperial stout is very strong and dry (not sweet), originally brewed for the

Russian czars. Irish stout is rather bitter, with a strong roasted barley flavor. Milk stout is, as the name suggests, milder than the Irish stout, and sweetened.

Trappist ale: Made since medieval times by the Trappist monks in Dutch and Belgian abbeys, these ales are strong, with a rich, fruity flavor, deep amber color, and high alcohol content.

------- **BELGIAN ALE** -------

Belgian ales are in a category all their own. Produced in the lambic style, they are made from wheat and barley, and are top-fermented, with wild airborne yeast for spontaneous fermentation. These sour beers are sometimes sweetened, such as the refreshing faro lambics or the winelike gueuze lambics, a complex blend of old and young lambics. Lambics are also flavored with fruits, such as the framboise lambics, made with raspberries, or the krick lambics, made with cherries.

------- **WHEAT BEER** -------

Also called Weissbier, Weizenbier, or white beer, this distinct style originated in Bavaria and is technically an ale, due to a top fermentation process. It is made from wheat grain and malted barley, to produce a light-colored, slightly tart ale with light hops. It comes in three basic varieties:

Hefeweizen: Named for a German term meaning "yeast-wheat," this is an unfiltered wheat beer that goes through a second fermentation in the bottle.

Kristalweizen: The yeast has been filtered out of this ale, to produce a clear beer.

Fruit wheat beers: Wheat beers that have been brewed with fruit.

------- **SERVING AND ENJOYING BEER** -------

Beer does not age well; the quality will diminish after six months in the bottle (three months in a can), and so it is best consumed as fresh as possible, soon after it is purchased. Affected by light and fluctuating temperatures, beer should be stored in a cool, dark place, ideally in the refrigerator.

Most light-style beers (such as lagers) should be served at about 45°F. Any colder and the beer will cloud and the flavor will suffer. Stronger ales should be served at about 55°F, so their more complex flavors can be savored. The British enjoy their ales at room temperature, which is a bit too warm for American tastes, as we typically prefer our beer and ale served ice cold. While many still find a light pilsner-style lager refreshing on a hot summer day, the pale ales and amber ales, especially those from the microbreweries, have become a very popular alternative.

Most beer is served in a glass beer mug, pilsner glass, or stein, ideally a frosty glass straight from the freezer. When poured into the center of the glass, it produces a frothy head, which helps to release the bouquet of the beer.

BEER DRINKS

Most people enjoy their beer in its unadulterated state, which is completely understandable; indeed, mixed beer drinks are an acquired taste. Steeped in history, mixed beer drinks go way back and are a part of beer's illustrious story through the centuries.

Ale Flip

1 ounce fresh lemon juice
12 ounces chilled ale
Pinch of ground ginger
1 tablespoon sugar
1 egg yolk
1 ounce brandy

In a saucepan, heat the lemon juice with 2 ounces of the ale, ginger, and sugar over moderate heat until the sugar dissolves. Beat the egg yolk into the brandy in a small bowl. Add the heated mixture to the egg yolk mixture, and beat until smooth. Pour into a beer mug, and slowly add the rest of the ale, stirring well.

Beer Buster

1½ ounces vodka (freezer-chilled)
2 to 3 dashes Tabasco sauce
8 to 12 ounces chilled lager or ale

In a chilled beer mug, combine the vodka and Tabasco sauce. Slowly pour in the beer.

Black and Tan   *This classic is always made with equal amounts dark, bitter stout, and pale, light lager or ale, which is why it is sometimes aptly called a Half and Half.*

6 ounces lager or pale ale
6 ounces stout

Slowly pour the lager into a chilled beer mug, and then slowly add the stout.

Black Velvet *Created in 1861 to commemorate Prince Albert's passing, this explosively effervescent combination is ideally served in a silver tankard.*

8 ounces Guinness (or other Irish stout)
4 ounces chilled champagne

Slowly pour the stout into a chilled beer mug, metal tankard, or collins glass. Slowly add the champagne, and gently stir.

Black Velveteen *Similar to the Black Velvet, this is made with hard cider instead.*

6 ounces stout
6 ounces hard cider

Slowly pour the stout and cider into a chilled beer mug or tall glass.

VARIATION: **For a Snake Bite,** substitute ale or lager for the stout.

Bloody Brew *A "hoppy" twist on the Bloody Mary.*

1½ ounces vodka
4 ounces tomato juice
4 ounces chilled beer
Dash of Tabasco sauce
Dill pickle spear

Pour the vodka and tomato juice into an ice-filled highball glass. Slowly add the beer and Tabasco, stirring gently. Garnish with a pickle spear.

Boilermaker *This macho drink from the 1920s is appropriately named after the men who repaired those huge, steaming monster boilers. Any whiskey of your choice can be used, such as Tennessee sour mash, bourbon, or Irish or blended Canadian whiskey.*

1½ ounces whiskey
8 ounces chilled lager or pale ale

Pour the whiskey into a shot glass. Pour the beer into a frosted beer mug. Drink down the shot of whiskey, and immediately drink the beer as a chaser. Or drop the whiskey-filled shot glass into a mug of beer and drink it down.

~ CONTINUED

VARIATION: Beer has always played a key role as the classic chaser for a shot of spirits. Feel free to choose a tequila, spicy flavored vodka, or schnapps in place of the whiskey.

Depth Charge

1½ ounces peppermint schnapps
12 ounces chilled ale or lager

Pour the schnapps into a chilled beer mug, and slowly add the beer.

VARIATION: **For a French version,** substitute 1 ounce Cointreau for the schnapps, pouring it into a shot glass and then dropping it into the mug of beer.

Dog's Nose   *Many prefer to use a pale ale in this combination, but a rich porter is also a fine choice.*

12 ounces chilled ale
1 ounce gin

Slowly pour the ale into a chilled beer mug. Pour the gin into the mug of beer. Or pour the gin into a chilled shot glass, and drop it into the mug of beer.

Lager and Black

1½ ounces black currant syrup
12 ounces chilled lager

Pour the syrup into a chilled beer mug, and slowly pour in the lager.

VARIATIONS: **For a Lager and Lime,** substitute Rose's lime juice for the black currant syrup.

For a Stout and Black, substitute stout for the lager.

Lemon Top

12 ounces chilled ale or lager
2 ounces chilled lemon-lime soda

Slowly pour the ale into a chilled beer mug, and top with the soda.

Michelada *Loosely translated as "my cold beer," this classic Mexican approach to enjoying a cold, frosty one on a hot summer day has many variations, which may include tequila and Tabasco, but the essential ingredients remain constant: citrus, salt, and beer over ice. Here are a few versions to choose from.*

MICHELADA #1

Lime wedge

Kosher salt

12 ounces chilled Mexican lager (such as Pacifica or Corona)

Rub the rim of a chilled Pilsner glass with the lime wedge and rim with kosher salt. Fill the glass with ice, squeeze the lime wedge over the ice, and drop it in. Slowly pour in the beer.

MICHELADA #2

4 ounces fresh lemon juice

1 teaspoon salt

1½ ounces tequila

12 ounces Mexican lager (such as Corona or Pacifica)

Pour the lemon juice into an ice-filled beer mug. Add the salt and tequila, stirring to combine. Slowly pour in the beer.

MICHELADA #3

½ lime (preferably a Key lime)

Kosher salt

2 dashes Worcestershire sauce

Dash of soy sauce

Dash of Tabasco sauce

Pinch of black pepper

12 ounces dark Mexican beer (such as Negra Modelo)

Rub the rim of a chilled beer mug with the lime half and rim with kosher salt. Fill the glass with ice and squeeze the lime half over the ice. Add the Worcestershire, soy sauce, Tabasco, and pepper. Slowly pour in the beer, and gently sir.

Red Eye

3 ounces tomato juice

12 ounces ale or lager

Pour the tomato juice into a chilled beer mug, and slowly pour in the ale.

Shandygaff
The name of this British concoction from the late 19th century is thought to be derived from the London slang for a pint of beer, "shant of gatter" (shant or shanter meaning "pub," and gatter being a word for "water"). This "pub water" was a refreshing way to lower the potency of the beer. Ginger ale can be substituted for the spicier ginger beer.

6 ounces chilled ginger beer

6 ounces chilled lager or pale ale

Pour the ginger beer into a chilled beer mug, and slowly add the beer.

VARIATION: **For a Shandy,** substitute lemonade or lemon-lime soda for the ginger beer.

Stout Sangaree
This is one intensely rich and heavy concoction.

2 teaspoons simple syrup

12 ounces stout

2 ounces ruby port

Pinch of freshly grated nutmeg

Pinch of ground cinnamon

Pour the simple syrup into a chilled beer mug, and slowly pour in the stout, bringing a full head of foam on top. Float the port on top and sprinkle with nutmeg and cinnamon.

SAKE

An ancient craft motivates the principal methods behind this fine Japanese brewed beverage. Sake is neither a rice wine nor a spirit, neither distilled nor created from fruit, but basically brewed like a beer. This supremely natural libation is made from a grain (rice) and brewed to produce a clear, uncarbonated beer with a higher alcohol content of 15 to 16 percent.

Truly fine sake is made by *toji*, sake brewmasters whose technical expertise is crucial to bringing together all the elements of rice, water, yeast, climate, and region, by a complex method involving precise subtleties. The process of brewing sake, in very simplified terms, begins with washing and steam-cooking the rice. Yeast and *koji* (rice cultivated with a starch-dissolving mold) are then added and allowed to ferment in a fermentation process called *shikomi*. In the following days more rice, water, and *koji* are added three more times. The mash sits anywhere from two weeks to a month, with crucial temperature adjustments to produce particular flavors. The sake is then pressed, filtered, and blended.

The best premium sake is made with just three ingredients—polished rice, water, and *koji*—to make junmai-shu, or pure sake. Using quality water and rice are key, as 80 percent of sake is made up of water. Some styles of sake have neutral alcohol added as a preservative. Most mash is pressed by machine, but the preferred method used by breweries making the best-quality sake is a more ancient method. They fill canvas bags with the mash (or *moromi*), which they squeeze, or leave to drip, to extract the fresh sake.

Most sake is pasteurized at least once, and some again after the aging, which kills off bacteria and stabilizes the flavor and color. The sakes that are not pasteurized, called namazake, have a distinctly fresh sake flavor, and must be refrigerated. Unlike wine, most sake is not aged any more than six months, just enough to smooth out the flavors. Nor does it age well in bottles—sake is meant to be consumed within seven to eight months of bottling, so don't even bother drinking it if it is more than a year old.

There are five basic types of sake, requiring different brewing methods and different degrees of rice milling. The rice ranges from unmilled (or unground) to having a specified amount that must be ground or polished away. The amount of milling influences the taste. All styles but namazake can be similar enough in flavor, and the differences are sometimes hard to discern. Although ginjo sake is considered the premium sake, it is closely followed by other high-quality sake styles such as honjozo and junmai.

------- **JUNMAI-SHU** -------

This is pure sake. No other grains, starches, or distilled alcohol are added. Brewed using rice with a minimum of 30 percent polished (ground) away, this is a full-bodied, slightly tart sake that is not as fragrant as other types.

------- **HONJOZO-SHU** -------

For this sake style, at least 30 percent of the rice is polished away and a tiny amount of distilled alcohol is added. Although heavier than ginjo-shu, due to the larger amount of the grain remaining, it is lighter than junmai-shu. It is also more fragrant and earthy due to the auspicious addition of alcohol. If you insist on warming your sake, this is the perfect style for doing so.

------- **GINJO-SHU** -------

This delicate, light sake is made with rice that has been polished at least 40 percent. Ginjo sake has added alcohol (whereas junmai ginjo does not) and is a premium sake made using intricate and intense methods that produce a complex and fragrant brew.

------- **DAIGINJO-SHU** -------

At least 50 percent of the outer layer of rice must be polished away for a sake to be labeled daiginjo-shu. Sakes made with added alcohol are simply labeled daiginjo; those without alcohol are labeled junmai daiginjo. Either way, this is a very fragrant, full-bodied style of sake.

An unpasteurized sake that can be made in any of the above styles. It should be stored cold; otherwise it loses its fresh, lively flavor.

SUBCATEGORIES OF SAKE

------- NIGORI-SAKE -------

This is a sweet, unfiltered sake that still has the *kasu* (or lees) in it, which are bits of rice that make it cloudy. Some brands are better than others. The lesser-quality brands have the lees added back in after processing to produce the cloudy effect.

------- NAMA -------

Similar to nigori-sake, this is also an unfiltered sake, but the lees are removed. It is typically not pasteurized, so if found in the United States, it more than likely has been pasteurized. Some will also have a natural carbonation due to the active yeasts still remaining.

Many of the high-quality sakes may be crystal clear and colorless, but there are also rough-filtered, cloudy sakes on the market today. Momokawa Pearl sake is a great example of this style. Emulating the traditional fresh and un-filtered sakes of Japan, it is actually produced in the United States. Sakes can be sweet or dry, soft or acidic, and the relatively light mouthfeel can sway from full-bodied to delicate. Whether you prefer a floral fruity sake, spicy and nutty, or one with a straightforward rice flavor, there are sakes for every taste to choose from today. Both imported and domestic sakes offer varying qualities, from an inexpensive domestic Hakusan sake, a moderately priced high-quality domestic Momokawa Diamond Junmai Ginjo, to a high-end superpremium Hakuryu Daiginjo sake from Japan. Many aficionados suggest that the best sakes for sipping include either an unfiltered sake such as Nigori Dreamy Clouds, said to be reminiscent of citrus, or a Dewazakura Izumi Judan, with tropical fruit notes.

Sake is best consumed soon after purchase, and it should be stored in a cool, dark area away from light, or kept stored in the refrigerator. Like wine, once sake is opened it begins to oxidize, which will change the taste. It is best enjoyed at the time of opening, but any remaining sake can be stored in the refrigerator and should be consumed within the next day or two.

Although the prevailing tradition is to serve sake warmed, contrary to popular belief, not all sakes are best consumed this way. Many premium sakes, like a ginjo, are best served slightly chilled (but not too chilled) or at room temperature (perfect for a junmai), as warming tends to cloud the intended flavor. If you insist, sakes such as a honjozo-shu can be warmed, but only slightly above body temperature (about 100 degrees).

The traditional way to serve sake is to pour it from a large serving vessel into small Japanese ceramic cups. This is performed in a charming sociable Japanese ritual, one that may be partially responsible for sake's purported reputation as an aphrodisiac. The very small cups are to promote numerous refillings from the large serving vessel, which is always held by the host with both hands while the person receiving the sake lifts his or her cup off the table, with one hand supporting the bottom and the other hand around it.

SAKE DRINKS

Although many sake connoisseurs think it sacrilegious to even consider using this refined beverage as a base for cocktails, sake has become the new darling of the creative cocktail bar scene. With a multitude of possibilities, from variations on classics such as the Sake Lemon Drop or Sake Cosmo to completely different concoctions, this may just be the tip of the creative iceberg. Innovative infusions, instilling botanical flavors such as grapefruit, lemon, black raspberry, or Asian pear into the sake, are enjoyed as shots. Sake's low alcohol content offers a nice perk when one is looking for a less potent cocktail, and it typically has no congeners, the trace elements that promote hangovers in other alcohol.

As a rule, a premium sake may be well suited for a Saketini, but for most mixed sake drinks with many different flavors at play, an inexpensive to moderately priced sake will do just fine. Most of the domestic filtered brands, such as Ozeki or Hakusan, are best suited for the drier cocktails, and a favorite choice for the more fruity concoctions is nigori-style sake, which is fruity, sweet, and unfiltered.

Asian Mary

4 ounces sake
3 ounces tomato juice
Tiny pinch of wasabi
Lime twist

Shake the sake, tomato juice, and wasabi vigorously with ice. Strain into an ice-filled highball glass. Twist the lime peel over the drink, and drop it in.

Mango Sake Sour

3 ounces nigori-sake
1 ounce sweet-and-sour
1 ounce puréed mango
Lemon twist

Shake the liquid ingredients vigorously with ice. Strain into a chilled sour glass. Twist the lemon peel over the drink, and drop it in.

Momokawa Mojito

3 ounces sake (preferably Momokawa Diamond)
½ ounce fresh lime juice
1 ounce simple syrup
5 to 6 fresh mint leaves (preferably Japanese *shiso* mint)
1 fresh mint sprig

Shake the sake, lime juice, simple syrup, and mint leaves vigorously with ice. Strain into a chilled cocktail glass, or over ice in a chilled highball glass. Garnish with the mint sprig.

Nigori Bellini

3 ounces nigori-sake
2 ounces puréed white peaches (or regular peaches)
1 ounce chilled champagne
Peach slice

Shake the sake and peach purée vigorously with ice. Strain into a chilled cocktail glass. Float the champagne on top. Garnish with the peach slice.

Orange Sake Mimosa

3 ounces sake
½ ounce mandarin-flavored vodka
½ ounce Grand Marnier
1 ounce fresh orange juice
Splash of chilled champagne
Orange slice

Shake all the liquid ingredients but the champagne vigorously with ice. Strain into a chilled champagne flute. Top with the champagne. Garnish with the orange slice.

Pearl Martini *A cocktail of modern minimalism, made with Momokawa Pearl sake, a rough-filtered nigori-style sake.*

3 ounces chilled premium sake
½ ounce vodka
2 to 3 thin slices fresh ginger
Slice of candied ginger

Shake the sake, vodka, and fresh ginger vigorously with ice. Strain into a chilled cocktail glass. Garnish with the candied ginger.

Sake Colada

3 ounces nigori-sake
1 ounce pineapple juice
½ ounce fresh lime juice
½ ounce Thai coconut milk
½ ounce simple syrup
Pineapple slice

Shake all the ingredients but the pineapple slice vigorously with ice. Strain into a chilled cocktail glass. Garnish with the pineapple slice.

Sake Cosmo

3 ounces sake
½ ounce Cointreau
1 ounce cranberry juice
½ ounce fresh lime juice
Lime twist

Shake the liquid ingredients vigorously with ice. Strain into a chilled cocktail glass. Twist the lime peel over the drink, and drop it in.

Sake Lemon Drop

3 ounces sake

1 ounce fresh lemon juice

¼ ounce fresh orange juice

½ ounce simple syrup

Lemon twist

Shake the liquid ingredients vigorously with ice. Strain into a chilled cocktail glass. Twist the lemon peel over the drink, and drop it in.

Saketini   *This is best with a good-quality sake such as Momokawa Diamond or Ozeki sake.*

4 ounces chilled sake

½ ounce high-quality gin (such as Bombay Sapphire)

½ teaspoon dry vermouth

Lemon twist

Shake the liquid ingredients vigorously with ice. Strain into a chilled cocktail glass. Twist the lemon peel over the drink, and drop it in.

VARIATION: Substitute ½ ounce of dry sherry for the gin.

Tokyotini   *East meets West in a sublime concoction of lemon vodka, sake, and aromatic ginger. If you can find it, a ginger liqueur called Canton Delicate ginger liqueur is a great substitute for the ginger syrup.*

Lemon wedge

Powdered sugar

1½ ounces citron vodka

½ ounce good-quality sake

1 ounce fresh lemon juice

½ tablespoon ginger syrup (page 73)

Slice of candied ginger

Rub the rim of a chilled cocktail glass with the lemon wedge and rim with powdered sugar. Shake the liquid ingredients vigorously with ice. Strain into the prepared glass and garnish with the candied ginger.

Zen Cucumber

4 ounces good-quality sake
1 ounce fresh lemon juice
1 ounce simple syrup
4 to 5 thin slices of cucumber (preferably English cucumber)

Shake all ingredients but the garnish vigorously with ice. Strain into a chilled cocktail glass. Garnish by floating a few cucumber slices on top of the drink.

VARIATION: Pour the entire contents of the shaker into a highball glass, ice and all. Top with chilled club soda.

Brandy

------   ------

THERE IS NOTHING QUITE LIKE A FINE COGNAC, unparalleled in its superiority and depth.

It inevitably conjures pleasant visions of an amber-hued spirit enjoyed as the evening is winding down, glowing in a snifter and warmed by the hand to release its sublimely rich bouquet, the moment made perfect by a heady sip that warms the soul.

Beyond Cognac and Armagnac, which are distilled from the fermented juice of grapes, the quintessential definition of brandy becomes broadly defined to encompass not only grape brandies but brandies distilled from other fruits as well. Generally speaking, brandies made from grapes and apples (such as Calvados) are aged in wooden casks, but other fruit brandies, such as the characteristically clear, colorless eaux-de-vie, typically are not. There is often confusion surrounding what makes a brandy; cachaça, for example, could, in broader terms, be considered a cane sugar brandy as well as a rum. Other brandy types include grappa, marc, kirsch, and other fruit eaux-de-vie. Fruit brandy has thus become a generic term used to describe any spirit distilled from a specific fruit, and it stretches even further to mean a neutral brandy spirit base that is flavored with fruit and sweetened. Although technically liqueurs, these are also called brandies, such as apricot or peach brandy.

The roots of the word "brandy" derive from *brandewijn,* a Dutch term for their "burned (distilled) wine," a grape-based spirit that they were exporting extensively by the 1500s. Although the French make the most world-renowned brandies, hailing from Cognac and Armagnac, and claim to have invented it (as do the Italians, Dutch, and Spanish), the archetypal roots of the spirit actually reach as far back as Egypt and the Middle East, and brandy was brought to the Andalusian area of Spain by the Moors in A.D. 900. Whether or not it was a refined, drinkable spirit is pure speculation, but it is highly unlikely.

COGNAC

Cognac is the most famous and well-known of the brandies and is the ultimate maxim to which all others aspire. Produced only in the Cognac region (north of Bordeaux) in France, Cognac must be made from the grapes from vineyards in the Charente and Charente-Maritime districts. It is made from a combination of white grape varieties, mainly ugni blanc but also folle blanche and colombard, among others, which produce an acidic white wine perfect for distilling into this smooth, aromatic brandy. The Cognac region is further subdivided into six areas: Grande Champagne, Petite Champagne, Borderies, Fins Bois, Bons Bois, and Bois Ordinaires. The significance of these areas with respect to labeling is discussed later in this section.

The process used to distill Cognac dates back to the 17th century. A double distillation takes place in the *alambic charentais,* a traditional Cognac pot still. The slightly cloudy liquid produced from the first distillation has an alcohol content of 30 percent (60 proof) and is called *brouillis,* with a second distillation producing a clear, young spirit called *bonne chauffe.* The "heads and tails" are the beginning and end of the second distillation; these are separated out from the middle running, called the *coeur,* or heart, which produces the best-quality Cognac. The raw Cognac typically comes out of the second distillation at 140 proof (or 70 ABV) and before bottling is diluted down to a minimum 80 proof with distilled water and low-proof Cognac. Most brandies and Cognacs are bottled at 80 proof.

The Cognac is then aged for at least two years and as long as twenty or more, starting out in new, toasted Limousin oak casks, or *barriques,* which give it color and tannins as well as imparting its characteristic vanilla flavor. Depending on the distillery house, the Cognac is moved after a year or two of aging from the new cask to an older cask, to avoid excessive tannins and to add complexity, transforming the young distillate into a mature, smooth, aromatic spirit.

With a few rare exceptions, Cognac is usually a blend of single Cognacs from various distillates from different regions, ages, and vintages. The mixing takes place frequently throughout the cask aging and bottling process, with each house bringing its own distinct character, style, and quality to the Cognac. Some distilleries may also add caramel coloring to the younger distillates to adjust and darken the spirits, keeping the colors consistent among the bottles.

------- **COGNAC LABELING** -------

Decoding Cognac labels, with their stars and abbreviations and regions, can be a daunting prospect. In the most basic terms, here are the meanings of the styles and subcategories and their corresponding symbolism.

Cognacs vary in quality depending on which region the grapes come from, with distinctions in the climate, chalky soil content, and even altitude affecting the character of the grapes and allowing for a diverse and rich selection from which the complex blends are made. The six districts of the Cognac region are categorized by the quality of the grapes grown in each. The highest-quality Cognacs come from the Grande Champagne and Petite Champagne regions, which, in this case, have nothing to do with sparkling wines and everything to do with the quality of the grapes grown in the area. The labels will often state the specific district but more frequently will simply state *fine champagne,* which means that more than 60 percent of the wines used to make the Cognac were from grapes grown in the Grande Champagne district.

------- **COGNAC DISTRICTS** -------

∾ **GRANDE CHAMPAGNE**   This district produces premium-quality wines for the best Cognacs, used primarily in Cognac blends, which are aged for extensive periods of time.

∾ **PETITE CHAMPAGNE**   This area produces wines that are a close second best, from a blend of both Grande Champagne and Petite Champagne Cognacs.

∾ **BORDERIES**   This area makes wines that produce mild Cognacs with rich bouquets.

∾ **FINS BOIS**   The greatest amount (40 percent) of Cognac is distilled from wines grown here, producing strong Cognacs ideal for relatively brief aging.

∾ **BONS BOIS**   Strong Cognacs of lesser quality come from wines produced in this area.

∾ **BOIS ORDINAIRES**   This area supplies the wine for only 3 percent of Cognac production.

------- **INDICATORS OF AGE** -------

The number of stars on a Cognac label indicate how long it was aged:

- One star: aged a minimum of three years
- Two stars: aged a minimum of four years
- Three (or more) stars: aged a minimum of five years

In addition to the stars, Cognac labels contain abbreviations that connote their superiority and quality and their minimum aging (many are aged beyond the minimum), meaning the number of years the youngest ingredient has aged in a cask. The following are the most commonly used, with a very broad and basic description of each.

V.S. (VERY SPECIAL)
Cognacs that have been aged for a minimum of two and a half years.

V.O. (VERY OLD)
Aged a minimum of four and a half years (which in terms of Cognac is relatively young).

V.S.O.P. (VERY SUPERIOR OLD PALE)
Aged as long as ten years.

V.V.S.O.P. (VERY VERY SPECIAL OLD PALE)
Aged longer than a V.S.O.P.

X.O. (EXTRA OLD)
Indicates a premium Cognac.

Different distillers assign names to further designate their best premium Cognacs, such as *Extra,* or *Napoleon X.O.* These also connote a respectable amount of aging, but they do not specifically designate an age. They also tend to represent quality, although in vague terms.

------- **A FEW FAMOUS COGNAC BRANDS** -------

Rémy Martin has a V.S.O.P. that is a light herbal Cognac with citrus tones, and a fine X.O. with citrus and spice. Hine is a tony choice, from the roasted spiciness of Antique to the complex bouquet of fruits and spices of Rare and Delicate and the delicate fruitiness of Triomphe. Courvoisier has a light V.S. and a woody and sweet V.S.O.P. Martell V.S. is spicy and clean, with a woody and fruity V.S.O.P. Hennessy offers a rich, well-aged Paradis.

ARMAGNAC

They say you can experience all the bountiful richness of the Armagnac region simply by partaking of the aromatic bouquet and flavors of its brandy. This French brandy may not be as well-known as Cognac, but it is held in equally high esteem as one of the great high-quality brandies, as well as one of the oldest. Armagnac predates Cognac by about two hundred years. This region is documented as the first producer of drinkable brandy, in the early 15th century, with historical speculation suggesting that it found its way through the Pyrenees from Spain. Distilled from wine produced only in the Gascony region of France, Armagnac is made mainly from three varieties of white grapes—colombard, folle blanche, and ugni blanc—and is distilled in the Bas Armagnac, Ténarèze, and Haut Armagnac cultivation areas.

Traditionally, the wine is distilled once at a low temperature in a small, continuous column still called an *alambic armagnaçaise.* This is significantly different from Cognac's double distillation process and results in a hearty, earthy, full-flavored brandy. Unlike Cognac, for which the blending takes place simultaneously with distillation and aging, the varying eaux-de-vie for Armagnac are kept separate up until the bottling, making it possible to also produce vintage brandy. Armagnac is traditionally aged in Monlezun oak (although Limousin oak is now frequently used) for anywhere from three to forty years. During this time, it is decanted (moved) periodically into older casks, a complex wood aging procedure that is crucial to a fine Armagnac. After forty years of aging in wood casks, select vintage Armagnac is moved to large glass jars capped with raffia tops and stored in a designated area, aptly called Paradis, where vintages reaching back a hundred years or so can be found.

Various vintages from the distillates produced in the three key Armagnac-producing regions may be kept separate for vintage bottling or blended together to maintain continuity in style and quality. Delicate and dry, rich, nutty, floral, and silky smooth, these brandies of the Armagnac region have a style all their own, with aromas and flavors conjuring their distinct *terroir,* which can indeed be experienced with one sip.

Three main regions produce the different styles and qualities of Armagnac. The Haut-Armagnac region produces brandy used mostly for blending. Premium-quality Armagnacs are produced in the Ténarèze region, with its characteristic light, aromatic, fruity brandy, and in the Bas Armagnac region, known for its smooth style. Premium Armagnacs from these regions will have the appellation on their label, the equivalent of a Grande Champagne Cognac. The basic Armagnac is a blend of brandies and will simply be labeled as "Armagnac." The age of the Armagnac is designated like that of Cognac, but unlike Cognac, Armagnac bottles may carry vintage dates.

- Aged a minimum of three years: V.S. or three stars
- Aged a minimum of four years: V.O.
- Aged a minimum of five years: Extra, Napoleon, X.O., Vielle Réserve
- Aged a minimum of seven years: V.S.O.P., Réserve
- Aged a minimum of ten years: Hors d'age, X.O.

The following well-known Armagnac brands also produce vintage brandies: Clés des Ducs, Janneau, Château de Laubade, Château du Tariquet, Marquis de Montesquiou, and Samalens (Bas Armagnac).

SPANISH BRANDY

The origins of brandy as a spirit began in Moorish Andalusia around A.D. 900 in Jerez, a city rich in ancient distillation practices. Brandy was originally made to fortify wine, thus making sherry, which is still the main focus of production in Jerez.

Spain's leading brandies, Lepanto and Fundador (the oldest producer), are mostly produced in Jerez de la Frontera by the large sherry houses, frequently using the same *solera* method that they use in making their equally superior sherry. However, the brandies are made with grapes from the La Mancha region farther north, rather than the regional Jerez grapes used for sherry. Spain is the second largest producer of brandy outside of France, and more than a few Spanish brandies compare with the French brandies in both quality and quantity. They are slightly sweet and pungently full flavored, with a defining sherry note acquired from aging in old sherry casks. The aging period is indicated on the label, from the youngest, Brandy de Jerez Solera, to the Solera Reserva, to the oldest, Solera Gran Reserva. Outside of Jerez, a few Catalonian producers make brandy; these are closer in style to Armagnac—not surprising, due to their relatively closer proximity. The best-known houses are Torres and Mascaro, with Mascaro offering a superior brandy comparable to a Cognac.

Other Spanish brandies include Sanches Romate's Cardenal Mendoza, Bobadilla, Pedro Domecq, Gran Duque d'Alba, and Osborne's Conde d'Osborne.

OTHER BRANDY STYLES

------- AGUARDIENTE -------

Meaning "burned water" in Spanish, aguardiente generically describes several styles of potent, low-quality spirits. The Spanish use it to describe their equivalent of a French marc, a brandy distilled from the husks and skins of pressed grapes.

Aguardiente is the Portuguese term for brandy. It encompasses various styles, from brandy that has been aged in port wine casks to other distillates from various fruits. In South America, mainly Brazil and Mexico, a young, rustic sugarcane spirit, sometimes flavored with aniseed, is referred to as *aguardiente de caña.*

A Brazilian brandylike rum made from the pressed raw juice of sugarcane, also called *pinga*. Hundreds of different cachaças are made in Brazil, but the brands most commonly found in the United States are Cachaça 51, Cachaça de Caricé, Néga Fulô, and Pitú.

(See also the discussion of cachaça in the rum section, page 243.)

------- **GRAPPA** -------

This Italian spirit is technically not a brandy, as it is distilled not from wine but from pomace, a vintner's term for the grape skins, husks, and stems that remain after the grapes have been pressed to make wine. Although grappa was previously regarded as a fiery and pungently raw unaged spirit, recently many wine producers have gotten savvy, using specific grape varieties and even aging the spirit in wooden casks for two to four years, to impart a bouquet and color ranging from cherrywood sweet to an oaky dryness. Some producers have also begun adding flavors or using designer bottles. In a long tradition, the best grappas come from Venice and the Friuli region.

------- **MARC** -------

Marc is a fine example of the vintner's ingenuity and entrepreneurial spirit of recycling. Like grappa, French marc is another "brandy" that is distilled from the skins and husks of pressed grapes, called the *marc* (the French term for pomace), as opposed to most brandies, which are distilled from wine. Typically yellowish or light in color and known as vintner's brandy or poor man's brandy, it can range in style from light and delicate, such as the Marc de Champagne, to a stronger, more aromatic spirit, such as Marc de Bourgogne. It is usually partaken as a digestif.

------- **METAXA** -------

The most famous brandy from Greece, Metaxa is made from red grapes, sweet muscat grapes, and white savatino grapes, giving it a winelike flavor that is enhanced by aromatic herbs and spices. The addition of sweeteners makes it much sweeter than Cognac and pushes it nearly into the realm of a liqueur, especially the younger three-star Metaxas. It is labeled under three grades of quality indicating age, from three stars to five stars to the seven-starred Golden Amphora—cask aged with a toffee, nutty flavor—and Grande Fine, with dark amber, rich sherry tones.

------- **PISCO BRANDY** -------

As cachaça is to Brazil, pisco is to Chile and Peru, and they are still at odds over who first produced this spicy brandy. A South American spirit thought to date back to the Incas, pisco is a colorless brandy with a distinctively fruity character. Made mostly from the wine of fragrant muscat grapes grown in the official region north of Santiago de Chile, it is often blended with wine from pedro ximénez and torontel grapes as well. It is aged in clay jars or ancient oak casks that have no color left to give the spirit, producing a light-colored brandy regardless of the age. The best pisco brandies, such as Control Gran Pisco, are refined, premium spirits, despite their reputation for being fiery and raw. The most popular brands are Pisco Control, Pisco Capel, and Don César (a Chilean marc).

------- **U.S. BRANDIES** -------

In the last thirty years, many brandy producers in America have worked hard to beat a bad rap for mediocrity, going from brandies that were not fit for anything but cooking, conveniently made from grapes unsuitable for wines for the table or for raisins, to more refined, aged spirits using a wide selection of wine-grade grapes, including such varieties as chenin blanc, pinot noir, chardonnay, and muscat. Made mostly in the Napa Valley wine region of California, most of these brandies are made using the Spanish style of distillation. However, a few exceptional boutique producers are distilling by the Cognac-style pot still method, producing world-class brandies equal to many of the best V.S.O.P. Cognacs.

American brandies are typically matured for at least two years in home-grown American oak barrels, producing a light and fruity brandy. Many of these, such as the E&J brandy from Gallo, are well suited for mixed drinks, but for sipping, choose a brandy from a top-quality small artisanal producer, such as Germain-Robin or Carneros Alambic, both from the Napa Valley.

------- **WEINBRAND** -------

This is the designated term used for German brandies, which must be aged for at least six months. When aged for more than twelve months, they are further distinguished as *Alter Weinbrand* (or V.S.O.P.). Many German brandies use wines purchased from other countries, but when specifically acquired from the Cognac and Armagnac regions, a quality brandy is usually guaranteed. Asbach Uralt is similar in style to French Cognac. Aged in oak barrels, it is one of the most popular brands of German brandy.

------- **FRUIT BRANDIES** -------

When used alone, the term "brandy" typically refers to brandies made from grape wine, such as Cognac or Armagnac. The term "fruit brandy" refers to brandies made from other fruits, as well as those made from pomace, or the grape remains of the winemaking process.

❧ **APRICOT BRANDY**   Any brandy distilled from apricots, including the sweetened versions, which are more like liqueurs. See also the description of apricot brandy in the section on liqueurs (page 238).

❧ **APPLE BRANDY**   Any brandy distilled from apples; also called cider brandy. Two well-known apple brandies are applejack and Calvados.

~ *APPLEJACK*   This apple brandy is the American version of French Calvados. Made from apple cider, it is aged for two to five years in wooden casks before it is bottled. This brandy is ideal for mixed drinks calling for apple brandy, as opposed to using a high-end Calvados.

~ *CALVADOS*   Made in Normandy, France, where the climate is more conducive to growing apples than grapes, this fine apple brandy has been produced since the 16th century. Calvados is made from fermented and distilled apple cider, with the occasional addition of pears for a more balanced complexity. The best Calvados is from the Pays d'Auge area, where it is produced in pot stills. Bottles from this area are labeled as such; all others are simply labeled "Calvados." The oak casks used for aging impart a dry, spicy, vanilla note to the more mature brandies, while the younger brandies still tend to have a distinct taste of apples. The method and indication of age on Calvados labels are similar to those for Cognac and Armagnac. Calvados, especially the Hors d'Age, which is aged for six or more years, is as refined and sippable as Armagnac and should be served in a brandy snifter rather than used for mixed drinks. Younger Calvados is often enjoyed over ice, with a splash of tonic. For mixed drinks calling for apple brandy, applejack is a better choice than squandering a fine Calvados.

✎ **EAUX-DE-VIE**   Pure fruit distillates, clear and colorless. Rather than being aged in wood like Cognacs, they rest and develop in glass. Eau-de-vie is a French phrase derived from the Latin *aqua vitae,* meaning "water of life," and is used to describe all spirits distilled from fermented fruits. Distilled from a variety of fruits, including strawberries (*fraise*), pears (*poire*), raspberries (*framboise*), yellow plums (*mirabelle*), and plums (*pruneau*), eaux-de-vie are usually high in alcohol, at 90 proof, and are usually dry, versus the sweet crème fruit liqueurs, which are not distilled from the fruit but are flavored with fruit essence and sweetened. Grappa, marc, and kirsch are also considered eaux-de-vie. All eaux-de-vie are best served well chilled and neat, in small amounts, given their high alcohol content. Although they blend well with club soda, they are lost when mixed with other flavored ingredients, which drown out the delicate fruit bouquet.

~ *KIRSCH*   This colorless, pure distillate is a cherry eau-de-vie, traditionally made from black morello cherries from Bavaria, but other red cherry varieties are also often used. The juice is pressed from the cherries and, for the initial fermentation, the stones are ground up and left in the juice, where they impart a slightly bitter, almond flavor. The kirsch undergoes a short period of aging in large, earthenware vats (rather than barrels), so it remains colorless. A great after-dinner brandy, kirsch should be served slightly chilled in a small liqueur glass. The best kirsch comes from Germany and is also called kirsch-wasser, or schwarzwalder when produced in the Black Forest region of Bavaria. It is also made in France, in the Alsace and Franche-Comté regions, as well as in Switzerland and Austria.

~ *MIRABELLE*   A French eau-de-vie with a light, spicy, and slightly sweet plum flavor, made from yellow mirabelle plums.

~ *POIRE WILLIAMS*   An eau-de-vie flavored with Williams pears. (See the description in the section on liqueurs, page 241.)

~ *A FEW OTHER EXAMPLES OF EAUX-DE-VIE*   Clear Creek, in the state of Oregon, makes a delightful eau-de-vie-style pear brandy, as well as other fruit brandies. Pascall, in France, produces LaVielle Prune, a plum-flavored brandy. Framboise Sauvage is a fine eau-de-vie flavored with wild raspberries.

BRANDY DRINKS

Brandy is not just to be savored as a fine vintage and served as a digestif after a meal. After all, it is the quintessential spirit from which the cocktail was born, courtesy of Peychaud's apothecary in New Orleans. From the very beginning, brandy was the preferred restorative beverage upon which mixed drinks were built. Its versatility has inspired many cocktail innovations and libations ever since.

A.J.   *The A.J. stands for applejack.*

1½ ounces applejack (or Calvados)
1½ ounces fresh grapefruit juice
4 dashes grenadine

Shake the ingredients vigorously with ice. Strain into a chilled cocktail glass.

Alabama   *Similar to a Sidecar but with lime juice instead of lemon juice.*

1 ounce brandy
1 ounce Cointreau
½ ounce fresh lime juice
½ teaspoon sugar
Orange twist

Shake the liquid ingredients and sugar vigorously with ice. Strain into a chilled cocktail glass. Twist the orange peel over the drink, and drop it in.

American Beauty   *A classic named after the American Beauty rose.*

½ ounce brandy
½ ounce dry vermouth
½ ounce fresh orange juice
¼ teaspoon grenadine
¼ teaspoon white crème de menthe
¾ ounce ruby port

~ CONTINUED

Shake all the ingredients but the port vigorously with ice. Strain into a chilled cocktail glass. Float the ruby port on top.

VARIATION: Substitute ¾ ounce each brandy, ruby port, and pineapple juice, and a dash each of grenadine and triple sec. Shake the ingredients vigorously with ice. Strain into a chilled cocktail glass.

Angel Face

¾ ounce brandy
¾ ounce gin
½ ounce apricot brandy
½ ounce apple brandy

Shake the ingredients vigorously with ice. Strain into a chilled cocktail glass.

Apple Brandy Highball

2 ounces Calvados
3 to 5 ounces chilled club soda
Apple peel spiral

Pour the Calvados into an ice-filled highball glass. Top with club soda, and garnish with the apple peel.

Apple Swizzle

½ ounce apple brandy
1 ounce light rum
¾ ounce fresh lime juice
2 to 4 dashes Angostura bitters
1 teaspoon sugar
Lime slice

Pour the liquid ingredients and sugar into an ice-filled highball glass. Stir well. Garnish with the lime slice.

Apricot Cocktail

1½ ounces apricot brandy
¼ ounce gin
¾ ounce fresh lemon juice
¾ ounce fresh orange juice

Shake the ingredients vigorously with ice. Strain into a chilled cocktail glass.

Au Currant Sidecar *A variation on the Sidecar using the rich, velvety tones of Metaxa, the Greek answer to a brandy-liqueur hybrid, and the sweet, black currant flavor of crème de cassis.*

Lemon wedge
Sugar
1½ ounces Metaxa
1 ounce fresh lemon juice
1 ounce fresh orange juice
½ ounce crème de cassis
1 ounce Grand Marnier
1 teaspoon superfine sugar
Lemon twist

Rub the rim of a chilled cocktail glass with the lemon wedge and rim with sugar. Shake the liquid ingredients and superfine sugar vigorously with ice. Strain into the prepared glass. Twist the lemon peel over the top of the drink, and drop it in.

VARIATION: The black raspberry flavor of Chambord liqueur is a fine option in place of the crème de cassis.

Barton Special Cocktail

1½ ounces Calvados or apple brandy
¾ ounce gin
¾ ounce scotch whisky
Lemon twist

Shake the liquid ingredients vigorously with ice. Strain into a chilled cocktail glass. Optional: Add an ice cube or two. Twist the lemon peel over the drink, and drop it in.

The Barujo   *This Nuevo Latino cocktail is a Colombian version of the Mojito. It is served at Baru, a Colombian restaurant located in Old San Juan, Puerto Rico. This cocktail is made with* agua ardiente, *meaning "fire water" or "hard water." A favorite Colombian liquor similar to Brazil's cachaça, it has a rumlike flavor with subtle overtones of anise.*

4 to 5 fresh mint leaves
1 ounce fresh lemon juice
1 teaspoon superfine sugar
1½ ounces agua ardiente
2 to 3 ounces chilled club soda

Muddle the mint, lemon juice, and sugar in the bottom of a chilled highball glass. Fill glass with ice and then add the agua ardiente. Stir, adding a splash of club soda, and serve.

Bermuda Highball

1 ounce brandy
1 ounce gin
1 ounce dry vermouth
2 to 3 ounces chilled ginger ale
Lemon twist

Pour the brandy, gin, and vermouth into an ice-filled highball glass. Top with the ginger ale and stir gently. Twist the lemon peel over the drink, and drop it in.

Betsy Ross

2 ounces brandy
1½ ounces ruby port
½ teaspoon Cointreau or triple sec

Stir the ingredients in a mixing glass with ice. Strain into a chilled cocktail glass.

Between the Sheets *A classic from the 1920s with a perfect balance of flavors.*

1 ounce brandy (or Cognac)
1 ounce light rum
1 ounce Cointreau
1 ounce fresh lemon (or lime) juice
Dash of simple syrup
Lemon twist

Shake the liquid ingredients vigorously with ice. Strain into a chilled cocktail glass. Twist the lemon peel over the drink, and drop it in.

Blackjack

1½ ounces brandy
1½ ounces very cold strong coffee
¾ ounce kirsch
Lemon twist

Shake the liquid ingredients vigorously with ice. Strain into an ice-filled highball glass. Garnish with the lemon twist.

Bombay Cocktail

1 ounce brandy
½ ounce dry vermouth
½ ounce sweet vermouth
½ teaspoon Cointreau
Dash of Pernod

Shake the ingredients vigorously with ice. Strain into a chilled cocktail glass.

Bosom Caresser

1½ ounces brandy
¾ ounce Madeira
½ ounce triple sec
1 teaspoon grenadine

Shake the ingredients vigorously with ice. Strain into a chilled cocktail glass.

Brandied Port

1 ounce brandy
1 ounce tawny port
½ ounce fresh lemon juice
1½ teaspoons maraschino liqueur
Orange slice

Shake the liquid ingredients vigorously with ice. Strain into an ice-filled old-fashioned glass. Garnish with the orange slice.

Brandy Alexander   *This classic was created during Prohibition, when many speakeasies served cheap brandy. They came up with this cocktail with cream to mask the biting taste.*

1 ounce brandy (or Cognac)
1 ounce brown crème de cacao
1 ounce heavy cream
Fresh grated or ground nutmeg

Shake the liquid ingredients vigorously with ice. Strain into a chilled cocktail glass. Sprinkle a dusting of nutmeg on top.

VARIATIONS: **For a blended ice cream version,** increase the brandy and crème de cacao to 2 ounces each, and substitute ½ cup vanilla ice cream for the cream. Combine in a blender until smooth. Sprinkle with nutmeg.

For a Panama Cocktail, substitute white crème de cacao for the brown crème de cacao.

Brandy Cassis

1½ ounces brandy
1 ounce fresh lemon juice
½ ounce crème de cassis
Lemon twist

Shake the liquid ingredients vigorously with ice. Strain into a chilled cocktail glass. Twist the lemon peel over the drink, and drop it in.

Brandy Cobbler

2 ounces brandy
½ ounce simple syrup
2 ounces chilled club soda
Maraschino cherry
Orange slice
Fresh mint sprig

Pour the brandy and syrup into an ice-filled wineglass. Top with club soda and stir gently. Garnish with the cherry, orange slice, and mint sprig.

Brandy Crusta   *A crusta always has a sugar rim and long citrus spiral, and is traditionally made with brandy. This New Orleans classic is similar to a Sidecar, and is served in a sour glass.*

Lemon wedge
Superfine sugar
2 ounces brandy
½ ounce Cointreau
½ ounce fresh lemon juice
Dash of maraschino liqueur
Lemon peel spiral

Rub the rim of a chilled sour glass with the lemon wedge and rim with sugar. Shake the liquid ingredients vigorously with ice. Strain into the prepared glass. Garnish with the lemon spiral.

Brandy Julep   *Also known as a Georgia Julep.*

8 to 10 fresh mint leaves
1 tablespoon sugar
¼ ounce peach brandy
1½ to 2 ounces brandy
Fresh mint sprig

Muddle the mint leaves, sugar, and peach brandy in the bottom of an old-fashioned glass. Fill the glass with ice, add the brandy, and stir briefly. Garnish with the mint sprig.

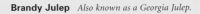

Brandy Rickey

2 ounces brandy
½ ounce fresh lime juice
3 to 5 ounces chilled club soda
Lime wedge

Pour the brandy and lime juice into an ice-filled highball glass. Top with club soda and stir gently. Squeeze the lime wedge over the drink, and drop it in.

Brandy Sangaree

½ teaspoon sugar
2 ounces brandy
2 to 3 ounces chilled club soda
½ ounce ruby port
Fresh grated or ground nutmeg

Combine the sugar and brandy in an old-fashioned glass, fill the glass with ice, and top with club soda. Float the port over the top, and sprinkle with nutmeg.

Brandy Sling

2½ ounces brandy
½ ounce Grand Marnier
½ ounce fresh lemon juice
2 to 4 ounces chilled club soda
Lemon wedge

Shake the brandy, Grand Marnier, and lemon juice vigorously with ice. Strain into an ice-filled highball glass. Top with club soda and stir gently. Squeeze the lemon wedge over the drink, and drop it in.

Brandy Sour

2 ounces brandy
¾ ounce fresh orange juice
½ ounce simple syrup
Maraschino cherry
Orange slice

Shake the liquid ingredients vigorously with ice. Strain into a chilled sour glass. Garnish with the cherry and orange slice.

VARIATIONS: **For a lemon-lime version,** use ¹/₂ ounce lime juice and ¹/₂ ounce lemon juice in place of the orange juice.

For an Apple Brandy Sour, substitute Calvados or applejack for the brandy, and add a dash of grenadine.

For a Fireman's Sour, add 1 ounce grenadine.

Calvados Car

Lemon wedge
Sugar
1 ounce Calvados (or other apple brandy)
1 ounce Cointreau (or triple sec)
½ ounce fresh orange juice
½ ounce fresh lemon juice

Rub the rim of a chilled cocktail glass with the lemon wedge and rim with sugar. Shake the liquid ingredients vigorously with ice. Strain into the prepared glass.

Charlie Chaplin

1 ounce apricot brandy
1 ounce sloe gin
1 ounce fresh lime juice
Lime wedge

Shake the liquid ingredients vigorously with ice. Strain into a chilled cocktail glass. Squeeze the lime wedge over the drink, and drop it in.

Cherry Blossom

1½ ounces brandy
1 ounce kirsch (or other cherry brandy)
½ ounce Cointreau (or triple sec)
¼ ounce fresh lemon juice
Dash of grenadine

Shake the ingredients vigorously with ice. Strain into a chilled cocktail glass.

Chicago Cocktail

Lemon wedge
Sugar
1½ ounces brandy
¼ ounce Cointreau
Dash of Angostura bitters

Rub the rim of a chilled cocktail glass with the lemon wedge and rim with sugar. Shake the liquid ingredients vigorously with ice. Strain into the prepared glass.

VARIATION: **For a Fantasio,** add ¼ ounce maraschino liqueur.

Corpse Reviver   *The flavor alone would raise the dead; potent and powerful, this drink was originally concocted as a hangover remedy. (See also a description in the Hangover Remedies and Pick-Me-Ups section, page 454.)*

CORPSE REVIVER #1

1 ounce brandy
1 ounce applejack
1 ounce sweet vermouth

Stir the ingredients in a mixing glass with ice. Strain into a chilled cocktail glass.

CORPSE REVIVER #2

1 ounce brandy
1 ounce Fernet Branca
1 ounce white crème de menthe

Stir the ingredients in a mixing glass with ice. Strain into a chilled cocktail glass

- -

Depth Bomb

¾ ounce Calvados (or applejack)
¾ ounce Cognac (or brandy)
¼ ounce fresh lemon juice
Dash of grenadine
Apple slice

Shake the liquid ingredients vigorously with ice. Strain into a chilled cocktail glass. Garnish with the apple slice.

- -

Dream

1½ ounces brandy
¾ ounce Cointreau (or triple sec)
½ teaspoon anisette

Shake the ingredients vigorously with ice. Strain into a chilled cocktail glass.

- -

East India

1½ ounces brandy
¼ ounce Cointreau
1½ ounces pineapple juice
Dash of Angostura bitters
Lemon twist
Maraschino cherry

Shake the liquid ingredients vigorously with ice. Strain into a chilled cocktail glass. Garnish with the lemon twist and cherry.

French Connection

2 ounces brandy

1 ounce amaretto

Pour the ingredients into an ice-filled old-fashioned glass. Stir well.

Harvard Cocktail

1½ ounces brandy

¾ ounce sweet vermouth

½ ounce fresh lemon juice

1 teaspoon grenadine

Dash of Angostura bitters

Shake the ingredients vigorously with ice. Strain into a chilled cocktail glass.

Harvard Cooler

2 ounces apple brandy

½ ounce fresh lemon juice

1 teaspoon simple syrup

3 to 5 ounces chilled club soda

Lemon peel spiral

Pour the liquid ingredients into an ice-filled highball glass. Stir well. Garnish with the lemon spiral.

VARIATION: **For a Moonlight,** skip the club soda. Shake the liquid ingredients vigorously with ice. Strain into a chilled cocktail glass.

Honeymoon

1½ ounces apple brandy

¾ ounce Bénédictine

¼ ounce Cointreau

1 ounce fresh lemon juice

Lemon twist

Shake the liquid ingredients vigorously with ice. Strain into a chilled cocktail glass. Twist the lemon peel over the drink, and drop it in.

Hoopla

¾ ounce brandy
¾ ounce Lillet Blanc
¾ ounce Cointreau (or triple sec)
1 ounce fresh lemon juice
Orange twist

Shake the liquid ingredients vigorously with ice. Strain into a chilled cocktail glass. Twist the orange peel over the drink, and drop it in.

International Cocktail

2 ounces Cognac (or brandy)
¼ ounce anisette
¼ ounce Cointreau
¼ ounce vodka

Shake the ingredients vigorously with ice. Strain into a chilled cocktail glass.

Is Paris Burning?

2 ounces brandy
½ ounce Chambord
Lemon twist

Shake the liquid ingredients vigorously with ice. Strain into a chilled cocktail glass. Twist the lemon peel over the drink, and drop it in.

Jack-in-the-Box

1½ ounces applejack
1½ ounces pineapple juice
Dash of fresh lemon juice
Dash of Angostura bitters

Shake the ingredients vigorously with ice. Strain into a chilled cocktail glass or over ice in an old-fashioned glass.

Kahlúa Toreador

2 ounces brandy
1 ounce Kahlúa
1 egg white

Shake the ingredients vigorously with ice. Strain into a chilled cocktail glass.

Lady Be Good

1½ ounces brandy
½ ounce white crème de menthe
½ ounce sweet vermouth

Shake the ingredients vigorously with ice. Strain into a chilled cocktail glass.

La Jolla

1½ ounces brandy
½ ounce crème de banane
¼ ounce fresh lemon juice
¼ ounce fresh orange juice

Shake the ingredients vigorously with ice. Strain into a chilled cocktail glass.

Liberty Cocktail

1 sugar cube
1 lime wedge
1 ounce Calvados
¾ ounce light rum

Muddle the sugar cube and lime wedge in the bottom of an old-fashioned glass. Fill with ice, pour in the liquor, and stir.

Metaxa Sidecar

Lime wedge
Sugar
1½ ounces Metaxa
½ ounce limoncello
1 ounce fresh orange juice
½ ounce fresh lime juice

Rub the rim of a chilled cocktail glass with the lime wedge and rim with sugar. Shake the liquid ingredients vigorously with ice. Strain into the prepared glass.

Metropolitan   *This is the classic recipe, similar to a Manhattan, not to be confused with a Nouveau Metropolitan, which is a variation on the Cosmopolitan (page 317).*

1½ ounces brandy
1½ ounces sweet vermouth
½ teaspoon simple syrup
2 dashes Angostura bitters
Maraschino cherry

Stir the liquid ingredients in a mixing glass with ice. Strain into a chilled cocktail glass. Garnish with the cherry.

Midnight Cocktail

1½ ounces apricot brandy
¾ ounce triple sec
¾ ounce fresh lemon juice

Shake the ingredients vigorously with ice. Strain into a chilled cocktail glass.

Mikado

1½ ounces brandy
½ ounce Cointreau (or triple sec)
¼ ounce crème de noyaux (or amaretto)
1 teaspoon grenadine
Dash of Angostura bitters

Shake the ingredients vigorously with ice. Strain into an ice-filled old-fashioned glass.

Montana

2 ounces brandy
1 ounce ruby port
½ ounce dry vermouth

Pour the ingredients into an ice-filled old-fashioned glass. Stir well.

Olympic

1 ounce brandy
1 ounce Cointreau (or triple sec)
1 ounce fresh orange juice
¼ ounce fresh lemon juice
Orange twist

Shake the liquid ingredients vigorously with ice. Strain into a chilled cocktail glass. Twist the orange peel over the drink, and drop it in.

Ostend Fizz

¾ ounce kirsch
¾ ounce crème de cassis
½ ounce fresh lemon juice
3 to 5 ounces chilled club soda
Lemon slice

Shake the kirsch, crème de cassis, and lemon juice vigorously with ice. Strain into an ice-filled highball glass. Top with club soda and stir gently. Garnish with the lemon slice.

Paradise

1 ounce apricot brandy
¾ ounce gin
¾ ounce fresh orange juice

Shake the ingredients vigorously with ice. Strain into a chilled cocktail glass.

VARIATIONS: Another version increases the gin to 1 ounce and adds ½ ounce fresh lime juice.

For a Royal Smile Cocktail, substitute ½ ounce lemon juice for the orange juice, and add a dash of grenadine.

Pear Dream   *The signature drink from the Hotel Belle Rive, the infamous Côte d'Azur hangout for Fitzgerald and Hemingway in Cap d'Antibes.*

1½ ounces pear brandy
2 ounces fresh pink grapefruit juice
2 ounces apricot nectar
Splash of grenadine
Lime slice

Shake the liquid ingredients vigorously with ice. Strain into a chilled cocktail glass. Garnish with the lime slice.

Picasso

1½ ounces brandy
1 ounce Dubonnet
¼ ounce fresh lemon juice
Lemon twist and orange twist

Pour the liquid ingredients into an ice-filled highball glass. Twist the lemon and orange peel over the drink, and drop them in.

VARIATION: **For a Phoebe Snow,** substitute Pernod (or anisette) for the lemon juice.

Pisco Punch

2 ounces pisco brandy
¼ ounce fresh lime juice
¼ ounce pineapple juice
2 dashes Angostura bitters
Lime slice

Combine the liquid ingredients with ½ cup crushed ice in a blender. Blend until smooth. Pour into a chilled wineglass. Garnish with the lime slice.

Pisco Sidecar

Lemon wedge
Sugar
1½ ounces pisco brandy
¾ ounce Cointreau
½ ounce fresh lemon juice
½ ounce fresh orange juice

Rub the rim of a chilled cocktail glass with the lemon wedge and rim with sugar. Shake the ingredients vigorously with ice. Strain into the prepared glass.

Pisco Sour

1½ ounces pisco brandy
¾ ounce fresh lemon juice
¼ ounce simple syrup
Maraschino cherry

Shake the liquid ingredients vigorously with ice. Strain into a chilled sour glass. Garnish with the cherry.

Polonaise

1½ ounces brandy
½ ounce blackberry brandy
½ ounce dry sherry
Dash of fresh lemon juice
Dash of orange bitters

Shake the ingredients vigorously with ice. Strain into an ice-filled old-fashioned glass.

VARIATION: **For a Poop Deck Cocktail,** substitute 1 ounce ruby port for the sherry. Shake and strain into a chilled cocktail glass.

Quakers Cocktail

¾ ounce brandy
¾ ounce rum
¾ ounce fresh lemon juice
¼ ounce raspberry syrup
Lemon twist

Shake the liquid ingredients vigorously with ice. Strain into a chilled cocktail glass. Twist the lemon peel over the drink, and drop it in.

Saratoga Cocktail

2 ounces brandy
¼ ounce pineapple juice
Dash of fresh lemon juice
Dash of maraschino liqueur
Dash of Angostura bitters

Shake the ingredients vigorously with ice. Strain into a chilled cocktail glass.

Sidecar

THIS CLASSIC PARISIAN COCKTAIL originated around the early 1900s, and although much speculation surrounds the conception of this gem, Harry Cipriani at Harry's New York Bar in Paris is attributed with the great honor. The cocktail was named for a favored patron, a Frenchman whose particular choice of transportation to and from the bar was a chauffeur-driven motorcycle sidecar. With the perfect balance of strong, sweet, and sour elements, the Sidecar is thought to be the original inspiration behind the Margarita and the Daiquiri. The sugar-coated rim and lemon twist are optional, but a well-chilled glass is highly recommended.

Lemon wedge
Superfine sugar
1½ ounces Cognac (or brandy)
¾ ounce Cointreau (or triple sec)
¾ ounce fresh lemon juice
Lemon twist

Rub the rim of a chilled cocktail glass with the lemon wedge and rim with sugar. Shake the liquid ingredients vigorously with ice. Strain into the prepared cocktail glass. Twist the lemon peel over the top of the drink, and drop it in.

VARIATIONS: **For a Mango Sidecar,** add 1 ounce mango purée.

For a Tuaca Sidecar, substitute Tuaca for the Cointreau and add 1/2 ounce fresh orange juice and 1/2 ounce fresh lime juice.

For a Boston Sidecar, reduce the brandy to 1 ounce, add 1 ounce light rum, and substitute fresh lime juice for the lemon juice.

For a Polish Sidecar, add 3/4 ounce blackberry brandy and garnish with a few fresh blackberries.

Stinger

ANOTHER POPULAR CLASSIC COCKTAIL from Prohibition days, the stinger used crème de menthe to mask the low-quality brandy available at the time. It has an illustrious list of fans, including many famous literary luminaries such as Ian Fleming, Evelyn Waugh, and Somerset Maugham. When it comes to cocktails made with an intense amount of crème de menthe, you're either a mint-flavor aficionado or you aren't—and this drink will certainly help determine which camp you fall into. Served as a nightcap, it is always made with the white (clear) crème de menthe, never the green. Technically, you can make a Stinger with any kind of liquor, whether it's rum, bourbon, Galliano, or tequila, just as long as it has the crème de menthe.

Classic Stinger

1½ ounces brandy
1½ ounces white crème de menthe

Stir the ingredients in a mixing glass with ice. Strain into a chilled cocktail glass. Or shake and pour into an ice-filled old-fashioned glass filled with crushed ice.

Contemporary Stinger

2 ounces brandy
¾ ounce white crème de menthe

Pour the ingredients over crushed ice in an old-fashioned glass, and stir.

Stirrup Cup

1½ ounces brandy
1½ ounces cherry brandy
¾ ounce fresh lemon juice
1 teaspoon simple syrup

Shake the ingredients vigorously with ice. Strain into an ice-filled old-fashioned glass.

VARIATION: **For a Vanderbilt,** omit the lemon juice and add 3 dashes Angostura bitters. Shake with ice and strain into a chilled cocktail glass.

Stone Fence

2 ounces applejack
2 dashes Angostura bitters
2 to 4 ounces chilled apple cider
Orange twist

Pour the liquid ingredients into an ice-filled old-fashioned glass. Stir well. Twist the orange peel over the drink, and drop it in.

Tiger's Milk

1 ounce brandy
1 ounce rum
1 teaspoon sugar
4 ounces half-and-half
Freshly grated or ground nutmeg

Shake the brandy, rum, sugar, and half-and-half vigorously with ice. Strain into a chilled wineglass, and sprinkle with nutmeg.

Tulip Cocktail

¾ ounce apple brandy
¾ ounce sweet vermouth
¼ ounce apricot brandy
Dash of fresh lemon juice

Shake the ingredients vigorously with ice. Strain into a chilled cocktail glass.

Valencia

2 ounces apricot brandy
1 ounce fresh orange juice
3 dashes orange bitters

Shake the ingredients vigorously with ice. Strain into a chilled cocktail glass.

Via Veneto

2 ounces brandy
½ ounce sambuca
½ ounce fresh lemon juice
1 teaspoon simple syrup
½ egg white (optional)

Shake the ingredients vigorously with ice. Strain into a chilled cocktail glass.

Widow's Kiss

1 ounce apple brandy
½ ounce Bénédictine
½ ounce yellow Chartreuse
Dash of Angostura bitters

Shake the ingredients vigorously with ice. Strain into a chilled cocktail glass.

Champagne & Sparkling Wines

THE VERY EMBODIMENT OF CELEBRATION, champagne is evocative of beauty and sophistication, romance and festive occasions, elegance and luxury, and all that is good in life. All these are captured in the tiny bubbles of this exquisitely enjoyable effervescent wine.

Strictly speaking, to be called champagne, an effervescent wine must be produced in the Champagne region of northeastern France. When produced anywhere else, it is called simply a sparkling wine. Non-champagne sparkling wines can be designated *méthode champenoise,* meaning that they were produced following the method used to make champagne. A complex and delicate process that is now called the "traditional method" (as the Champenois objected even to the use of the term "Champagne method"), the *méthode champenoise* is widely copied due to its huge popularity and success, and many claim to have achieved quality comparable to French champagne.

To make champagne, the pale juices from pinot noir, pinot meunier, and chardonnay grapes are vigorously fermented. The fermentation is then slowed down and finally stopped by cooling the wine in damp underground cellars or with air-conditioning (more prevalent these days). The wine spends a winter chilling and then is bottled and referments in the spring as it warms back up. Premature bottling is essential to the process, as the wine continues to ferment in the bottle. This fermentation produces a gas that dissolves in the wine. The natural effect is encouraged by a bit more sugar and yeast, added to the light, pale wine, and after two or so years in the bottle (for nonvintage champagnes the minimum is fifteen months, three years for vintage champagne), it acquires a distinct character, strength, and effervescence.

This intricate process of double fermentation was inadvertently invented in the seventeenth century by a French monk, Dom Pérignon, who very auspiciously began bottling his wine, rather than following the centuries-old practice of storing it in large oak barrels, only to find, as it refermented, that by spring's thaw, the thin, fine French glass bottles had all exploded from the effervescent gases.

The main difference in champagne brands lies in the making of the cuvée, or the blends that come together in one bottle of champagne, by expertly blending the young wines and occasionally adding the character and depth of an older, reserve wine.

Nonvintage champagne is a blend containing wines from multiple past harvests, which controls consistency. Champagnes come in luxury cuvées that are of either specially selected vintage wines or multivintage blends. The established champagne houses have a reputation to uphold (from the delicacy of Taittinger champagnes to the classic style of Clicquot and the boldness of Bollinger), which requires that their distinct style stay consistent in quality and flavor from year to year. If champagne vineyards experience a particularly great grape year, the best grapes will become a vintage champagne, pressed and fermented from a single year's grapes, and that year will be stated on the label.

CHAMPAGNE LABELING

∞ **BLANC DE BLANCS**   A champagne made entirely from white chardonnay grapes, usually light, dry, and refreshing.

∞ **BLANC DE NOIRS**   A light, dry champagne made exclusively from dark-skinned pinot noir and pinot meunier (red) grapes.

∞ **CUVÉE**   The blend used to make a particular champagne.

∞ **CRÉMANT**   A gently sparkling champagne.

∞ **NONVINTAGE (NV)**   Champagne containing wines from more than one year.

∞ **RICH**   Very sweet.

∞ **RESERVE**   A much-used but meaningless term.

∞ **VINTAGE**   Containing wines from only a single year, stated on the label.

∞ **ROSÉ**   A blend of still red wine with the sparkling white wine from the Champagne region.

∞ **GRAND CRU**   Wines from one or more of the top 17 villages; used for blending.

SWEETNESS LEVELS

Champagne styles are categorized and labeled according to the level of sweetness:

- Extra brut: bone dry
- Brut: exceptionally dry
- Sec: medium dry in champagne terms, but has a trace of medium sweetness
- Demi-sec: medium-sweet
- Doux: sweet to medium-sweet

CHAMPAGNE BOTTLE SIZES

Connoisseurs insist that the use of larger bottles greatly improves flavor.

- Split: 187 ml
- Standard bottle: 750 ml
- Magnum: 1.5 liters (equivalent of 2 bottles)
- Jeroboam (or double magnum): 3 liters (equivalent of 4 bottles)
- Rehoboam: 4.5 liters (equivalent of 6 bottles)
- Methuselah: 6 liters (equivalent of 8 bottles)
- Salmanazar: 9 liters (equivalent of 12 bottles)
- Balthazar: 12 liters (equivalent of 16 bottles)
- Nebuchadnezzar: 15 liters (equivalent of 20 bottles)

OTHER SPARKLING WINES

∾ **FRENCH CRÉMANT**   A gently sparkling wine made in Champagne.

∾ **GERMAN SEKT**   A sparkling wine made from riesling and chardonnay grapes.

∾ **ITALIAN ASTI SPUMANTE**   *Spumante* meaning "sparkling" in Italian, this is a popular sweet sparkling white wine made from muscat (*moscato*) grapes from the Asti, Piedmont, region of Italy. Relatively low in alcohol, it is typically served as a dessert wine as well as an aperitif.

∾ **ITALIAN PROSECCO**   A light, dry Italian sparkling wine made from the white prosecco grapes grown in Veneto, Italy.

∾ **SPANISH CAVA**   Produced in the Catalonian region, these fine sparkling wines are made using the traditional *méthode champenoise.* This region is one of the largest producers of bubbly.

U.S. SPARKLING WINES Mostly produced in Northern California, but also in the Northwest, American sparkling wines are made from pinot noir and chardonnay grapes, using the traditional *méthode champenoise*.

CHAMPAGNE'S FUNNY STUFF, I'M USED TO WHISKEY. WHISKEY IS A SLAP ON THE BACK, AND CHAMPAGNE'S A HEAVY MIST BEFORE MY EYES.
            —JIMMY STEWART, American actor (from the film The Philadelphia Story)

SERVING CHAMPAGNE

Champagnes and sparkling wines do not benefit from aging and should be enjoyed reasonably soon, whatever the vintage, as they can go flat in the bottle if left too long. To preserve the bouquet, store champagne in a cool, dry place, at room temperature. Do not keep it in the refrigerator for long periods of time. Champagne should, however, always be served chilled. Place it in the refrigerator only two to three hours before serving, or quickly chill it down by placing it in a bucket filled with equal amounts of ice and water. The best champagne (fine vintage champagnes) should be chilled to no more than 46°F, whereas nonvintage champagnes can be further chilled to 43°F, and sparkling wines, such as sekt and cava, can be chilled to 39°F.

Once champagne is uncorked, the bubbles slowly dissipate, and rather than using dubious techniques to preserve the fizz, such as hanging a silver spoon down in the neck or using a champagne stopper, it is best to just enjoy the entire bottle at its most effervescent.

The volatile effervescence held in a bottle of champagne packs enough pressure to be very dangerous if pointed in the wrong direction, and bottles should be opened with care (the corks have even been known to pop off without any provocation). As much as the sound of a cork popping seems cinematically celebratory and festive, it is not the correct way to open a bottle of champagne, as it allows too much of the effervescence to escape. The best method is to firmly hold the cork and twist it, with the help of a towel over the top of the bottle, while slowly turning the bottle until the cork is loosened, and to remove it with a minimum loss of fizz.

The glamorous and iconic saucer-shaped coupe, a legendary glass modeled after Marie Antoinette's breast, is ideal for grand party celebrations and wedding toasts, as its design both allows for quicker pouring than a flute (which needs a slower pour to avoid froth overflow) and adds a retro glamour to the occasion. For sipping fine champagne and smaller gatherings, the more contemporary champagne flute is best, as it is better designed than the coupe for preserving the effervescence.

MIXING CHAMPAGNE COCKTAILS

Champagne cocktails are, by their very bubbly nature, refreshing drinks, fizzy and energizing. Typically low in alcohol content, some are slightly sweet, some are tart, and many are made with fresh juices. Because of champagne's delicate flavor, the best champagne cocktails are made predominantly with champagne, accentuated and enhanced with minimal amounts of other ingredients. And save your expensive champagne for sipping and appreciating; a moderate to inexpensively priced good, dry sparkling wine or champagne is more appropriate for mixed drinks.

When making champagne (or sparkling wine) cocktails, all other ingredients should precede the champagne. Pour the champagne in very slowly, as the last ingredient added. Otherwise, it will quickly overflow. The champagne's effervescence will naturally blend the ingredients together.

∽ *CHAMPAGNE, IF YOU ARE SEEKING THE TRUTH, IS BETTER THAN A LIE DETECTOR.* —GRAHAM GREENE, *English novelist*

CHAMPAGNE AND SPARKLING WINE DRINKS

Alcazar

1 ounce vodka
1 ounce apricot purée
Dash of apricot liqueur
3 to 5 ounces chilled champagne

Shake all ingredients but the champagne vigorously with ice. Strain into a chilled champagne flute, and slowly top with champagne.

Alfonso   *This classic is best when the ingredients are prechilled.*

1 sugar cube
Dash of Angostura bitters
1¼ ounces Dubonnet
3 to 5 ounces chilled champagne
Lemon twist

In the bottom of a chilled champagne flute, soak the sugar cube with the bitters. Pour in the Dubonnet, add an ice cube, and slowly top with champagne. Run the lemon peel around the rim, twist it over the drink, and drop it in.

Ambrosia

Dash of fresh lemon juice
Dash of triple sec
¾ ounce brandy
¾ ounce Calvados
3 to 5 ounces chilled champagne

Shake all ingredients but the champagne vigorously with ice. Strain into a chilled champagne flute, and slowly top with champagne.

Bellini ------

ONE OF THE MOST FAMOUS SPARKLING APERITIFS was created in the 1940s in Venice, at Harry's Bar, in honor of the Venetian Renaissance painter Giovanni Bellini. It is traditionally, and ideally, made with puréed fresh white peaches and prosecco, an Italian dry sparkling wine. White peaches are somewhat difficult to find, with a seasonally narrow window, but any variety of ripe peach or even nectarine can be used. If peaches are unavailable, you can substitute 1 ounce of peach nectar; although not as flavorful, it will do in a pinch. Peach brandy or schnapps has occasionally been used as well but is not recommended from a purist's point of view.

----

3 ounces white peach purée (or peach nectar)
4 to 6 ounces chilled prosecco (or other dry sparkling wine)
Peach slice

Pour the peach purée into a chilled champagne flute. Slowly add the prosecco, stirring gently. Garnish with a fresh peach slice.

Bombay Bellini

2 ounces white peach purée
2 ounces mango purée
¼ ounce peach brandy
Dash of fresh lemon juice
3 to 5 ounces chilled champagne

Pour all ingredients but the champagne into a chilled champagne flute. Slowly top with champagne.

American Flyer

1½ ounces light rum
½ ounce fresh lime juice
½ teaspoon sugar
3 to 5 ounces chilled champagne

Shake all ingredients but the champagne vigorously with ice. Strain into a chilled champagne flute, and slowly top with champagne.

Barracuda

½ ounce white rum
½ ounce Galliano
½ ounce pineapple juice
¼ ounce fresh lime juice
¼ ounce grenadine
3 to 5 ounces chilled champagne

Shake all ingredients but the champagne with ice. Strain into an ice-filled collins glass or into a chilled champagne flute. Slowly top with champagne.

Black Velvet
This drink was created in commemoration of the death of Prince Albert. It's also known as a Bismarck or Champagne Velvet.

3 ounces chilled Guinness
3 ounces chilled champagne

Slowly pour the ingredients, in the order given, into a chilled champagne flute. Don't stir.

Blue Champagne

1 ounce vodka (or gin)
¼ ounce fresh lemon juice
¼ ounce blue curaçao
Dash of triple sec
3 to 5 ounces chilled champagne

Pour all ingredients but the champagne into a chilled champagne flute. Slowly top with champagne.

Brandy Champagne Cocktail

1 sugar cube
2 dashes Angostura bitters
½ ounce brandy
3 to 5 ounces chilled champagne
Lemon twist

In the bottom of a chilled champagne flute, soak the sugar cube with the bitters. Pour in the brandy, and slowly top with champagne. Run the lemon peel around the rim, twist it over the drink, and drop it in.

Campari Champagne Cocktail

1 ounce Campari
3 to 5 ounces chilled champagne
Orange twist

Pour the Campari into a chilled champagne flute. Slowly add the champagne, stirring gently. Run the orange peel around the rim, twist it over the drink, and drop it in.

VARIATION: **For a Due Campari,** add ½ ounce Cordial Campari and ¾ ounce fresh lemon juice.

Caribbean Fizz

1 ounce dark rum
1 ounce banana purée
1 ounce pineapple juice
3 to 5 ounces chilled champagne

Shake all ingredients but the champagne vigorously with ice. Strain into a chilled champagne flute, and slowly top with champagne.

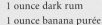

Caribbean Royale

½ ounce light rum
½ ounce crème de banane
3 to 5 ounces chilled champagne
Dash of orange bitters
Banana slice

Pour all liquid ingredients but the champagne into a chilled champagne flute. Slowly top with champagne. Garnish with the banana slice.

Casanova

½ ounce apple juice
½ ounce raspberry purée
3 to 5 ounces chilled champagne
2 fresh raspberries

Pour all liquid ingredients but the champagne into a chilled champagne flute. Slowly top with champagne. Drop the raspberries into the drink.

Champagne Cooler

1 ounce Grand Marnier
½ ounce Cognac
2 dashes Angostura bitters
3 to 5 ounces chilled champagne
Orange slice

Pour all liquid ingredients but the champagne into a chilled champagne flute. Slowly top with champagne. Garnish with the orange slice.

VARIATION: **For a Dynamite,** add 1 ounce fresh orange juice.

Champagne Cosmo

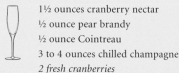

1½ ounces cranberry nectar
½ ounce pear brandy
½ ounce Cointreau
3 to 4 ounces chilled champagne
2 fresh cranberries

Shake the cranberry nectar, pear brandy, and Cointreau vigorously with ice. Strain into a chilled champagne flute. Slowly top with the champagne, and garnish with the cranberries.

Champagne Julep

6 to 8 small fresh mint leaves
1 teaspoon superfine sugar
¼ ounce fresh lemon juice
Dash of Cognac
3 to 5 ounces chilled champagne
Fresh mint sprig

Muddle the mint leaves, sugar, lemon juice, and Cognac together in the bottom of a collins glass. Add a few ice cubes, and slowly top with champagne. Garnish with the mint sprig.

Chicago

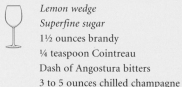

Lemon wedge
Superfine sugar
1½ ounces brandy
¼ teaspoon Cointreau
Dash of Angostura bitters
3 to 5 ounces chilled champagne

Rub the rim of a chilled wineglass with the lemon wedge, and rim with sugar. Shake all ingredients but the champagne vigorously with ice. Strain into the prepared glass, and slowly top with champagne.

Citron Sparkler *Sometimes the most sumptuous libations are the essence of simplicity.*

2 tablespoons softened lemon sorbet
½ ounce Galliano
3 to 5 ounces chilled prosecco (or champagne)
2 fresh cranberries

Combine the lemon sorbet and Galliano in the bottom of a chilled champagne flute. Slowly pour in the champagne. Skewer or drop the cranberries into the drink.

VARIATION: **For a fruity alternative,** substitute 1 ounce Chambord for the Galliano, and serve with a mint sprig.

Corpse Reviver No. 3 *Originating at the Cambon Bar, in the Ritz Hotel, Paris, this libation was created by Franck Meier in 1926.*

1½ ounces Pernod
3 to 5 ounces chilled champagne
¼ lemon wedge

Pour the Pernod into a chilled champagne flute. Slowly top with champagne. Squeeze the lemon wedge over the top.

Death in the Afternoon *Also known as the Hemingway, this was one of Hemingway's favorite pick-me-ups. While hanging out with other artistic illuminati of the 1920s on Paris's Left Bank, he enjoyed the popular absinthe enough to concoct his own signature drink, and aptly named it Death in the Afternoon, not to be confused with his Death in the Gulf Stream cocktail (found in the gin section, page 180).*

1½ ounces absinthe (or Pernod)
3 to 5 ounces chilled brut champagne

Pour the absinthe or Pernod into a chilled champagne flute. Swirl to coat the inside of the flute, and slowly top with the champagne.

Classic Champagne Cocktail

ALTHOUGH AN INEXPENSIVE CHAMPAGNE is suitable for most champagne-based cocktails, this classic is intended for a good-quality dry champagne, perfected with the sugar, bitters, and lemon.

- -

1 sugar cube
2 to 3 dashes Angostura bitters
3 to 5 ounces chilled dry champagne
Lemon twist

In the bottom of a chilled champagne flute, soak the sugar cube with the bitters. Slowly top with champagne. Run the lemon peel around the rim, twist it over the drink, and drop it in.

VARIATIONS: **For a London Special,** substitute a long orange peel spiral for the lemon peel; place half in the cocktail and leave half hanging over the edge of the glass.

For an Irish Champagne Cocktail, add 1 ounce Irish whiskey.

Dream

1 ounce Dubonnet
½ ounce Cointreau (or triple sec)
½ ounce fresh grapefruit juice
3 to 5 ounces chilled champagne

Shake all ingredients but the champagne vigorously with ice. Strain into a chilled champagne flute, and slowly top with champagne.

Épernay

1 ounce crème de framboise
¼ ounce Midori melon liqueur
3 to 5 ounces chilled champagne

Pour all ingredients but the champagne into a chilled champagne flute. Top slowly with champagne.

Fellini

½ ounce limoncello
½ ounce Mandarine Napoléon liqueur (or triple sec)
1 ounce fresh mandarin juice
3 to 5 ounces chilled champagne

Shake all ingredients but the champagne vigorously with ice. Strain into a chilled champagne flute, and slowly top with champagne.

Flying

¾ ounce gin
¾ ounce fresh lemon juice
¼ ounce Cointreau (or triple sec)
1 teaspoon sugar
3 to 5 ounces chilled champagne

Shake all ingredients but the champagne vigorously with ice. Strain into a chilled champagne flute, and slowly top with champagne.

Fraises Royale

1 ounce crème de fraise
1 ounce limoncello
3 to 5 ounces chilled champagne
1 fresh strawberry, hulled

Shake the crème de fraise and limoncello vigorously with ice. Strain into a chilled champagne flute, and slowly top with champagne. Garnish with the strawberry.

French Champagne Cocktail

1 sugar cube
2 dashes Angostura bitters
½ ounce crème de cassis
3 to 5 ounces chilled champagne

In the bottom of a chilled champagne flute, soak the sugar cube with the bitters. Pour in the crème de cassis, and slowly top with champagne.

French Kiss

⅔ ounce raspberry purée
1 ounce ginger beer
Dash of apricot brandy
3 to 5 ounces chilled champagne
2 fresh raspberries

Pour all liquid ingredients but the champagne into a chilled champagne flute, and stir. Slowly top with champagne. Garnish with the raspberries.

French Sherbet

1 ounce Cognac
½ ounce kirsch
2 tablespoons softened lemon sherbet
3 to 5 ounces chilled champagne

Pour all ingredients but the champagne into a chilled champagne flute, and stir. Slowly top with champagne.

French 75

THIS CLASSIC COCKTAIL WAS POPULAR at Harry's New York Bar in Paris, purportedly named after a French-made 75 mm howitzer cannon used in World War I. It was originally served over ice, but is now more frequently served up in a champagne flute and, in keeping with its French roots, many recipes replace the gin with Cognac. The gin version is often found served under the name Diamond Fizz.

1 ounce gin
½ ounce fresh lemon juice
1 teaspoon sugar
5 ounces chilled brut champagne
Orange peel spiral

Shake the gin, lemon juice, and sugar with ice, and strain into an ice-filled collins glass or a chilled champagne flute. Slowly top with champagne. Garnish with the orange peel spiral.

French 125 *A Cognac version of the French 75.*

¾ ounce Cognac
1½ ounces sweet-and-sour
3 to 5 ounces chilled champagne

Shake all ingredients but the champagne vigorously with ice. Strain into an ice-filled collins glass or a chilled champagne flute, and slowly top with champagne.

OTHER VARIATIONS ON THE FRENCH 75:

For a Soixante-Neuf, omit the sugar, and add a lemon twist.

For a King's Peg, omit the sugar and lemon juice.

For a French 69, add ¼ ounce Pernod.

For a French 76, substitute vodka for the gin.

For a French 95, substitute bourbon for the gin.

Ginger Fizz

1 ounce bourbon
1 ounce pineapple juice
2 to 3 thin slices fresh ginger
3 to 5 ounces chilled champagne

Shake all ingredients but the champagne vigorously with ice. Strain into a chilled champagne flute, and slowly top with champagne.

James Bond

1 sugar cube
Dash of Angostura bitters
¾ ounce vodka
¼ ounce Lillet
3 to 5 ounces chilled champagne
Lemon twist

In the bottom of a chilled champagne flute, soak the sugar cube with the bitters. Pour in the vodka and Lillet. Slowly top with champagne. Run the lemon peel around the rim, twist it over the drink, and drop it in.

Jumping Jellybean

1 ounce tequila
1 ounce Grand Marnier
1 ounce fresh lemon juice
3 to 5 ounces chilled champagne

Shake all the ingredients but the champagne vigorously with ice. Strain into a cocktail glass, and slowly top with champagne.

Juniper Royale

1 ounce gin
½ ounce fresh orange juice
½ ounce cranberry juice
Dash of grenadine
3 to 5 ounces chilled champagne

Shake all ingredients but the champagne vigorously with ice. Strain into a chilled champagne flute, and slowly top with champagne.

Kentucky Champagne Cocktail

1 sugar cube
2 to 3 dashes Peychaud's bitters
1 ounce bourbon
½ ounce peach liqueur
3 to 5 ounces chilled champagne
Lemon twist

In the bottom of a chilled champagne flute, soak the sugar cube with the bitters. Pour in the bourbon and peach liqueur. Slowly top with champagne. Run the lemon peel around the rim, twist it over the drink, and drop it in.

Kir Royale

½ ounce crème de cassis
4 to 6 ounces chilled champagne
Lemon twist

Pour the crème de cassis into a chilled champagne flute. Slowly top with champagne. Run the lemon peel around the rim, twist it over the drink, and drop it in.

La Dolce Vita

1 ounce vanilla-flavored vodka
1 ounce apricot nectar
½ ounce Cointreau
½ ounce fresh lime juice
1 to 2 ounces chilled prosecco (or champagne)

Shake all ingredients but the prosecco vigorously with ice. Strain into a chilled champagne coupe. Float the prosecco on top.

Lady Macbeth

3 to 5 ounces chilled champagne
1 ounce ruby port
Lemon twist

Pour the champagne into a chilled champagne flute. Slowly pour in the port. Do not stir. Run the lemon peel around the rim, twist it over the drink, and drop it in.

Lee Miller's Frobisher   *Named after Lee Miller, the famous World War II photographer who was also Man Ray's infamous muse and model.*

2 ounces gin
Dash of Angostura bitters
4 to 6 ounces chilled champagne
Lemon twist

Pour the gin and bitters into an ice-filled highball glass. Slowly add the champagne, stirring gently. Run the lemon peel around the rim, twist it over the drink, and drop it in.

Mexican Fizz

1 ounce tequila
1 ounce crème de cassis
1 ounce champagne

Pour the tequila and crème de cassis into an ice-filled highball glass. Slowly add the champagne, stirring gently.

Mimosa   *Freshly squeezed orange juice is crucial for a great mimosa—America's favorite brunch cocktail. Legend gives credit for this creation to the Ritz Hotel, Paris, 1925; the original calls for the juice of half an orange.*

2 ounces fresh orange juice

¼ ounce Cointreau

3 to 5 ounces chilled champagne

Pour the orange juice and Cointreau into a chilled champagne flute. Top slowly with champagne, stirring briefly.

Monte Carlo Imperial

¾ ounce gin

¼ ounce white crème de menthe

½ ounce fresh lemon juice

3 to 5 ounces chilled champagne

Shake all ingredients but the champagne vigorously with ice. Strain into a chilled champagne flute, and slowly top with champagne.

VARIATION: **For a Monte Carlo Highball,** increase the gin to 1¾ ounces, increase the lemon juice to 1 ounce, and serve in a highball glass.

Never on Sunday

2 ounces Metaxa

1 ounce ouzo

¼ ounce fresh lemon juice

Dash of Angostura bitters

3 ounces chilled champagne

3 ounces ginger beer

Lemon wedge

Pour the Metaxa, ouzo, lemon juice, and bitters into an ice-filled highball glass. Slowly add the champagne and ginger beer, stirring gently. Garnish with the lemon wedge.

Ohio

¾ ounce rosso (sweet) vermouth
¾ ounce Canadian whisky
Dash of triple sec
Dash of Angostura bitters
3 to 5 ounces chilled champagne

Pour all ingredients but the champagne into a chilled champagne flute. Slowly top with champagne.

Old Cuban   *This champagne variation on the Mojito is from Bemelmans Bar at the Carlyle Hotel in New York.*

1½ ounces good-quality rum
¾ ounce fresh lime juice
Dash of Angostura bitters
1 ounce simple syrup
6 fresh mint leaves
1½ ounces chilled champagne
Half a vanilla bean

Shake the rum, lime juice, bitters, simple syrup, and mint vigorously with ice. Strain into a chilled champagne flute. Slowly top with champagne, and stir gently. Garnish with the vanilla bean.

Paradis

1 ounce strained raspberry purée
½ ounce Cointreau
½ ounce crème de banane
3 to 5 ounces chilled champagne
1 fresh raspberry

Pour the raspberry purée, Cointreau, and crème de banane into a chilled champagne flute. Slowly top with champagne. Drop in the raspberry.

Passion

1 ounce aged Bacardi (8 years old)
½ ounce crème de pêche
1 ounce fresh lime juice
½ ounce simple syrup
1 ounce passion fruit purée
3 to 5 ounces chilled champagne

Shake all ingredients but the champagne vigorously with ice. Strain into an ice-filled highball glass, and slowly top with champagne.

Pimm's Royal

1½ ounces Pimm's No. 1
4 to 5 ounces chilled champagne
Lemon twist
Strip of cucumber peel

Pour the Pimm's into an ice-filled highball glass or chilled champagne flute. Slowly add the champagne, stirring gently. Run the lemon peel around the rim, twist it over the drink, and drop it in. Garnish with the cucumber peel.

Pineapple Flirtini

1½ ounces vodka
1½ ounces chilled champagne
¼ ounce pineapple juice
Pineapple slice

Stir the liquid ingredients gently in a mixing glass with ice. Slowly strain into a chilled cocktail glass. Garnish with the pineapple slice.

Pink Framboise Dream

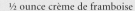

½ ounce crème de framboise
½ ounce Cointreau
1 ounce fresh pink grapefruit juice
3 to 5 ounces chilled champagne

Shake all ingredients but the champagne vigorously with ice. Strain into a chilled champagne flute, and slowly top with champagne.

Prince of Wales

1 ounce brandy
1 ounce Madeira
¼ ounce Cointreau
2 dashes Angostura bitters
3 to 5 ounces chilled champagne
Orange slice

Shake the brandy, Madeira, Cointreau, and bitters vigorously with ice. Strain into a chilled champagne flute, and slowly top with champagne. Garnish with the orange slice.

Poire Williams Champagne Cocktail

1½ ounces Poire Williams (or other pear brandy)
1 teaspoon simple syrup
3 to 5 ounces chilled champagne
Pear slice

Pour the Poire Williams and simple syrup into a chilled champagne flute. Slowly top with champagne. Garnish with the pear slice.

Ritz

¾ ounce fresh orange juice
¾ ounce Cognac
¼ ounce Cointreau
3 to 5 ounces chilled champagne

Shake all ingredients but the champagne vigorously with ice. Strain into a chilled champagne flute, and slowly top with champagne.

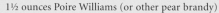

Ritz 75 *From the Ritz Hotel Bar in Paris.*

½ ounce gin
½ ounce fresh lemon juice
½ ounce fresh mandarin juice
1 teaspoon sugar
4 ounces chilled brut champagne

Shake all ingredients but the champagne vigorously with ice. Strain into an ice-filled collins glass or a chilled champagne flute, and slowly top with champagne.

Royal Gin Fizz

2 ounces gin
1 ounce fresh lemon juice
1 egg
¼ ounce simple syrup
3 to 5 ounces chilled champagne

Shake all ingredients but the champagne vigorously with ice. Strain into an ice-filled collins glass. Slowly add champagne, stirring gently.

Typhoon

1 ounce gin
Dash of Pernod
½ ounce fresh lime juice
4 ounces chilled champagne
Lime twist

Shake the gin, Pernod, and lime juice vigorously with ice. Strain into an ice-filled highball glass. Slowly top with champagne, and stir gently. Garnish with the lime twist.

Valencia Royale

1 ounce apricot brandy
1 ounce fresh orange juice
3 to 5 ounces chilled champagne
Orange slice

Pour the apricot brandy and orange juice into a chilled champagne flute. Slowly top with champagne. Garnish with the orange slice.

Violet Champagne d'Amour

1 ounce Parfait Amour
½ ounce fresh lemon juice
¼ ounce Cointreau
3 to 5 ounces chilled champagne
2 fresh violets

Pour all liquid ingredients but the champagne into a chilled champagne flute. Slowly top with champagne. Float the violets on top of the drink.

Volcano

¾ ounce raspberry liqueur
¾ ounce blue curaçao
3 to 5 ounces chilled champagne
Orange twist

Shake the raspberry liqueur and curaçao vigorously with ice. Strain into a chilled champagne flute, and slowly top with champagne. Run the orange peel around the rim, twist it over the drink, and drop it in.

GIN IS THE QUINTESSENTIAL COCKTAIL LIQUOR and the original inspiration for many classic cocktails, from the Martini and the Negroni to the fizzes, rickeys, and collinses. Historically infamous, gin has swung between extremes, from London gin houses and the bathtub gins of Prohibition to being the darling of the golden age of cocktails, used in glamorous libations ritualized by the literary set and Hollywood.

Gin's origins are deeply rooted in juniper-based medicinal cures. It was first distilled by monks around 1150 in Italy, and by the fourteenth century, the Italians were using a juniper-based elixir as a remedy for kidney complications. This elixir is generally thought to be the prototype for gin. But it was the Dutch who refined the distillation process, making the apothecary's tonic into a recreational tipple, and by the 1650s they were producing *genever,* with its intense juniper bouquet. The word "gin" was derived from *genever,* the Dutch term for juniper.

Gin was not only used by the Dutch as a cure for upset stomachs, but it also gained a reputation for the "numbed fearlessness" it gave soldiers going into battle. The English mercenaries who aided the Dutch during the Thirty Years War (1618–1648) came back home with tales of the Dutch courage, along with a few bottles of *genever*. Although originally used as a health tonic, gin has no official medicinal value today; nonetheless, Martini drinkers claim a variety of positive effects.

The popularity of gin as the English spirit of choice began with Dutch William III of Orange, who assumed the British throne in 1689. His preference for Holland gin was conspicuously evident through the restrictive tariffs he placed on England's favorite spirit at the time, French brandy, along with other spirits. It was inevitable that this "ginesque" spirit, made basically of grain alcohol with the addition of juniper, would quickly gain favor, and soon the ports of Bristol, Plymouth, and London became major distilling centers. From the fashionable Banqueting House at Hampton Court Palace, which was dubbed the gin temple, to the slums of London, gin became the perfect numbing distraction from reality and poverty.

By 1690, with lenient distillation laws and heavy taxes on beer, making gin was a cheap option, and by 1730, with millions of gallons being imbibed, the laws had changed to allow intoxicating liquors to be consumed only in dwelling houses. This further promoted the infamous "gin shops," found in one-fifth of London's houses. This low moment in gin's history, when industrious and mostly amateur distillers produced unregulated and dangerously bad distillates masked with strong juniper flavor, resulted in a bad reputation that took decades to shake. Regulation ensued, and Alexander Gordon, one of the more reputable producers, was one of the first to obtain a license to distill gin, in 1769, assisting in the beginning of a restored and regulated quality gin.

Gin's popularity is steeped in the cultural history of the Martini—from the turn-of-the-century bar scene, strictly for sophisticated urbanites, dry and otherwise, to Prohibition and the decadent 1920s and '30s, inspiring the era of home-distilled, "bathtub" gin, produced simply by adding essence of juniper to the base alcohol, masking the harsh taste and harking back to the infamous London gin shop days.

Franklin Roosevelt, a Martini aficionado, ushered in the first "legal" Martini in 1933, further perpetuating the already popular Martini ritual that eventually evolved into the maximum-dryness fetish of the 1950s and '60s.

By the late 1950s, gin had been eclipsed by vodka, with James Bond and Smirnoff simultaneously promoting a stylish preference for Russian vodka into the mainstream of popular culture. When it comes to the Martini, however, gin is still the spirit of choice.

The quality of gin varies depending on the raw ingredients, the purity of the added water, and the method of distillation. Beyond the usual flavors of juniper and cilantro (coriander), distillers strive for distinctly individual gins by adding their own combination of botanicals—from clove and lemon and orange rind to licorice, anise, angelica, juniper, orrisroot, almonds, cardamom, and cassia bark—to give each variety an individual complexity.

This colorless, light-bodied spirit, like vodka, is distilled from grain (wheat or rye) or cane (molasses), but it parts company with vodka once the base spirit is flavored. Gin is distilled in column stills, producing a clean, light-bodied, high-proof spirit, and is then redistilled with botanical flavoring, usually in an Old World pot still. The best-quality brands are redistilled with the flavorings, by suspending and vaporizing them into the spirit for complexity, while the mass-market brands infuse the botanicals by soaking them in the base spirit and then redistilling the spirit. The low-end brands, known as compound gins, simply add essences and extracts to the base spirit later.

GIN STYLES

When people refer to gin, they usually mean London dry gin, which is most often used in cocktails, but there is a wide spectrum of styles of gin to choose from, including a new generation of gins available on the market that have taken a departure from the classic juniper flavor.

From the intensely pungent gins to the softer styles, and many aromatic variations in between, each distiller strives for its own distinct signature of delicate complexity. This section clarifies the differences with a few brand examples, but of course, the best way to form a preference is to taste them.

------- OLD TOM GIN -------

One of the few remaining examples of old-style gin, Old Tom is representative of a slightly sweetened style popular in 18th-century England. It's no longer made in the old way, however, but is a neutral grain spirit with botanical flavorings, sweetened with sugar syrup.

------- PLYMOUTH GIN -------

By British law, Plymouth gin may be produced only in the city of Plymouth. Although similar to London dry gin, it is intensely fragrant and fuller-bodied, slightly fruity, citrusy, very dry, and very aromatic—and makes a perfectly acceptable Martini.

------- LONDON DRY GIN -------

The classic dry gin is a quintessentially English style, bone-dry, mildly perfumed to pungent, and lacking the sweetness of the original 18th-century old-style Old Tom gin. London dry gin is typically made by the more refined process, in which botanicals are distilled into the gin, not added later.

This light, aromatic gin is the most popular style, great for mixing as well as Martinis.

Examples of London dry gin:

- Beefeater: pungent, with lime, orange, and lavender notes
- Beefeater Crown Jewel: lighter and more delicate, with citrus
- Bombay and Bombay Sapphire: delicate, with pine forest tones
- Classic Tanqueray: heavy on the juniper and cilantro, rich and pungent
- Tanqueray No. TEN: a smoother, softer style
- Van Gogh, from Denmark: a fine classic dry gin
- Boodles, Booth's High & Dry and House of Lords, Gilbey's, and Miller's

------- **U.S. DRY GIN** -------

These gins tend to be softer and less flavorful than the London dry gins, and are great for mixing. Brands include Junipero and Fleischmann's.

------- **HOLLAND GIN** -------

Also known as *genever,* this Dutch-style gin is highly aromatic, with intense juniper flavor. Distilled from malted grain mash, the old-style, or "oude genever," is similar to England's Old Tom gin (but much higher in quality due to a refined distillation process)—pungent, slightly sweet, and fuller-bodied, with a light yellow hue. The *jonge* (young) *genevers,* similar to London dry gins, are lighter-bodied and drier, and the wood-aged *genever* is called *korenwijn.*

With their intense flavor, Holland gins are best served neat or over ice; they are not ideal for mixed drinks.

Bols, Bokma, and De Kuyper are famous Dutch brands.

------- **MID-PUNGENCY GINS** -------

A few gins of note fall into the mid-pungency range; these hover between the intense pungency of Beefeater and the softer, smoother Tanqueray No. TEN.

Old Raj: includes saffron for a golden hue

Citadelle: a premium gin from France, well-balanced with lime tones

Magellan: tinted blue by roots and herbs

------- **NEWER GINS** -------

The newer "second generation" gins are a distinct departure from the classic juniper style, flavored with a broad spectrum of aromatic botanicals such as orange, clove, mixed citrus, and pear, and even colored blue (Magellan gin) and bottled in trendy signature bottles:

- Zuidam, from Holland: flavored with vanilla and spice

- Wet, from Beefeaters: flavored with pears

- Damrak, a gin from Denmark: with citrus notes

- Hendrick's, from Scotland: rose petals and cucumbers

Other newer styles of flavored gin include:

- Almond gin: mixed with bitter almond

- Apple gin: mixed with apple

- Black currant gin: mixed with black currant

- Lemon gin: mixed with lemon and/or lemon peel extract

- Orange gin: mixed with bitter orange

SERVING AND MIXING GIN

↬ *THE PROPER UNION OF GIN AND VERMOUTH IS A GREAT AND SUDDEN GLORY; IT IS ONE OF THE HAPPIEST MARRIAGES ON EARTH, AND ONE OF THE SHORTEST LIVED.* —BERNARD DE VOTO, 1897–1955, American critic and historian

The aromatic, delicate, and unobtrusive characteristics of gin make it the quintessential spirit for mixed drinks, in concordance with just about any ingredient, from juices to liqueurs to vermouth. When it comes to multi-ingredient mixed drinks, using a moderate or cheaper gin such as Gordon's or Seagram's is perfectly appropriate.

For preparing a Martini or Gin and Tonic, where good-quality gin is most appreciated, you will enjoy the subtlety of a dry, aromatic premium gin such as Citadelle, Tanqueray, or Bombay Sapphire. Chilling the gin before-hand is a popular practice, as it helps to keep the ice from diluting the drink too quickly. However, the flavor of the gin's aromatic botanicals is improved with a bit of dilution, so it becomes a matter of preference.

Abbey Cocktail

1½ ounces gin
¾ ounce Lillet Blanc
¾ ounce fresh orange juice
2 dashes Angostura bitters
Maraschino cherry

Shake the liquid ingredients vigorously with ice. Strain into a chilled cocktail glass. Garnish with the cherry.

Alexander   *Dating from the 1920s, the original Alexander was made with gin, but the brandy version has become more popular (page 124).*

1 ounce gin
¾ ounce white crème de cacao
¾ ounce heavy cream
Pinch of freshly grated nutmeg

Shake the liquid ingredients vigorously with ice. Strain into a chilled cocktail glass, and sprinkle with nutmeg.

VARIATION: **For an Avalanche,** substitute brown crème de cacao for the white.

Antibes

1½ ounces gin
½ ounce Bénédictine
2 ounces fresh grapefruit juice
Orange slice

Shake the liquid ingredients vigorously with ice. Strain into an ice-filled old-fashioned glass, and garnish with the orange slice.

Arcadia

1½ ounces gin
½ ounce Galliano
½ ounce crème de banane
½ ounce fresh grapefruit juice

Shake the ingredients vigorously with ice. Strain into a chilled cocktail glass.

Bali Highball

1½ ounces gin
2 ounces guava nectar
½ ounce fresh lime juice
1 ounce pomegranate syrup
3 to 4 ounces chilled club soda
Lime wheel
Orange blossom (or other edible flower)

Shake the gin, guava nectar, lime juice, and pomegranate syrup vigorously with ice. Strain into an ice-filled highball glass. Top with club soda. Garnish with the lime wheel and orange blossom.

Beauty Spot

2 ounces gin
½ ounce white crème de cacao
1 egg white
½ teaspoon grenadine

Shake the gin, crème de cacao, and egg white vigorously with ice. Strain into a chilled cocktail glass. Drop the grenadine in the center of the drink; do not stir.

Bella, Bella

1 ounce gin
⅔ ounce Campari
½ ounce limoncello
½ ounce Mandarine Napoléon (or other orange liqueur)
⅔ ounce fresh orange juice
Lime peel spiral

Shake the liquid ingredients vigorously with ice. Strain into a chilled cocktail glass. Garnish with the lime peel spiral.

Blue Monday

1 ounce gin
1 ounce Cointreau (or triple sec)
Dash of blue curaçao
3 to 4 ounces chilled club soda

Pour the gin and Cointreau into an ice-filled highball glass. Add the curaçao. Top with club soda and stir.

Boston Cocktail

1½ ounces gin
1½ ounces apricot brandy
½ ounce fresh lemon juice
Dash of grenadine

Shake the ingredients vigorously with ice. Strain into a chilled cocktail glass.

Bramble

4 to 5 fresh blackberries
1 teaspoon sugar
1 ounce fresh lime juice
1½ ounces gin
½ ounce crème de mûre (blackberry liqueur)
3 to 4 ounces chilled club soda
Lime wedge

In the bottom of a chilled highball glass, muddle together the black-berries, sugar, and lime juice. Fill the glass with ice and add the gin and crème de mûre. Top with club soda and stir briefly. Garnish with the lime wedge.

- -

Bronx Cocktail   *Invented in 1906 by Waldorf Astoria barman Johnny Salon after a visit to the Bronx Zoo.*

1½ ounces gin
¼ ounce dry vermouth
¼ ounce sweet vermouth
¾ ounce fresh orange juice
Orange slice

Shake the liquid ingredients vigorously with ice. Strain into a chilled cocktail glass. Garnish with the orange slice.

- -

Capri Cocktail

1½ ounces gin
½ ounce limoncello
¼ ounce peach schnapps
1 ounce fresh grapefruit juice
1 ounce mango juice
Dash of orgeat (or almond) syrup

Shake the ingredients vigorously with ice. Strain into a chilled cocktail glass.

- -

Caribbean Sunset

1 ounce gin
1 ounce crème de banane
1 ounce blue curaçao
1 ounce fresh lemon juice
½ ounce heavy cream
Dash of grenadine
Orange slice
Maraschino cherry

Shake the liquid ingredients vigorously with ice. Strain into an ice-filled highball glass. Garnish with the orange slice and cherry.

Chelsea Sidecar   *This variation on the Sidecar is made with gin instead of Cognac. Also known as the Chelsea Hotel or Gin Sidecar, it is a signature drink from the Chelsea Hotel in New York.*

Lemon twist

2 ounces gin

¾ ounce Cointreau

½ ounce fresh lemon juice

Rub the rim of a chilled cocktail glass with the lemon peel. Shake the liquid ingredients vigorously with ice. Strain into the prepared cocktail glass. Garnish with the lemon twist.

Cherry Cobbler

2 ounces gin

¾ ounce Cherry Heering

¼ ounce crème de cassis

¼ ounce fresh lemon juice

¼ ounce simple syrup

2 to 3 ounces chilled club soda (optional)

Lemon slice

Maraschino cherry

Fresh mint sprig

Shake all the liquid ingredients except the club soda vigorously with ice. Strain into a chilled old-fashioned glass. Top with club soda, if using. Garnish with the lemon slice, cherry, and mint sprig.

Coco Chanel

1 ounce gin

1 ounce Kahlúa

1 ounce heavy cream

Shake the ingredients vigorously with ice. Strain into a chilled cocktail glass.

Costa del Sol

2 ounces gin
1 ounce Cointreau
1 ounce apricot brandy

Shake the ingredients vigorously with ice. Strain into a chilled cocktail glass.

Crimson

1½ ounces gin
½ ounce fresh lemon juice
¼ ounce grenadine
¾ ounce ruby port

Shake the gin, lemon juice, and grenadine vigorously with ice. Strain into a chilled cocktail glass. Float the port on top.

VARIATION: Float ½ ounce tawny port instead of ruby port for a slightly drier version.

Dawn

1 ounce gin
¾ ounce Campari
1¾ ounces fresh orange juice
Orange slice

Shake the liquid ingredients vigorously with ice. Strain into an ice-filled old-fashioned glass. Garnish with the orange slice.

Death in the Gulf Stream

Ernest Hemingway created this hangover remedy, although there is a bit of speculation as to the exact time and place. Some attribute it to the Hotel Ritz in London, in 1922, others to a drink of his dated later, from 1937 in Key West. Hemingway's preference was for the more intensely pungent Holland gin, but a good-quality London dry gin is equally suitable. Either way, according to Hemingway, "it's tart and bitter—reviving and refreshing."

2 ounces gin
1½ ounces fresh lime juice
Pinch of superfine sugar
3 to 4 splashes Angostura bitters
Lime peel spiral

Pour the gin and lime juice into an ice-filled highball glass. Add the sugar and bitters and stir to combine. Twist the lime peel spiral over the drink, and drop it in.

Delmonico Number 1

This is the house cocktail from New York's famous Delmonico Restaurant, a classic that predates Prohibition. Traditionally served in a Delmonico glass (similar to a sour glass), it can be garnished with either a lemon or orange twist.

1 ounce gin
½ ounce brandy (or Cognac)
½ ounce dry vermouth
½ ounce sweet vermouth
2 dashes Angostura bitters
Orange twist

Shake the liquid ingredients vigorously with ice. Strain into a chilled cocktail glass. Garnish with the orange twist.

Desert Healer Cocktail

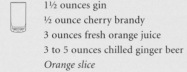

1½ ounces gin
½ ounce cherry brandy
3 ounces fresh orange juice
3 to 5 ounces chilled ginger beer
Orange slice

Shake the gin, cherry brandy, and orange juice vigorously with ice. Strain into an ice-filled highball glass. Top with ginger beer and stir gently. Garnish with the orange slice.

Dolomint

1 ounce gin
1 ounce Galliano
1 ounce fresh lime juice
3 to 5 ounces chilled club soda
Fresh mint sprig

Shake the gin, Galliano, and lime juice vigorously with ice. Strain into an ice-filled highball glass. Top with club soda and stir gently. Garnish with the mint sprig.

Flamingo

1½ ounces gin
½ ounce apricot brandy
½ ounce fresh lime juice
¼ ounce grenadine

Shake the ingredients vigorously with ice. Strain into a chilled cocktail glass.

Florida

¾ ounce gin
¼ ounce kirsch
¼ ounce triple sec
1½ ounces fresh orange juice
1 teaspoon fresh lemon juice
Orange twist

Shake the liquid ingredients vigorously with ice. Strain into a chilled cocktail glass. Garnish with the orange twist.

Foghorn

2 ounces gin
½ ounce fresh lime juice
3 to 5 ounces chilled ginger ale or ginger beer
Lime wedge

Pour the gin and lime juice into an ice-filled old-fashioned glass. Top with ginger ale and stir gently. Squeeze the lime wedge over the drink, and drop it in.

VARIATIONS: **For a Dragonfly** (also known as Prohibition Champagne), squeeze the lime wedge only, omitting the lime juice.

For a Leap Frog (basically a Gin Buck), substitute 2 ounces lemon juice for the lime juice.

Gibson *See the Martini section.*

Gin and Sin

2 ounces gin
¼ ounce fresh orange juice
¼ ounce fresh lemon juice
2 dashes grenadine

Stir the ingredients in a mixing glass with ice. Strain into a chilled cocktail glass.

Gin and Tonic *The quintessential English summertime libation. Many prefer theirs with a lot of fresh lime.*

2 ounces good-quality gin
4 ounces chilled tonic water
1 or 2 lime wedges

Pour the gin and tonic water into an ice-filled old-fashioned glass. Stir well. Squeeze the lime wedges over the drink and drop them in.

Gimlet

THIS CLASSIC COCKTAIL WAS ORIGINALLY CONCEIVED by the British navy as a remedy for avoiding scurvy, combining their rations of gin and lime juice. The name was inspired by a "gimlet," the corkscrew-like device used to tap into the lime juice kegs. A key ingredient in the Gimlet is Rose's lime juice (otherwise known as lime cordial), introduced by Lauchlin Rose of Scotland as yet another preventative for scurvy in 1867. In *The Long Goodbye,* writer Raymond Chandler glamorized the drink for the masses when his character, detective Philip Marlowe, pontificated on his favorite cocktail: "A real gimlet is half gin and half Rose's lime juice and nothing else." The classic recipe from the 1930s Savoy Hotel bar is indeed made of equal parts Plymouth gin and Rose's lime juice. Of course, there are many variations according to personal preference, from different ratios of gin to lime juice to the addition of water or club soda, and, for those who desire fresh lime juice instead of Rose's, a teaspoon of sugar or ½ teaspoon simple syrup is needed. Many also enjoy a sugar rim, first moistened with lime juice.

Classic Gimlet

1¼ ounces gin
1¼ ounces Rose's lime juice
Lime wedge

Stir the gin and lime juice in a mixing glass with ice. Strain into a chilled cocktail glass. Squeeze the lime wedge into the drink.

Contemporary Gimlet

2½ ounces gin
½ ounce Rose's lime juice
Lime wedge

Stir the gin and lime juice in a mixing glass with ice. Strain into a chilled cocktail glass. Squeeze the lime wedge over the drink.

Gin Fizz   *Made popular during Prohibition, this classic highball has many variations but is always shaken.*

2 ounces gin
1 ounce fresh lemon juice
1 teaspoon sugar
2 to 3 ounces chilled club soda

Shake the gin, lemon juice, and sugar vigorously with ice. Strain into an ice-filled highball glass. Top with club soda and stir gently.

VARIATIONS: **For a Silver Fizz,** add an egg white.

For a Golden Fizz, add an egg yolk.

For a Royal Gin Fizz, use champagne in place of the club soda.

For a Grand Royal Fizz, add 1 teaspoon maraschino liqueur, 1 ounce orange juice, and ¼ ounce half-and-half.

For a Gina, add ½ ounce crème de cassis.

Gin Julep

8 to 10 fresh mint leaves
¼ ounce fresh lime juice
¼ ounce fresh lemon juice
1 teaspoon sugar
2 ounces gin
Fresh mint sprig

Muddle the mint leaves, lime juice, lemon juice, and sugar in the bottom of an old-fashioned glass. Add ice and the gin, stirring briefly. Garnish with the mint sprig.

Gin Rickey   *A fizzy concoction similar to a collins or a fizz, made with lime juice instead of lemon juice.*

2 ounces gin
1 ounce fresh lime juice
3 to 5 ounces chilled club soda
Lime wedge

Pour the gin and lime juice into an ice-filled highball glass. Top with club soda and stir gently. Squeeze the lime wedge over the drink, and drop it in.

Gin Sling

2 ounces gin
½ ounce Cointreau
½ ounce fresh lemon juice
3 to 5 ounces chilled club soda
Lemon wedge

Shake the gin, Cointreau, and lemon juice vigorously with ice. Strain into an ice-filled highball glass. Top with club soda and stir gently. Squeeze the lemon wedge over the drink, and drop it in.

Golden Dawn *A classic aperitif from 1930.*

1 ounce gin
1 ounce apricot brandy
1 ounce Calvados
Dash of fresh orange juice
Dash of grenadine

Shake the gin, apricot brandy, Calvados, and orange juice vigorously with ice. Strain into a chilled cocktail glass. Float the grenadine on top.

Gold Martini

1½ ounces gin
½ ounce citron vodka
1 ounce Cointreau
¼ ounce brandy
3 to 4 thin slices of fresh ginger
Candied ginger slice

Shake all the ingredients except the candied ginger vigorously with ice. Strain into a chilled cocktail glass. Garnish with the candied ginger slice.

Grass Skirt

1½ ounces gin
1 ounce Cointreau
1 ounce pineapple juice
½ teaspoon grenadine

Shake the ingredients vigorously with ice. Strain into a chilled cocktail glass.

Green Devil   *Also known as a Greenback.*

1½ ounces gin
¾ ounce crème de menthe
½ ounce fresh lime juice
2 to 3 ounces chilled club soda (optional)

Shake the gin, crème de menthe, and lime juice vigorously with ice. Strain into an ice-filled old-fashioned glass. Top with club soda, if desired.

Guggenheim   *A gin variation on the classic Between the Sheets cocktail.*

1 ounce gin
1 ounce brandy
1 ounce Cointreau

Shake the ingredients vigorously with ice. Strain into a chilled cocktail glass.

Honolulu

2 ounces gin
½ ounce orange curaçao
¼ ounce fresh lime juice
¼ ounce fresh orange juice
Lemon twist

Shake the liquid ingredients vigorously with ice. Strain into a chilled cocktail glass. Twist the lemon peel over the drink, and drop it in.

VARIATION: Add ¼ ounce pineapple juice and a dash of Angostura bitters.

Imperial Gin

2 ounces gin
1 ounce fresh lemon juice
1 ounce fresh lime juice
2 to 3 ounces chilled club soda
Lemon peel spiral

Shake the gin, lemon juice, and lime juice vigorously with ice. Strain into an ice-filled highball glass. Top with club soda and stir gently. Garnish with the lemon peel spiral.

Jamaica Glow

1½ ounces gin
½ ounce dry red wine
½ ounce dark rum
½ ounce fresh orange juice

Shake the ingredients vigorously with ice. Strain into a chilled cocktail glass.

Jet Black

1½ ounces gin
2 teaspoons sweet vermouth
¼ ounce black sambuca (such as Opal Nera)

Shake the ingredients vigorously with ice. Strain into a chilled cocktail glass.

Jewel of the Nile

1½ ounces gin
½ ounce green Chartreuse
½ ounce yellow Chartreuse

Stir the ingredients in a mixing glass with ice. Strain into a chilled cocktail glass.

Jockey Club

2 ounces gin
¼ ounce crème de noyaux
¼ ounce white crème de cacao
¼ ounce fresh lemon juice
Dash of orange bitters

Shake the ingredients vigorously with ice. Strain into a chilled cocktail glass.

Juniper Royale

1 ounce gin
½ ounce fresh orange juice
½ ounce cranberry juice
Dash of grenadine
3 to 4 ounces chilled champagne

Shake all ingredients except the champagne vigorously with ice. Strain into a chilled champagne flute. Top with champagne, and stir gently.

Jupiter Cocktail

1½ ounces gin
½ ounce dry vermouth
¼ ounce Parfait Amour
¼ ounce fresh orange juice

Shake the ingredients vigorously with ice. Strain into a chilled cocktail glass.

Key Lime Martini

Lime wedge
Sugar
1½ ounces gin
1 ounce Tuaca
1 ounce fresh Key lime or other lime juice
1 teaspoon superfine sugar
Thinly sliced lime wheel

Rub the rim of a chilled cocktail glass with the lime wedge and rim with sugar. Shake all the ingredients except for the garnish vigorously with ice. Strain into the prepared glass. Garnish by floating the lime wheel on top.

Kyoto Cocktail

1½ ounces gin
½ ounce dry vermouth
½ ounce melon liqueur
Dash of fresh lemon juice

Shake the ingredients vigorously with ice. Strain into a chilled cocktail glass.

VARIATION: **For an Evergreen,** top with a splash of blue curaçao, and garnish with a maraschino cherry.

Lady Diana

1 ounce gin
1 ounce Campari
⅔ ounce fresh lime juice
Dash of simple syrup
Lime twist

Shake the liquid ingredients vigorously with ice. Strain into a chilled cocktail glass. Twist the lime peel over the drink, and drop it in.

L'Amour

2 ounces gin
Dash of cherry brandy
Dash of grenadine
Dash of fresh lemon juice
2 fresh mint sprigs

Shake the liquid ingredients vigorously with ice. Strain into a chilled cocktail glass. Garnish with the mint sprigs.

The Martini

~ *DO NOT ALLOW CHILDREN TO MIX DRINKS. IT IS UNSEEMLY AND THEY USE TOO MUCH VERMOUTH.* —STEVE ALLEN, *American humorist*

THE ILLUSTRIOUS AND FAMOUS MARTINI, a symbol of pure mixological alchemy and glamour, is structured on the perfect botanical balance between gin's juniper berry and dry vermouth's herbal qualities.

The origins of this famous cocktail are rather murky, with plenty of stories claiming the inception. Some believe the dry Martini was invented by the English in the late 1800s and was named after the Martini-Henry rifle, a favorite of the royal army. Another story insists that it originated in the town of Martinez, where it was mixed by a bartender named Richelieu or, conversely, that "professor" Jerry Thomas of San Francisco's Occidental Hotel created it for a miner who was on his way to the town of Martinez. Yet another legend attributes the creation to Martini di Arma di Traggi, a bartender at New York's Knickerbocker Hotel in 1910. Evolving from a popular drink called Gin and French made with London dry gin and Noilly Prat dry vermouth, Martini's variation was to stir with lots of ice and strain, and the Knickerbocker regulars are credited with changing the lemon twist garnish to an olive.

We may never know the real story, but we do know that the original ratio of equal parts London dry gin and Noilly Prat dry French vermouth, and a dash of orange bitters, is not dry enough for modern tastes. Dryness is a relative term, as the proportions of a 1930s Martini have slowly evolved, drying out to the absurdly dry extreme of straight chilled gin by the 1950s.

The Martini is a cult of mixological purism upon which many seek to wreak havoc with variations ranging from minuscule to colossal. It has an illustrious list of devotees, all advocating their particular stances, each of which, of course, is the correct way. As the Martini became progressively more dry, the ritual of controlling the vermouth also became more ridiculous and elaborate, from special syringes (such as Gorham's "martini spike") to dispense the exact calibrated amount of vermouth to atomizers that sent a mere fog of vermouth hovering above the cocktail glass of chilled gin. Whatever the ratio—even if it comes down to an atomized mist of Noilly Prat—it must have vermouth to be a Martini.

Then there are the two camps—the shaken versus the stirred.

While Harry Craddock, author of the 1930s *Savoy Cocktail Book,* after the famed London Savoy Hotel, was unyielding in his stance that Martinis should be vigorously shaken, retaining the chill factor with an infusion of fine slivers of ice, and James Bond may have made it stylish to shake, purists still insist on stirring. W. Somerset Maugham, a firm believer that Martinis should never be shaken, poetically stated, "Martinis should always be stirred, not shaken, so that the molecules lie sensuously on top of each other." Stirring also avoids the excessive dilution from melting ice inherent in a shaken Martini.

The Martini has endured many transmutations, from rinsing the glass with a variety of liqueurs or juices, such as Cointreau or Pernod, port or sake, to the Cold War Vodka Martini trend made fashionable by James Bond and Smirnoff. A true Martini, whether it's shaken or stirred, has only two liquid ingredients—gin and dry vermouth—anything more, or less (such as the straight gin cocktails Churchill enjoyed as he bowed toward France in lieu of the vermouth), no matter the posturing, is not a classic Martini.

The traditional dry vermouth is the French Noilly Prat, but Martini & Rossi is a very popular alternative. When it comes to choosing a gin, which is the main ingredient, it stands to reason that a premium-quality gin is the only guarantee of a perfect Martini. A subpar gin could ruin the drink. Many fine, ultrapremium gins are available, with nuanced differences in flavor, that have served to glamorize the Martini even further.

------- **THE SUPERLATIVE MARTINI** -------

Icy coldness is a must, so store both the gin and glasses in the freezer. Stir your liquid ingredients with cracked ice or ice cubes (never crushed ice) in a glass martini pitcher or a metal mixing cup (part of a metal cocktail shaker). Stir gently for a few revolutions, until the glass (or metal) turns frosty, and strain into a chilled cocktail glass. Garnish with either an olive or a small spiral of lemon peel, which should be twisted over the drink to disperse the tart bitter oil from the rind into the Martini.

Classic Martini

2 ounces gin
½ ounce dry vermouth
Lemon twist or green cocktail olive

Stir the gin and vermouth in a mixing glass with ice. Strain into a chilled cocktail glass. Run the lemon peel around the rim, twist it over the drink, and drop it in, or simply drop in the olive.

Dry Martini

2 ounces gin
¼ ounce dry vermouth
Lemon twist

Stir the gin and vermouth in a mixing glass with ice. Strain into a chilled cocktail glass. Run the lemon peel around the rim, twist it over the drink, and drop it in.

Extra-Dry (or Very Dry) Martini   *Whether the vermouth is administered via a dash, eyedropper, or atomizer, or is swirled around the glass just to coat it with a vaguely vermouthian flavor, this can be as dry as you like it.*

2 ounces gin
½ teaspoon dry vermouth
Green cocktail olive or lemon twist

Stir the gin and vermouth in a mixing glass with ice. Strain into a chilled cocktail glass. Drop in the olive, or run the lemon peel around the rim, twist it over the drink, and drop it in.

Perfect Martini   *Here the definition of "perfect" is a Martini made with equal parts sweet and dry vermouth.*

2 ounces gin
½ ounce dry vermouth
½ ounce sweet vermouth
Orange slice

Stir the liquid ingredients in a mixing glass with ice. Strain into a chilled cocktail glass. Garnish with the orange slice.

Dirty Martini   *A favorite of Franklin Delano Roosevelt, who historically served one up to Joseph Stalin in 1943.*

2 ounces gin
½ ounce extra-dry vermouth
½ ounce brine from cocktail olives
Green cocktail olive

Stir the liquid ingredients in a mixing glass with ice. Strain into a chilled cocktail glass. Garnish with the olive.

Naked Martini   *For those who insist on drinking straight gin and calling it a Martini, whose idea of an extra-dry or bone-dry Martini includes such posturing as a Winston Churchillesque bow toward France, or simply letting the sun shine through a bottle of Noilly Prat onto a cocktail glass of straight gin, this is the Martini for you. There is, however, a variation even for this, which redeems its Martini standing by infusing the olive with dry vermouth before dropping it in.*

3 ounces premium-quality gin
Lemon twist or green cocktail olive (optionally infused with dry vermouth)

Stir or shake the gin in a mixing glass with ice. Strain into a chilled cocktail glass. Run the lemon peel around the rim, twist it over the drink, and drop it in, or simply drop in the olive.

Fino Martini

2 ounces gin
2 dashes fino sherry
Lemon twist

Shake the gin and sherry vigorously with ice. Strain into a chilled cocktail glass. Twist the lemon peel over the drink, and drop it in.

Knickerbocker   *This Martiniesque cocktail is the epitome of old New York elegance.*

2 ounces gin
1 ounce dry vermouth
½ ounce sweet vermouth
Dash of orange bitters
Lemon twist

Stir the liquid ingredients in a mixing glass with ice. Strain into a chilled cocktail glass. Run the lemon peel around the rim, twist it over the drink, and drop it in.

Smoky Martini

2 ounces gin
¼ ounce single-malt scotch
½ teaspoon dry vermouth
Lemon twist

Shake the liquid ingredients vigorously with ice. Strain into a chilled cocktail glass. Twist the lemon peel over the drink, and drop it in.

Picasso Martini   *Invented by bartender Colin Peter Field at the Ritz, Paris, in 2000. In this Cubist-inspired Martini, the dry vermouth is added via an ice cube made with distilled water and dry vermouth.*

2½ ounces chilled gin
1 cube Noilly Pratt dry vermouth

Pour the chilled gin into a chilled cocktail glass. Drop in the vermouth ice cube.

Gibson   *The signature characteristic of the Gibson is a pickled cocktail onion for garnish, and it has a following all its own, apart from the Martini. Originally made with equal parts gin and dry vermouth, with a maraschino cherry garnish, as cocktail lore tells it, the modern Gibson was created in the 1940s at the Players Club in Manhattan for American artist Charles Dana Gibson, creatively substituting a white pearl onion in place of the maraschino cherry or usual martini olive.*

2 ounces gin
¼ ounce dry vermouth
Pearl cocktail onion

Stir the gin and vermouth in a mixing glass with ice. Strain into a chilled cocktail glass. Garnish with the onion.

VARIATION: For an ultra-dry Gibson, pour 2 ounces chilled dry gin into a chilled cocktail glass misted with an atomizer spray of Noilly Prat dry vermouth.

Maiden's Prayer   *This classic is a delightful cross between a Chelsea Sidecar and a Lemon Drop.*

1 ounce gin
1 ounce Cointreau
½ ounce fresh lemon juice
½ ounce fresh orange juice
Orange twist

Shake the liquid ingredients vigorously with ice. Strain into a chilled cocktail glass. Twist the orange peel over the drink, and drop it in.

Mandarine Martini

¼ ounce Mandarine Napoléon
Dash of Cointreau
1½ ounces gin
½ ounce vodka
Mandarin or orange peel spiral

Pour the Mandarine Napoléon and the Cointreau into a chilled cocktail glass, swirl to coat the inside of the glass, and discard. Shake the gin and vodka vigorously with ice. Strain into the prepared glass, and garnish with the mandarin peel spiral.

Martinez   *One of the assumed predecessors to the Martini, this is a much sweeter concoction than the modern dry Martini. The original, first created in California during the Gold Rush of the 1850s, was made with equal parts sweet vermouth and Old Tom gin (a sweeter gin) and was usually sweetened further with maraschino or orange liqueur.*

2 ounces Old Tom gin
½ ounce sweet vermouth
¼ ounce maraschino liqueur
Dash of orange bitters

Shake the ingredients vigorously with ice. Strain into a chilled cocktail glass.

Milano

1½ ounces gin
1½ ounces Galliano
1 ounce fresh lemon juice

Shake the ingredients vigorously with ice. Strain into a chilled cocktail glass.

Monkey Gland

1½ ounces gin
1 ounce fresh orange juice
1 teaspoon Bénédictine
2 to 4 dashes grenadine

Shake the ingredients vigorously with ice. Strain into a chilled cocktail glass or over ice in an old-fashioned glass.

Moonshot

1½ ounces gin
3 ounces clam juice
Dash of red pepper sauce

Stir the ingredients in a mixing glass with ice. Strain into a chilled sour glass.

Newport Cooler

1½ ounces gin
½ ounce brandy
½ ounce peach liqueur
Dash of fresh lime juice
3 to 5 ounces chilled ginger ale

Pour all the ingredients but the ginger ale into an ice-filled collins glass. Top with the ginger ale and stir gently.

Negroni

THIS TURN-OF-THE-CENTURY IMPORT FROM ITALY was purportedly created by Florentine count Camillo Negroni, who requested that gin be added to his Americano cocktail, and the result is this complex triangulation of gin, bitter Campari, and sweet vermouth. Traditionally served over ice to slightly dilute the intensity, some prefer adding a splash of club soda, but it is equally enjoyable shaken and served up. The classic recipe dictates equal parts gin, Campari, and sweet vermouth, with variations that include lighter versions closer to a Martini, which are more suitably stirred than shaken.

Classic Negroni

1 ounce gin
1 ounce Campari
1 ounce sweet vermouth
2 to 3 ounces chilled club soda (optional)
Orange slice

Shake the gin, Campari, and vermouth vigorously with ice. Strain into an ice-filled highball glass. Top with club soda, if desired. Garnish with the orange slice.

Negroni Cocktail   *This version is shaken and served up.*

Shake the gin, Campari, and vermouth vigorously with ice. Strain into a chilled cocktail glass. Omit the club soda. Garnish with an orange twist instead of the orange slice.

VARIATIONS: **For a Punt e Mes Negroni,** substitute 1/2 ounce Punt e Mes for the Campari.

For a Cardinal, substitute 1 ounce dry vermouth for the sweet vermouth. Club soda is optional.

For a Dirty Dick's Downfall (after Nixon), a lighter, drier version, use 2 ounces gin, 1/2 ounce dry vermouth, and 1/2 ounce Campari. Garnish with a lemon twist.

Orange Blossom   *This classic cocktail has gone through a few transmutations, from the Waldorf-Astoria version made with equal parts gin, orange juice, and sweet vermouth to a basic gin version of the Screwdriver made with equal parts gin and orange juice, also known as an Adirondack. Here is the classic version that keeps surfacing and rings true.*

1½ ounces gin
1½ ounces fresh orange juice
¼ ounce Cointreau
1 to 2 dashes orange flower water
Orange slice

Shake the liquid ingredients vigorously with ice. Strain into an ice-filled old-fashioned glass. Garnish with the orange slice.

Orchid

Lemon wedge
Sugar
2 ounces gin
1 ounce crème de noyaux
½ ounce Tuaca
½ ounce Parfait Amour
1 ounce fresh lemon juice

Rub the rim of a chilled cocktail glass with the lemon wedge and rim with sugar. Shake the ingredients vigorously with ice. Strain into the prepared glass.

Oriental

1½ ounces gin
1 ounce Alizé de France passion fruit liqueur
¼ ounce limoncello
Lemon twist

Shake the liquid ingredients vigorously with ice. Strain into a chilled cocktail glass. Garnish with the lemon twist.

Pall Mall

1½ ounces gin
½ ounce dry vermouth
½ ounce sweet vermouth
1 teaspoon white crème de menthe
Dash of Angostura bitters

Stir the ingredients in a mixing glass with ice. Strain into a chilled cocktail glass.

Parisian Cocktail

1 ounce gin
1 ounce crème de cassis
1 ounce Noilly Prat dry vermouth

Stir the ingredients in a mixing glass with ice. Strain into a chilled cocktail glass.

Passion Cocktail

¼ ounce Alizé de France passion fruit liqueur
2 ounces Bombay Sapphire gin
Lemon peel spiral

Coat a chilled cocktail glass with the liqueur and discard. Stir the gin in a mixing glass with ice. Strain into the prepared glass. Garnish with the lemon peel spiral.

Pink Gin *A classic cocktail "remedy" from the early days of the British Empire in India, popular with the British officers for its purported ability to soothe the stomach. Often referred to as Gin and Bitters, and similar to a Gin Cocktail with orange bitters, this was a favorite of writer Ian Fleming, of James Bond fame. The classic method is to rinse a sherry glass with the bitters first, and then to add the chilled gin. It is traditionally served with a glass of water on the side.*

4 to 5 dashes Angostura or Peychaud's bitters
2½ ounces chilled gin
Lemon twist

Pour the bitters into a chilled sherry or cocktail glass, and swirl to coat the glass. Discard the excess. Pour in the gin. Garnish with the lemon twist.

VARIATION: **For a Gin and Pink,** add 5 ounces tonic water and serve over ice in a highball glass, with a lemon twist.

Pink Martini

2 ounces good-quality gin
½ ounce guava nectar
½ ounce fresh orange juice
Orange twist

Shake the liquid ingredients vigorously with ice. Strain into a chilled cocktail glass. Run the orange peel around the rim, twist it over the drink, and drop it in.

Pink Pamplemousse

1½ ounces gin
¾ ounce Mandarine Napoléon (or other orange liqueur)
1½ ounces fresh pink (or regular) grapefruit juice
Lemon twist

Shake the liquid ingredients vigorously with ice. Strain into a chilled cocktail glass. Twist the lemon peel over the drink, and drop it in.

Rendezvous

1½ ounces gin
½ ounce kirsch
½ ounce Campari
Lemon twist

Shake the liquid ingredients vigorously with ice. Strain into a chilled cocktail glass. Twist the lemon peel over the drink, and drop it in.

Ramos Gin Fizz

THE RAMOS BROTHERS USHERED THIS CLASSY COCKTAIL into popularity in the 1890s, when it became the signature libation at the New Orleans Imperial Cabinet Saloon. This Gin Fizz is a Gulf Coast variation that calls for the Ramos Brothers' secret/essential ingredient—orange flower water (found in most specialty food shops). Tradition calls for this to be well shaken in a cocktail shaker for about 5 minutes (held with a bar towel); however, you may prefer the more expedient modern option of using a blender to mix this frothy cocktail, also known as the New Orleans Fizz.

------

2 ounces gin

1 ounce fresh lemon juice

½ ounce fresh lime juice

1 teaspoon vanilla extract

2 to 3 dashes orange flower water

1 egg white (optional)

1½ ounces heavy cream

1 tablespoon superfine sugar

2 to 4 ounces chilled club soda

Lemon slice

Shake all the ingredients except the club soda and lemon slice vigorously with ice for 3 to 4 minutes. Strain into a chilled highball glass. Top with club soda and stir gently. Garnish with the lemon slice.

Rocco *From Bayswater Brasserie, in Sydney, Australia.*

1½ ounces gin
½ ounce Campari
½ ounce Mandarine Napoléon liqueur
½ ounce fresh mandarin orange juice
½ ounce apple juice

Shake the ingredients vigorously with ice. Strain into a chilled cocktail glass.

Rose Martini

2½ ounces good-quality gin
Dash of Cointreau
Dash of rose water
2 or 3 rose petals

Stir the liquid ingredients in a mixing glass with ice. Strain into a chilled cocktail glass. Float rose petals on top.

Seville

1½ ounces gin
½ ounce sherry
½ ounce fresh orange juice
½ ounce fresh lemon juice
2 teaspoons sugar

Shake the ingredients vigorously with ice. Strain into a chilled cocktail glass.

Silver Bullet

1½ ounces gin
¾ ounce kümmel
¾ ounce fresh lemon juice
Lemon twist

Shake the liquid ingredients vigorously with ice. Strain into a chilled cocktail glass. Twist the lemon peel over the drink, and drop it in.

Tasmanian Twister Cocktail

1½ ounces gin
½ ounce Campari
½ ounce sweet vermouth
1 ounce fresh pink grapefruit juice
Orange twist

Shake the liquid ingredients vigorously with ice. Strain into a chilled cocktail glass. Twist the orange peel over the drink, and drop it in.

Tom Collins   *The epitome of 1950s suburbia, this classic drink was actually created in the mid-1800s by John Collins, barman at Limmer's Hotel in London, as a variation on his Holland gin–based John Collins cocktail. The original drink was named after the slightly sweet Old Tom gin, as opposed to the later version made with London dry gin, which became much more popular, catching on here after World War I vets brought it back home to America.*

2 ounces gin
1 ounce fresh lemon juice
½ ounce simple syrup
3 ounces chilled club soda
Lemon slice
Maraschino cherry

Pour the gin, lemon juice, and simple syrup into an ice-filled collins glass. Top with club soda and stir gently. Garnish with the lemon slice and cherry.

VARIATIONS: **For a Tex Collins,** substitute 3 ounces fresh grapefruit juice and 1 tablespoon honey for the lemon juice and sugar syrup.

For a Raspberry Collins, add ¾ ounce crème de framboise and 3 ounces raspberry purée, and garnish with a few raspberries.

Singapore Sling ......

THIS INTERNATIONAL CLASSIC was created at the Raffles Hotel in Singapore in 1915, by bartender Ngiam Tong Boon. The immense popularity of this famous drink inspired a multitude of variations throughout the Pacific, making it difficult to actually pin down the original recipe, but the one that seems to prevail is made with gin, cherry brandy, lime juice, and Bénédictine. Other variations include a splash of soda or for the cherry brandy to be floated on top. This recipe encompasses all the best aspects of a great Singapore Sling.

1½ ounces gin
¾ ounce cherry brandy
¾ ounce Bénédictine
¾ ounce Cointreau
1 ounce fresh orange juice
¾ ounce fresh lime juice
2 to 3 ounces chilled club soda
Pineapple wedge
Orange slice
Maraschino cherry

Shake all the liquid ingredients but the club soda vigorously with ice. Strain into an ice-filled highball glass. Top with club soda and stir gently. Garnish with the pineapple, orange slice, and cherry.

Venus

2 ounces gin
1 ounce Cointreau
¼ ounce simple syrup
Dash of Peychaud's bitters
8 fresh raspberries

Shake the liquid ingredients and 6 of the raspberries vigorously with ice. Strain into a chilled cocktail glass. Garnish with the remaining 2 raspberries.

Vesper Martini

Vesper Martini   *Conjured straight from Ian Fleming's* Casino Royale, *this infamous Martini was James Bond's cocktail of choice, named after Vesper Lynd, Bond's doomed double-agent girlfriend. This very potent cocktail appropriately calls for Russian vodka, symbolic of Vesper Lynd's allegiance to the Russians, served with an orange twist to complement the Lillet, a delicious replacement for vermouth, in Bond's preferred glass, a champagne coupe. Of course, this drink is shaken, not stirred.*

2 ounces gin
¼ ounce Russian vodka
⅓ ounce Lillet Blanc
Large orange twist (or a traditional lemon twist)

Shake the liquid ingredients vigorously with ice. Strain into a champagne coupe or chilled cocktail glass. Twist the orange peel over the drink, and drop it in

Liqueurs

LIQUEURS, BY THEIR VERY NATURE, are amazing feats of complex botanical mixology, and although many were originally created as remedies, these aromatically assertive elixirs were destined to be sipped and savored, and inevitably utilized as an integral and crucial component enhancing many cocktails.

Many of the traditional liqueurs were first formulated in monasteries, as the medicinal ingredients used were often grown in their gardens, and the coveted recipes were closely guarded secrets, known only to the monks involved in the process. The Bénédictine monks of France, who made the first liqueur from a complex formula of 75 different herbs and spices, have kept their secret since 1510. They may have been the first, but the Carthusian monks get the prize for alchemy in sheer numbers, bringing together 130 different botanicals to make Chartreuse, back in the sixteenth century. The Italians were also known for their liqueur-making expertise, and once Catherine de Medici married the future French king Henry II in 1533, this union further promoted the art of liqueurs in France.

Liqueurs eventually became soothingly palatable after-dinner digestifs, especially popular with those who were not fond of the stronger alternatives, such as Cognac. Served in the traditionally appropriate small and delicate glass, liqueurs were often seen as a "ladylike" drink. Although today they are no longer thought to have health-giving properties and are simply considered flavorful libations, some still hold on to the belief of their curing powers. By the 1920s and '30s, bars from London to Paris and Berlin to Venice were concocting libations utilizing these flavor-intense elixirs, to transform the old straightforward drinks into much more exciting and potent cocktails.

The term "liqueur" encompasses a wide spectrum of spirits (such as brandy, Cognac, gin, and rum) that have been flavored, infused, or distilled with an even wider roster of botanicals (ranging from anise seed, bitter orange peels, and violets to fruits and nuts) and then usually sweetened with a sugar syrup. With a seemingly endless number of combinations, hundreds of liqueurs are available, differing not only in color and flavor, but in sweetness, dryness, and bitterness as well as alcohol content, which can range from a mild Baileys Irish Cream at 34 proof to Chartreuse at 110 proof.

Ideally, most liqueurs are to be enjoyed neat, savored slowly and sipped from a cordial glass or snifter while the warmth of the hand brings out the fragrant botanical aromas. They also play a crucial role in the mixology of many classic cocktails: without the orange liqueur, a Margarita wouldn't be a Margarita, and although the Sazerac uses only a mere rinsing of Pernod, without the added whisper of anise flavor, it's just a bourbon with bitters.

The drinks in this section are a sampling of classic cocktails as well as more modern concoctions that showcase a liqueur as their main ingredient. There is also an extensive liqueur glossary to assist in clarifying the different varieties of liqueur possibilities out there.

LIQUEUR DRINKS
(INCLUDING BITTER LIQUEURS)

Alabama Slammer

1 ounce Southern Comfort
1 ounce amaretto
½ ounce sloe gin
Dash of fresh lemon juice
Maraschino cherry
Lemon slice

Shake the liquid ingredients vigorously with ice. Strain into an ice-filled highball glass. Garnish with the cherry and lemon slice.

Alfonso Special Cocktail

1½ ounces Grand Marnier
¾ ounce gin
¾ ounce dry vermouth
¼ ounce sweet vermouth
2 dashes Angostura bitters

Shake the ingredients vigorously with ice. Strain into a chilled cocktail glass.

Amaretto Alexander

2 ounces amaretto
1½ ounces white crème de cacao
1 ounce heavy cream

Shake the ingredients vigorously with ice. Strain into a chilled cocktail glass.

Amaretto Sour

2 ounces amaretto
1 ounce fresh lemon juice
Maraschino cherry

Shake the liquid ingredients vigorously with ice. Strain into a chilled sour glass. Garnish with the cherry.

Angel's Tit

2 ounces chilled white crème de cacao
½ ounce heavy cream
Maraschino cherry

Pour the crème de cacao into a chilled champagne coupe. Float the cream on top, and garnish with the cherry.

B-52 *This is a layered pousse-café drink (see page 219 for technique).*

½ ounce Kahlúa
½ ounce Irish cream liqueur
½ ounce Grand Marnier

Slowly pour each liqueur into a chilled pousse-café glass in the order given.

B&B

½ ounce Bénédictine
½ ounce Cognac

Pour the Bénédictine into a cordial glass. Float the Cognac on top; do not mix.

Banshee *Also known as a Capri.*

1 ounce white crème de cacao
1 ounce crème de banane
1 ounce heavy cream

Shake the ingredients vigorously with ice. Strain into a chilled cocktail glass.

THE NOTORIOUS ABSINTHE, which scandalized late 19th-century Europe, was embraced by the literary and artistic café society of the mid-1800s. Purportedly addictive, it was the drink of choice for artists, writers, and poets, most notably Toulouse-Lautrec, Van Gogh, Baudelaire, Oscar Wilde, Rimbaud, and Verlaine. All had quite the passion for the "Green Fairy," so named for the signature cloudy green color and alleged hallucinogenic properties. Wormwood is the ingredient in absinthe that was thought to be the cause of such visionary inspiration, as well as the insane actions of creative types. Van Gogh evidently was partaking of the aperitif at the time of the infamous ear incident.

Eventually, its scandalous reputation along with the lack of quality control by unscrupulous producers, caused absinthe to be banned from production and distribution by the end of World War I.

Potent, at 75 percent alcohol by volume, absinthe has an intense licorice flavor, tinged with an herbal aftertaste. When mixed with cold water, it begins to *louche*, or turn a cloudy white, sage green. Although unobtainable in the United States, other fine anise-flavored liqueurs are available, such as Pernod (the producers of the original), Herbsaint, and Absente, a newly refined form of absinthe without the wormwood.

- -

Traditional Café-Style Absinthe

1½ ounces Pernod (or other absinthe substitute)
1 sugar cube
5 ounces cold filtered water
1 perforated spoon

Pour the Pernod into a pousse-café or sour glass. Place the perforated spoon across the top of the glass, resting it on the rim. Position a sugar cube on the spoon, and slowly pour the water over the sugar cube, until the sugar is dissolved and the mixture in the glass turns cloudy.

Blue Angel

½ ounce blue curaçao
½ ounce brandy
½ ounce Parfait Amour
½ ounce heavy cream
Dash of fresh lemon juice

Shake the ingredients vigorously with ice. Strain into a chilled cocktail glass.

Bocci Ball

2 ounces amaretto
4 ounces fresh orange juice
1 to 2 ounces chilled club soda
Orange slice

Shake the amaretto and orange juice vigorously with ice. Strain into an ice-filled highball glass. Top with club soda and stir gently. Garnish with the orange slice.

Buttered Toffee

1 ounce amaretto
1 ounce Baileys Irish Cream
1 ounce Tia Maria (or other coffee liqueur)
2 ounces heavy cream

Pour the amaretto, Baileys, and Tia Maria into an ice-filled wineglass, top with the cream, and stir briefly.

Butterfinger

2 ounces butterscotch schnapps
1½ ounces Baileys Irish Cream
6 ounces milk
½ ounce chocolate syrup

Shake all ingredients but the chocolate syrup vigorously with ice. Strain into a chilled cocktail glass. Float the chocolate syrup on top.

Café Romano

1 ounce sambuca
1 ounce Kahlúa or Tia Maria
1 ounce heavy cream

Shake the ingredients vigorously with ice. Strain into a chilled cocktail glass.

VARIATION: **For a Cara Sposa,** substitute 1 ounce triple sec for the sambuca.

Chocolate Almond

¾ ounce amaretto
¾ ounce Baileys Irish Cream
¾ ounce dark crème de cacao

Shake the ingredients vigorously with ice. Strain into an ice-filled old-fashioned glass.

Death by Chocolate

¾ ounce Baileys Irish Cream
¾ ounce dark crème de cacao
¾ ounce vodka
¼ cup chocolate ice cream
Chocolate shavings

Combine all ingredients but the chocolate shavings in a blender with ½ cup ice. Blend until smooth. Pour into a chilled wineglass. Garnish with the shaved chocolate.

Dreamsicle

1 ounce amaretto
½ ounce orange curaçao
½ ounce vanilla-flavored vodka
2 ounces fresh orange juice
2 ounces heavy cream

Shake the ingredients vigorously with ice. Strain into an ice-filled old-fashioned glass.

Duchess

1 ounce Pernod
1 ounce dry vermouth
1 ounce sweet vermouth

Shake the ingredients vigorously with ice. Strain into a chilled cocktail glass.

Golden Cadillac

1½ ounces white crème de cacao
¾ ounce Galliano
1½ ounces heavy cream

Shake the ingredients vigorously with ice. Strain into a chilled cocktail glass.

Grasshopper

1 ounce green crème de menthe
1 ounce white crème de cacao
1 ounce heavy cream

Shake the ingredients vigorously with ice. Strain into a chilled cocktail glass.

Hairy Navel   *This potent variation on the Fuzzy Navel is made with vodka.*

2 ounces peach schnapps
1 ounce vodka
4 ounces fresh orange juice
Orange slice
Peach slice

Shake the liquid ingredients vigorously with ice. Strain into an ice-filled highball glass. Garnish with the orange and peach slices.

Liquid Cocaine *Here are two of the many versions of this drink. They can also be served as a shooter (page 423).*

LIQUID COCAINE #1

½ ounce dark rum
½ ounce root beer schnapps
½ ounce Jägermeister
½ ounce Rumple Minze

Shake the ingredients vigorously with ice. Strain into an ice-filled old-fashioned glass.

LIQUID COCAINE #2

½ ounce dark rum
½ ounce Rumple Minze
½ ounce Jägermeister
½ ounce Goldschläger

Shake the ingredients vigorously with ice. Strain into an ice-filled old-fashioned glass.

Lollipop

¾ ounce green Chartreuse
¾ ounce Cointreau
¾ ounce kirsch
¼ teaspoon maraschino liqueur

Shake the ingredients vigorously with ice. Strain into a chilled cocktail glass.

London Fog *This drink has been described as tasting like Good & Plenty candy.*

1½ ounces amaretto
1½ ounces white crème de menthe
2 dashes Angostura bitters
Thin lemon slice

Shake the liquid ingredients vigorously with ice. Strain into a chilled cocktail glass. Float the lemon slice on top of the drink.

McClelland Cocktail

1½ ounces sloe gin
¾ ounce triple sec
2 dashes orange bitters

Shake the ingredients vigorously with ice. Strain into a chilled cocktail glass.

Melon Alexander *This is a melon-flavored variation on the classic Brandy Alexander.*

1½ ounces melon liqueur
1 ounce brandy
1 ounce heavy cream

Shake the ingredients vigorously with ice. Strain into a chilled cocktail glass.

Merry Widow *This is a sweet version of the classic.*

1½ ounces cherry brandy
1½ ounces maraschino liqueur
Maraschino cherry

Shake the liquid ingredients vigorously with ice. Strain into a chilled cocktail glass. Garnish with the cherry.

Milano

1½ ounces Galliano
1½ ounces gin
1 ounce fresh lemon juice

Shake the ingredients vigorously with ice. Strain into a chilled cocktail glass.

Mind Eraser

1½ ounces Kahlúa
1½ ounces vodka
2 to 3 ounces chilled club soda

Pour the Kahlúa into an ice-filled old-fashioned glass. Slowly float the vodka on top, then slowly top with club soda; don't mix.

Mocha Mint

¾ ounce Kahlúa (or other coffee-flavored liqueur)
¾ ounce white crème de menthe
¾ ounce white crème de cacao

Shake the ingredients vigorously with ice. Strain into a chilled cocktail glass.

Moulin Rouge

1½ ounces sloe gin
¾ ounce sweet vermouth
2 dashes Angostura bitters

Stir the ingredients in a mixing glass with ice. Strain into a chilled cocktail glass.

Nutty Irishman

1½ ounces Baileys Irish Cream
1½ ounces Frangelico

Shake the ingredients vigorously with ice. Strain into an ice-filled old-fashioned glass.

Oatmeal Cookie

1 ounce butterscotch schnapps
1 ounce Jägermeister
1 ounce Baileys Irish Cream
¼ ounce pastis
½ ounce heavy cream
Freshly grated or ground nutmeg

Shake all liquid ingredients but the cream vigorously with ice. Strain into an ice-filled old-fashioned glass. Float the cream on top, and dust with nutmeg.

Peppermint Stick

1½ ounces white crème de cacao
1 ounce peppermint schnapps
1 ounce heavy cream

Shake the ingredients vigorously with ice. Strain into a chilled champagne flute.

Pernod Cocktail

½ ounce water
½ teaspoon sugar
2 dashes Angostura bitters
2 ounces Pernod

Combine the water, sugar, and bitters in an old-fashioned glass. Fill with crushed ice, add the Pernod, and stir.

Pimm's Cup *A favorite drink of cricket spectators, this classic is made with Pimm's No. 1, a gin-based herbal liqueur invented by James Pimm and first served as a digestive tonic back in the 1880s, in his London oyster bar.*

3 ounces Pimm's No. 1
3 to 4 ounces chilled club soda
Cucumber spear
Lemon slice

Pour the Pimm's No. 1 into an ice-filled highball glass. Top with club soda and stir gently. Garnish with the cucumber spear and lemon slice.

VARIATION: Instead of the club soda, top with a splash of ginger ale, lemonade, or lemon-lime soda.

Pink Squirrel *This classic creamy drink traditionally uses crème de noyaux, with amaretto being a favored alternative, and is frequently blended with vanilla ice cream.*

1 ounce white crème de cacao
1 ounce crème de noyaux (or amaretto)
1 ounce heavy cream

Shake the ingredients vigorously with ice. Strain into a chilled cocktail glass.

Pousse-Café Drinks

LITERALLY MEANING "PUSH THE COFFEE," these drinks were invented in France as after-dinner drinks in the early 1800s, and had worked their way to New Orleans by about the 1840s. One of the most labor-intensive, technique-driven drinks, a pousse-café's multiple layers of liqueurs are sometimes more visually pleasing than the end flavor. The point is to be able to enjoy each liqueur separately as you sip through the layers.

The method of layering liqueurs, usually with equal amounts of three to six liqueurs, involves slowly pouring one on top of another, from the heaviest on the bottom to the lightest on top, for visually dramatic strata of colorful liqueurs. After pouring the first (and heaviest) liqueur into a stemmed pousse-café or other straight-sided glass, slowly pour the next layer over the rounded back of a bar spoon, as close to the layer below as possible without the spoon touching the liquid in the glass. Pousse-cafés can be made ahead of time and refrigerated. Here are a few classic pousse-café drinks.

Pousse-Café #1

¼ ounce grenadine
¼ ounce yellow Chartreuse
¼ ounce crème de cassis
¼ ounce white crème de menthe
¼ ounce green Chartreuse
¼ ounce brandy

Pousse-Café #2

¼ ounce raspberry syrup
¼ ounce anisette
¼ ounce Parfait Amour
¼ ounce crème de violette
¼ ounce yellow Chartreuse
¼ ounce green Chartreuse
¼ ounce brandy

Angel's Kiss

¼ ounce crème de cacao
¼ ounce crème de violette
¼ ounce brandy
¼ ounce heavy cream

Pour the first liqueur into a pousse-café glass or sherry glass. Slowly and carefully layer the other ingredients, one on top of the other, in the order given.

Here are a few more popular pousse-café drinks. The ingredients are listed in the order of pouring, from the first in the glass to the last layer.

Angel's Blush

½ ounce each: maraschino liqueur, crème de violette, Bénédictine, and heavy cream.

Fifth Avenue

1 ounce dark crème de cacao, 1 ounce apricot brandy, and ½ ounce heavy cream.

Fourth of July

¾ ounce each: grenadine, Cointreau, and blue curaçao.

French Tricolor

¾ ounce each: grenadine, maraschino liqueur, and crème de violette.

Havana Rainbow

¼ ounce each: grenadine, anisette, Parfait Amour, green crème de menthe, yellow Chartreuse, and rum.

Jersey Lily

½ ounce each: green Chartreuse and Cognac. Top with 10 dashes Angostura bitters.

Liquid Symphony

½ ounce each: crème de rose, yellow Chartreuse, green crème de menthe, and brandy.

Mexican Flag

½ ounce each: grenadine, green crème de menthe, and silver tequila.

Paris Rainbow

¼ ounce each: crème de violette, crème de cassis, maraschino liqueur, green crème de menthe, yellow Chartreuse, curaçao, and cherry brandy.

Queen Elizabeth Wine

1½ ounces Bénédictine
¾ ounce dry vermouth
¾ ounce fresh lemon juice
Lemon twist

Stir the liquid ingredients in a mixing glass with ice. Strain into a chilled cocktail glass. Run the lemon peel around the rim, twist it over the drink, and drop it in.

San Francisco Cocktail

2 ounces sloe gin
1 ounce dry vermouth
1 ounce sweet vermouth
Dash of Peychaud's bitters
Maraschino cherry

Shake the liquid ingredients vigorously with ice. Strain into a chilled cocktail glass. Garnish with the cherry.

Screaming Orgasm

¾ ounce Kahlúa
¾ ounce Irish cream liqueur
¾ ounce amaretto
¾ ounce vodka

Shake the ingredients vigorously with ice. Strain into a chilled cocktail glass.

Skinny Dipper

2 ounces melon liqueur
6 ounces cranberry juice
Lemon twist

Pour the melon liqueur and cranberry juice into an ice-filled collins glass. Stir well. Twist the lemon peel over the drink, and drop it in.

Slippery Nipple

1½ ounces Baileys Irish Cream
1½ ounces sambuca

Shake the Baileys and sambuca vigorously with ice. Strain into an ice-filled old-fashioned glass.

Sloe Gin Fizz

2 ounces sloe gin
1½ ounces fresh lemon juice
½ ounce simple syrup
3 to 4 ounces chilled club soda
Maraschino cherry

Shake all the liquid ingredients but the club soda vigorously with ice. Strain into an ice-filled highball glass. Top with club soda and stir gently. Garnish with the cherry.

Sloe Screw

1½ ounces sloe gin
1½ ounces fresh orange juice

Pour the ingredients into an ice-filled old-fashioned glass. Stir well.

Sombrero

2 ounces coffee liqueur
1½ ounces heavy cream

Pour the ingredients into an ice-filled old-fashioned glass. Stir well.

Toasted Almond

1 ounce amaretto
1 ounce Kahlúa
1 ounce heavy cream

Shake the ingredients vigorously with ice. Strain into an ice-filled old-fashioned glass.

Velvet Hammer *Another version of this drink, made with vodka, is also known as a Russian Bear (page 325).*

1 ounce Cointreau
1 ounce white crème de cacao
½ ounce brandy
1 ounce heavy cream

Shake the ingredients vigorously with ice. Strain into a chilled cocktail glass.

Yellow Parrot Cocktail

¾ ounce yellow Chartreuse
¾ ounce Pernod
¾ ounce apricot brandy

Shake the ingredients vigorously with ice. Strain into a chilled cocktail glass.

GLOSSARY OF LIQUEURS AND BITTERS

Liqueurs and bitters can be a bit mysterious. With a multitude of flavors and styles available in a seemingly endless array of jewel-hued bottles imported from all over the world, the options can be daunting, to say the least. This glossary covers many, but of course not all, of the liqueurs that are available. Use it as an illuminating liqueur "dictionary" of flavors and styles.

Generally speaking, a liqueur is any spirit-based drink to which flavoring elements have been added, usually by infusion. In most cases it is also sweetened. What separates the different styles from one another besides a flavor or color is the specific process by which the various flavors of these drinks are obtained. Some spirits gain their flavors of fruit, flowers, herbs, spices, or nuts through infusion, meaning that the flavoring ingredients are soaked and heated or macerated in the alcohol base. Others add flavors to neutral spirits during distillation for a more potent liqueur.

Sometimes the line between a liqueur and a spirit gets blurry. Kirsch is considered a spirit, because it is a straight, unsweetened distillate of cherries. Cherry brandy, on the other hand, is a liqueur because it is a neutral spirit from other sources to which cherry flavor has been added by an infusion of fruit. Liqueurs originated through the practice of adding aromatic ingredients (herbs, fruit extracts, seeds, spices, nuts, roots, flowers, etc.) to the earliest distilled spirits, to give them medicinal value by extracting the ingredients' beneficial qualities.

There also tends to be some confusion over the difference between "crème" liqueurs and "cream" liqueurs. Whereas cream liqueurs are emulsions combining a liqueur with dairy cream—for example, Baileys—crème liqueurs are made by infusing a neutral, unaged brandy with flavors ranging from fruits to nuts, seeds, and herbs. The French term "crème" is used to differentiate between the brandy-based flavored and sweetened liqueurs, such as crème de cassis, and the dry, unsweetened distilled spirits such as Calvados or Cognac.

With the colossal selection of liqueurs on the market, this glossary lists the most classically popular, along with a few of the more exotic that have found their way into contemporary drinks.

------- **BITTERS AND BITTER LIQUEURS** -------

As the name suggests, the term "bitters" refers to any number of spirits that have a bitter or bittersweet taste acquired from the use of bitter roots and herbs—berries, seeds, flowers, and bark—as flavoring agents. Traditionally used as a digestif, appetite stimulant, and hangover cure, many bitters began as complex herbal remedies. They frequently include extracts of cinchona bark, a source of quinine, which is known for its medicinal aid and ability to soothe digestive distress. Numerous herbs and roots impart bitterness to these spirits, from gentian root to quinine to Seville oranges, which lend a bitter, aromatic flavor.

Perfect for mixing with other ingredients, enhancing whiskey-based drinks, juices, and sparkling and fortified wines, bitters vary in their level of alcohol content, from the intense, high-alcohol cocktail bitters, which come in a variety of flavors, to the sippable variety, with much lower alcohol levels.

The bitters covered here are a selection, from the most popular to the not so well-known. They range from the sippable, such as Campari, which can be enjoyed like any other spirit, served either over ice or with an added splash of club soda, to those so bitter and concentrated that they are added only a few drops at a time to flavor another drink.

COCKTAIL BITTERS

So intense, a few drops is all you will need.

ANGOSTURA AROMATIC BITTERS

This is the bitter most widely used in cocktails. It is a concentrated elixir containing an infusion of gentian root, a flowering alpine plant, that is rendered down to a bright yellow essence and combined with herbs on a strong rum base. Gentian has been used for centuries as a tonic, antifever remedy, and cure for malaria in folk medicine. Angostura bitters was formulated by a German doctor (Johann Gottlieb Benjamin Siegert), who was in Angostura, Venezuela, in 1818, serving as surgeon general in Simón Bolívar's army. He administered his creation as a tonic to stimulate the appetite and improve the health of the troops. Now made in Trinidad, it is still taken as a digestif as well as used as a flavoring in foods and drinks, and at a potent 90 proof, a dash will do you.

PEYCHAUD'S BITTERS

A closely guarded family recipe made with a number of botanicals. It was originally made in New Orleans by Antoine Peychaud, an apothecary in the late 1800s, who is credited with making the first cocktail by mixing his bitters with French brandy. This relatively sweet anise- and orange-flavored bitter is the essential ingredient for the Sazerac, the New Orleans classic cocktail.

ORANGE AND PEACH BITTERS

Essential ingredients in many of the classic cocktails mixed in the early 1900s. Abbott's in the United States makes an orange bitter, and English bitters such as Holloway's orange bitters are still a popular choice. Peach bitters are no longer in such high demand and can be hard to find.

BITTERS SERVED AS APERITIFS AND DIGESTIFS

AMER PICON

This dark, maroon-hued, orange-flavored French bitter is an aromatized wine similar to vermouth, with a bitter taste. When mixed with club soda it is enjoyed as an aperitif, but it is also used in cocktails. Invented as an antimalarial remedy by an army officer serving in Algeria, it is made from spices, gentian, orange, and cinchona bark, the base for quinine.

APEROL

An Italian bitter with herbs, produced by Martini. It is lighter and slightly sweeter than its cousin, Campari.

CALISAY

A popular aperitif from Barcelona, Spain, that falls into the liqueur/bitter hybrid category, a sweet, herbal, and bitter digestif made from chinchon bark, herbs, bitter orange, and wormwood, and enjoyed as an alternative to absinthe. A similar but sweeter aperitif from Spain is Chinchon, made from the extract of anise and cinchona bark, a botanical yielding quinine, that is native to South America. It is part bitter, part liqueur, and part anise drink.

CAMPARI

Italy's most famous bitter aperitif, created in the 1860s in Milan by bartender and restaurateur Gaspare Campari. It is spicy, with bitter orange undertones from the peel of Seville oranges and a jewel-like bright red color created by the addition of cochineal, a natural colorant. Bitter Campari, or Campari Aperitivo, has an astringent, bittersweet flavor; there is also a sweeter version. For a refreshing aperitif, it is usually served chilled and over ice, or with a splash of club soda. Once it is opened, store Campari at room temperature or, better yet, in a cool, dark place for up to a year. Campari is a crucial ingredient in many cocktails, such as the Negroni and the Americano.

CHINA MARTINI

Made by the famous Martini & Rossi, this popular Italian bitter liqueur has a distinctive herbal-quinine flavor. It is bittersweet and syrupy and is typically served as an aperitif or after-dinner drink.

CYNAR

This Italian bitter is made with artichoke hearts (and leaves) and several herbs, and is relatively light and sweet for a bitter. Enjoyed either as an aperitif or a digestif, it is usually sipped on the rocks with a slice of orange. It is also used in mixed drinks.

FERNET BRANCA

An intense bitter from Italy that dates back to 1845, this slightly peppermint-accented bitter is enjoyed not only as an aperitif to stimulate the appetite, but also as a digestif that is highly regarded as a hangover cure, settling digestive distress. A deep brown liquid with an extremely aggressive bitter flavor, Fernet Branca is made from 40 herbs and spices, including cinchona bark, gentian root, rhubarb, cardamom, cloves, angelica, myrrh, chamomile, and peppermint. It is taken straight or on the rocks, as well as in mixed drinks, and can be added to coffee after a meal.

GAMMEL DANSK

Very popular in Denmark, this dark-amber bitter is made from herbs and fruit and has an intensely herbal, peppery flavor that is extremely dry, not at all sweet.

JÄGERMEISTER

A favorite German aperitif since its conception in 1878, made with a complex aromatic melding of 56 herbs, roots, and fruits. It is usually consumed as an aperitif or after-dinner drink but is also used in cocktails.

PUNT E MES

An aromatic aperitif categorized partway between a vermouth and a bitter, although it is softer and sweeter than other bitters. Frequently used in a variation of the Manhattan.

UNDERBERG

Made from a secret recipe (aren't they all?), this intensely pungent digestive bitter from Germany reportedly works wonders as a hangover remedy. Another German bitter popular as a digestif is Stonsdorfer.

UNICUM

This deeply colored bitter was originally a Hungarian specialty but is now made in Vienna (by Zwack, since 1840). It balances its bitterness with a slight sweetness.

OTHER BITTERS

AMARO MONTENEGRO

An Italian digestif bitter given a boost with sweetened wine.

AVERNA

A digestif from Italy.

BRANCA MENTA

A bitter Italian liqueur flavored with peppermint.

ABSINTHE

ABSINTHE MAKES THE TART GROW FONDER.

—HUGH DRUMMOND, *British aristocrat*

This distinctly anise-flavored drink, made from the bitter aromatic herb wormwood, is technically both a pastis and an anisette. Popular during the nineteenth century, it is no longer available, being illegal in the United States and much of Western Europe. Banned since the turn of the century due to the toxic, potentially lethal effects of thujone, a chemical found in, and extracted from, wormwood leaves, it was believed to cause madness and death. Before being outlawed, it had quite a following, as it was reputed to be an aphrodisiac and a hallucinogen. Aptly called the "Green Muse" or "Green Fairy," it has a distinctive green color that becomes milky white when diluted with water. It is high in alcohol, at 75 percent by volume.

There are equally fine anise-flavored substitutes that are wormwood-free; these include Herbsaint, Pernod, ouzo, anisette, and Absente.

- -

ADVOCAAT

Popular in the Netherlands, this Dutch brandy-based eggnog-flavored liqueur with a thick, velvety texture is also available in flavored versions with oranges, lemons, cherries, or vanilla. Very mild and low in alcohol, it is traditionally served cold with lemonade or as a nog with milk and nutmeg, and sometimes with hot chocolate or strong coffee.

- -

ALIZÉ DE FRANCE

This Cognac-based liqueur is flavored with tart passion fruit. It has a bright yellow hue and a refreshing flavor. Another style, with the addition of cranberry juice, is the rich red-hued Alizé Red Passion. They both must be refrigerated after opening.

AMARETTO

One of the most famous and popular liqueurs, with almond and apricot flavors, amaretto has a history to match. Legend has it that it was created in the sixteenth century by the widow who modeled for the Madonna in the Adoration of the Magi fresco in the Santa Maria Delle Grazie sanctuary in Saronno, and that she gave the recipe to the Italian painter Bernardo Luini.

This complex, deep-brown liqueur is made from almond extract along with apricot stones and seeds, steeped in brandy and sweetened with sugar syrup. It is sweet, with intense almond flavors reminiscent of marzipan. With such strong flavors, it is best used in small amounts. The Italian brand, Disaronno Amaretto, is the most famous, but France makes a similar liqueur, crème d'amandes.

ANIS AND ANISETTE

Thought to be good for ailments of the stomach, anis is flavored with anise berries and sometimes the seeds of star anise fruit. Lower in alcohol than pastis (a similar French anise-flavored liqueur), anis is flavored through a maceration of anise seed, which keeps the alcohol level down. Popular around the Mediterranean as an aperitif or digestif, both anis and anisette get cloudy when water is added, as does absinthe.

Anis is made in Spain, with both sweet and dry varieties available. French anis is dry. Anisette from France is stronger than anis, and is sweetened. The most famous brand is Marie Brizard.

OTHER ANISE-FLAVORED LIQUEURS:

- Herbsaint: from New Orleans.
- Anesone: an Italian liqueur often used as an absinthe substitute.
- Danziger Goldwasser, Opal Nera, ouzo, pastis, Pernod, Ricard, raki, sambuca, anisados.

ARAK

An Arabic term used to describe a potent liquor distilled from a variety of ingredients from the Middle East and Asia, such as dates, grains, grapes, or sundry palm saps. Some have a strong licorice flavor. Not to be confused with a rum from Java with the same name.

ARGENTARIUM

Still produced by a religious order in a monastary in the Lazio region of Italy, this brandy-based liqueur is flavored with a collection of herbs growing wild on the surrounding hillside and gathered by the monks. It is mostly consumed locally.

AURUM

Made in the Abruzzi mountains in eastern Italy, this Italian liqueur is named for its golden color, which is enhanced with saffron. It is made with top-quality aged brandy, infused with orange peel and whole oranges and triple distilled. The basic formula dates back to antiquity, and it may originally have been made with genuine particles of gold, possibly making it the true forerunner of Goldwasser. This digestif is best served up in a snifter at room temperature, and sipped like a fine Cognac.

B&B

A spicy, herbal liqueur made from a melding of brandy and Bénédictine. It is topaz in color, relatively dry, and similar to a flavored brandy.

BAILEYS IRISH CREAM

This is the archetypal Irish cream liqueur, inspiring all the other cream liqueurs that followed. Consisting of a pasteurized mixture of cream, eggs, chocolate, and Irish whiskey, this popular holiday drink is best served in a brandy glass on ice, given the heavy texture and sweetness. Store open bottles in the refrigerator.

BÄRENJÄGER

German for "bear hunter," this is a honey-flavored vodka-based liqueur.

BÉNÉDICTINE D.O.M.

A Cognac-based herbal liqueur from Normandy, France, named after the Bénédictine monks of the Abbey of Fécamp, who formulated it in around 1510 and produced it there until recently. Known as the world's oldest liqueur, it is made with Cognac and flavored with a multitude of aromatics, a complex balance of as many as 75 botanicals, including citrus peel, honey, basil, rosemary, and sage. The exact formula is cloaked in secrecy, with only three people being privy to it at any given time. The D.O.M. on the bottle stands for the Bénédictine dedication *Deo optimo maximo,* "To God most good, most great."

Tasting of herbs and spices, with a honeyed sweetness and a golden color, this liqueur should be served straight, in a large liqueur glass. It is also a great mixing ingredient, adding sweetness to drinks.

BUCKSHOT

An amber-colored liqueur flavored with chile pepper and having a spicy peach taste. Labeled the "original Wild West liqueur."

CHAMBORD

This lush, sweet liqueur is produced in France, made from Cognac and an infusion of small black raspberries, along with flavors of currants, black-berries, and red raspberries.

CHARTREUSE

This fine herbal liqueur from a monastary near Grenoble, France, was created in the 16th century by Carthusian monks. La Grande Chartreuse is still made by monks of this order, which is a silent order, helping to keep the recipe a secret. With a staggering number of more than 130 herbs and plants used to flavor the grape brandy base, it has an intensely aromatic and powerful flavor.

Chartreuse is infused, distilled, and aged in casks for up to five years. Several styles are produced, including green Chartreuse, the original and most intense at 110 proof, and yellow Chartreuse (the color attributed to the addition of saffron), which is lighter and sweeter, honeyed, slightly minty, and less strong at 80 proof. A premium version, the original Carthusian elixir, is called Élixir Végétal, the original recipe for which dates back to 1605. Packaged in a miniature bottle, this elixir is concentrated and very high strength at 142 proof. The French enjoy Chartreuse served neat, mixed with tonic or soda, or on the rocks with lots of ice. They also use the green variety to flavor their hot chocolate and add the yellow to coffee.

COCONUT-FLAVORED LIQUEURS

~ *MALIBU*   The most popular of the coconut-flavored liqueurs is from the Caribbean, made with Caribbean white rum flavored with the dried pulp and milk of the coconut, and slightly sweetened.

~ **BATIDA DE COCO**   Originally from Brazil, this is a coconut milk emulsion liqueur with a neutral spirit base.

- -

COINTREAU

Created in 1849 by Edward and Adolphe Cointreau, this brandy-based triple sec curaçao was originally called triple sec white curaçao, but in a market saturated with similarly named curaçaos, they wisely used the family name instead. Wildly popular for its rich, sweet, brandied fresh-orange flavor, Cointreau is the number one liqueur at the bar as an integral component in many mixed drinks, and is the orange liqueur of choice. Produced in Angers, France, and also in the Americas, this crystal clear liqueur is made by a double distillation of grape brandy, infused with a blend of bitter green Seville-style orange varieties from the Caribbean and sweeter types from the south of France. It is then sweetened and further aromatized with other secret plant ingredients to give it an herbal note. Cointreau is easily found in the signature square dark-brown bottle and is typically served in a snifter over ice to moderate the sweetness a bit and release the orange flavor. It is also great for mixing, upgrading any drink that calls for curaçao or triple sec.

- -

CRÈME LIQUEURS

"Crème" is a French term to describe sweet liqueurs or cordials, as opposed to drier versions. They have a high sugar content, are usually syrupy thick, and are excellent for adding sweetness and flavor to drinks. Most are 50 to 60 proof. A few popular brands are Marie Brizard, from France, as well as Bols and De Kuyper of Holland.

~ **CRÈME DE BANANE**   This banana-flavored liqueur comes in both white and brown versions.

OTHER BANANA LIQUEURS:

- 99 Bananas: has a heavy, intense banana flavor.

- Caymana: made in Ireland; a rich, cream-colored, banana-flavored liqueur.

~ **CRÈME DE CACAO**   A syrupy liqueur flavored with cocoa, chocolate, and vanilla beans, available in a clear "white" or dark-brown variety.

~ **CRÈME DE CAFÉ**   A coffee-flavored liqueur, similar to Kahlúa (page 237) but not nearly as rich or complex.

OTHER COFFEE-FLAVORED LIQUEURS:

- Capucello: a creamy, nutty, coffeelike liqueur, likened to cappuccino, from Holland.

- Tia Maria (page 242), Pasha (from Turkey).

~ *CRÈME DE MENTHE* A peppermint-flavored liqueur used in a multitude of drinks, available in green or white varieties.

OTHER MINT-FLAVORED LIQUEUR:

- Centerbe: an Italian liqueur made with more than 100 herbs, with an intensely assertive peppermint flavor (also called Mentuccia).

OTHER CRÈME FRUIT LIQUEURS:

- Crème d'ananas: pineapple flavored.

- Crème de cassis: black currant liqueur; most come from Dijon, France.

- Crème de fraise, such as fraise des bois: made with flavors of wild strawberries and herbs.

- Crème de framboise: raspberry flavored.

- Crème de mandarine: tangerine flavored.

- Crème de mûre: blackberry flavored.

- Crème de myrtille: blueberry flavored.

- Crème de noisette: hazelnut flavored.

- Crème de noyaux: a subtle almond-flavored liqueur, made from the oils of peach and apricot kernels (or pits).

- Crème de pêche: peach flavored.

- Crème de prunelle: prune, raisin, and plum flavored.

- Crème de violette: violet flavored.

CUARENTA Y TRES

A Spanish liqueur also sold under the name Licor 43 (see Licor 43, page 238).

CURAÇAO

Curaçao is a general term for orange-flavored liqueurs produced in the Dutch West Indies made from dried sour orange peels. Well-known varieties include white (clear), red-orange, and blue curaçao, which is used to tint drinks a blue hue, as well as to sweeten them.

- Triple sec: similar in style to curaçao, but not as sweet.

- Van der Hum: an orange and tangerine curaçao from South Africa.

- Crystal Comfort: a slightly sweet, clear, tangerine-flavored liqueur made in the United States.

DAMIANA

This legendary aphrodisiac from Baja California, Mexico, is a sweet, flowery, herbal liqueur marketed under the name Liqueur for Lovers, with a signature bottle in the shape of an Incan fertility goddess. According to legend, it was the first liqueur used in the Mexican Margarita.

DRAMBUIE

Originally made on the Scottish isle of Skye, back in 1892, and now made near Edinburgh, Drambuie is a whisky-based liqueur with a name derived from the Gaelic *an dram buidheach* ("the drink that satisfies"). Made from a blend of scotch whisky flavored with heather honey and Scottish herbs.

FRANGELICO

An Italian liqueur based on a 300-year-old recipe that includes hazelnuts and an infusion of berries and flowers.

GALLIANO

This very popular golden-hued Italian liqueur was created in 1896 by Armando Vaccari, who named it in tribute to the Italian hero Giuseppe Galliano. Neutral spirits are flavored with a mixture of 80 herbs, flowers, and other botanicals, including assertive vanilla, licorice, and anise notes. Extremely sweet, Galliano is not only enjoyed as an after-dinner sipper, but is also a great addition to many mixed drinks and is the signature ingredient in the Harvey Wallbanger (page 319).

GLAYVA

A scotch whisky–based liqueur made near Edinburgh, flavored with heather honey, orange peel, and other herbs. Similar to Drambuie, it is discernibly fruitier.

GODIVA LIQUEUR
A rich, chocolate-flavored liqueur with the addition of bitter orange; slightly minty. It comes in a white chocolate version as well.

OTHER CHOCOLATE LIQUEUR:

- Royal Mint Chocolate: a French liqueur that tastes like an after-dinner mint.

GOLDWASSER
The original version of this liqueur was concocted by Arnaldo Vilanova, a Catalan physician, whose advanced alchemic mixology created this "tonic" containing flakes of gold that cured the pope of a life-threatening illness, saving Vilanova from the Inquisition. A similar liqueur from France is liqueur d'or or eau d'or.

GRAND MARNIER
Created in France in 1880, this popular Cognac-based liqueur is made with bitter oranges from the Caribbean and is further refined through cask aging for a mellow and sweet product. It is best enjoyed like a fine brandy—sipped at room temperature from a snifter.

OTHER BRANDY AND COGNAC-BASED ORANGE-FLAVORED LIQUEURS:

- Cointreau, Harlequin orange liqueur, Aurum, Mandarine Napoléon.

IRISH MIST
A whisky-based herb- and honey-flavored liqueur from Ireland.

KAHLÚA
A rich, popular coffee liqueur made in Mexico from cane spirit, flavored with coffee, herbs, and vanilla. Some production is in England.

KEKE BEACH
This sweet-tart lime-flavored creamy liqueur from the Netherlands has a taste reminiscent of Key lime pie and adds a creamy consistency to drinks.

KÜMMEL
A popular digestif, this herbal liqueur is made from a neutral spirit flavored with anise and caraway seeds. It was created in 1575 by the Dutch distiller Lucas Bols.

A similar liqueur is Allasch, an extremely sweet Latvian liqueur flavored with almonds, aniseed, and cumin.

LICOR 43

Also called Cuarenta y Tres (Spanish for 43), this is Spain's favorite liqueur, produced and blended according to an ancient recipe dating back to 200 B.C. It contains a variety of 43 fruits and herbal elements. This extremely sweet and viscous liqueur has a predominant vanilla-citrus flavor and a bright yellow hue.

LIMONCELLO

An Italian lemon-flavored liqueur that dates back many centuries, based on an age-old method of combining an infusion of lemon peel, sugar, and water with a neutral spirit. A similar liqueur is CapriNatura, a lemony flavored, sweetly tart Italian liqueur.

LIQUEUR BRANDIES

Some spirits that are called fruit brandies are technically "crème" liqueurs, as they are based on a neutral grape brandy macerated with the addition of fruit juice and syrup for sweetener, rather than being distilled directly from the fruit itself. They are usually around 60 proof.

The following "brandies" fall into this category:

- *APRICOT BRANDY* A brandy wine flavored with apricot, such as the French Apry and Cusenier, both by Marie Brizard, Abricotine, and Bols apricot brandy.

- *BLACKBERRY BRANDY* A blackberry-flavored brandy liqueur (such as Echte Kroatzbeere).

- *CHERRY BRANDY* A brandy wine flavored with cherry, such as the popular Cherry Heering, Peter Heering's cherry liqueur from Denmark (page 240).

- *PEACH BRANDY* A brandy made with peach flavor; the one made by Bols is a popular brand.

There is also Peachtree, a peach brandy liqueur made in Holland (see also Southern Comfort, page 242).

MANDARINE NAPOLÉON

This fragrant Belgian brandy-based liqueur, created in 1892, is made from the peels of tangerines, as opposed to bitter orange peels from the Caribbean, imparting a candied orange flavor, and is frequently used in place of Cointreau or triple sec in mixed drinks.

MARASCHINO

A sour cherry liqueur that is more dry than sweet. The Italian word for cherry is *marasca*.

> *OTHER MARASCHINO LIQUEUR:*
>
> - Luxardo, a famous brand of cherry liqueur from Italy, made from a combination of cherry distillate infused with pressed cherry skins, which are further distilled and then aged. This clear liqueur has aromatic bitter cherry notes with nutty overtones from the cherry stones.

MIDORI

Produced by Suntory in Japan, this pale-green melon-flavored liqueur is made from sweet muskmelon, and is a popular addition to many cocktails. De Kuyper makes an inexpensive version.

NOCELLO

An Italian walnut-flavored liqueur.

> *OTHER NUT LIQUEURS:*
>
> - Amaretto, crème de noyaux, crème d'amande, Frangelico, Kahana Royale, Praline.

OPAL NERA

An Italian liqueur with aromatic flavors of anise and berries, a satiny texture, and a distinct, signature purple-black color.

OUZO

This intense licorice-flavored liqueur from Greece is crystal clear and flavored with herbs such as coriander, chamomile, and essences of aniseed and licorice.

Similar to other pastis liqueurs, it turns milky when combined with water or ice.

It is served cold either in a thick-bottomed shot glass or with water, pastis style, in a short glass, or poured over a few ice cubes in an old-fashioned glass.

PASTIS

A generic term for clear, strong 90-proof liqueurs, flavored with licorice or aniseed, that become cloudy or milky when mixed with water or ice. A very popular European aperitif, pastis is available from many sources; examples include Pernod (from France), Ricard (from Marseilles, France), ouzo (from Greece), and ojen (from Spain). This French spirit is distilled from the ingredients themselves and is higher in alcohol content than the usual anisettes, which may also be made with anise and/or licorice but which simply add flavor through maceration.

PARFAIT AMOUR (OR PARFAIT D'AMOUR)

The name of this French violet-hued liqueur translates as "perfect love," which is apt, as it was purportedly once served in Parisian brothels as an aphrodisiac. It is available in two styles, both of which are very sweet; the European version is curaçao based and delicate, fragrantly flavored with rose petals, violets, almonds, spices, and vanilla pods. The American version has a much more pronounced citrusy flavor, along with the spices and violets. It is similar to crème de violette.

PERNOD

A pastis made by the French producer of the original absinthe, often used as an absinthe substitute, with the same licorice, anise flavors. Like other pastis, this clear, yellow-green liqueur turns cloudy white when mixed with water or ice, usually in a ratio of 4 to 5 parts water to 1 part Pernod.

PETER HEERING

A popular cherry brandy made in Denmark, named after its inventor. This ruby-red liqueur flavored with black cherries and aged in wood casks is much more complex and drier than most fruit liqueurs.

PIMM'S NO. 1

This aromatic, herbal, bittersweet, liqueur-like drink was invented in the 1880s by Englishman James Pimm, a London restaurateur, and is purportedly the original Gin Sling. The most popular of the Pimm's liqueurs, Pimm's No.1 has a gin base, flavored with herbs, spices, quinine, and fruit, and is the liqueur used when someone orders a "Pimm's Cup." With the popularity of the original, Pimm went on to produce Pimm's No. 2 (whiskey based), No. 3 (brandy), No. 4 (rum), No. 5 (rye), and No. 6 (vodka). The vodka-based version is the only other one still produced.

POIRE WILLIAMS

Named after a variety of pear, this sweet, clear, pear-flavored liqueur is not a true eau-de-vie but a brandy-based fruit-infused liqueur. It is made in France, Switzerland, Germany, and Italy. A few premium-quality brands, such as Poire Prisonnière, have the whole pear inside the bottle. This feat of creative packaging is achieved by attaching bottles over the pear tree branches, so that the pear actually grows inside the bottle. Marie Brizard produces a nice one. It can be served as an aperitif, well chilled and with one ice cube.

OTHER PEAR-FLAVORED LIQUEUR:

- Pearle de Brillet: a French liqueur that imparts a perfumy pear flavor.

PUNSCH

Known in England as "Swedish punch" (originally a British colonial concoction). Made in Sweden, this cask-aged punch is a rum-based liqueur flavored with wine, spiced with cinnamon and cloves, and sweetened. Traditionally, it is to be gently heated and served warm in a heat-proof mug, but it is also enjoyed chilled and even poured over ice.

ROCK AND RYE

A citrus-flavored rye-whiskey-based liqueur flavored with a variety of fruit emphasizing the citrus. There is a piece of rock candy in each bottle.

SAMBUCA

Made in Italy, this predominantly licorice-flavored liqueur is made from an infusion of witch elder and licorice. It is similar to anisette, but relatively dry. This popular liqueur is traditionally served with three coffee beans floating on the surface, inspiring the phrase *con mosca,* "with flies." Available in white (clear) and black varieties.

SCHNAPPS

Technically, schnapps is an aquavit (a vodkalike spirit) and not a liqueur, but it is used like liqueurs in mixed drinks. Usually made from neutral spirits and flavored with fruit or peppermint, schnapps are less sweet and more potent than liqueurs.

SLOE GIN

The name is deceptive, as this is a liqueur made from sloe berries from the blackthorn shrub but is not really a gin. The English product is sweet and gin based. A similar liqueur called Prunelle is made in France, but it is brandy based.

SOUTHERN COMFORT

This bourbon-based peach-flavored American liqueur has more than 100 ingredients. It was created in 1874 by a New Orleans bartender trying to improve the whiskey he served.

STREGA

Italian for "witch," this is the name of an herbal liqueur from Benevento in southern Italy.

SUZE

A French aperitif made from the gentian root, a bitter plant used throughout history for medicinal purposes. Some are wine based and tend to be dry and bitter.

Other gentian liqueurs: Enzian from Germany, Gentiane from France.

TIA MARIA

A rich, rum-based coffee-flavored liqueur, first made in the 1600s, originally from Jamaica. This emulsion liqueur, made with sugarcane alcohol, tastes of rich coffee with a chocolate finish.

TRIPLE SEC

See curaçao, page 235.

Rum

------- *Rum* -------

RUM IS, LITERALLY AND FIGURATIVELY, the spirit of the Islands, with a sweet complexity characteristic of this sugarcane-based liquor. Christopher Columbus introduced sugarcane to the Caribbean in 1493, having gathered a few samples in the Canary Islands during his travels. The local islanders soon found a quasi-medicinal use for the fermented cane juice, as did the Brazilians a bit later. Columbus also brought sugarcane to Cuba, where the fermented juice was regarded as a medicinal cure for the flu, chills, home-sickness, and love. Early distillation of rum can also be traced to Brazil, where as far back as the early 1500s, the Portuguese settlers were making "sugarcane syrup wine," or *cachaça,* discovering that they could distill a spirit from the molasses sitting in the sugar factories, naturally fermenting from the heat.

America's history is intrinsically linked to the influence of rum. Long before whiskey or bourbon gained favor, rum was America's spirit of choice, and by the mid-1700s, millions of gallons were being imbibed in the colonies, and drunkenness was rampant. The first commercially distilled spirit in the colonies was rum made from West Indies molasses, which they acquired through ignoble and notorious means called the "triangular trade." New England's sailing ships would carry locally made rum, which they traded for slaves in Africa. From there they would head into the Caribbean, trading the slaves, who would work the sugarcane fields, for raw Caribbean molasses.

Not surprisingly, rum also became a smuggling commodity, and pirates earned a reputation as "rumrunners," which evolved into the nefarious moniker "rummy" that was eventually attached to rum drinkers and drunken sailors. Not only was rum used as political leverage, distributed among Virginia voters by George Washington to get elected to the House of Burgesses in 1758, but a 1765 tax levied against any non-British molasses used for rum production further fueled the uprising against the British.

Rum's reputation for inducing inebriation and causing strife on a wide scale in many American homes inevitably helped spark the Prohibition movement, led by Carry Nation, of the Women's Christian Temperance Union. Nation's infamous yell, "Smash the demon rum!" incited riots of rum-bottle smashing.

Today, far removed from a history steeped in notorious politics and debauchery, rum's rich, warm flavor is unlike any other bottled spirit, and it can instantly transport your palate to a balmy place.

The lovely sweetness inherent in rum comes from sugarcane, boiled down to a rich molasses, which is then fermented and distilled. Produced wherever there is sugarcane, rum is primarily from the world's tropical regions, with a large percentage made in Puerto Rico. By law, rum must be distilled from the fermented juice of the sugarcane, sugarcane syrup, and sugarcane molasses, but it can vary in color, weight, and sweetness. Full-bodied rums, such as Jamaican rum, involve longer and more elaborate fermentation and double-distillation processes, producing darker, sweeter rums. In the Caribbean, each island has its own distinctly different and perfected style of rum, from the molasses-flavored dark rums of Haiti, Jamaica, and Martinique to the silver, white, and lighter rums of Trinidad, Cuba, Puerto Rico, and the Virgin Islands, which retain very little molasses taste and tend to be drier. The following guide offers insight into the various types of rum available.

LIGHT RUMS

Labeled either white, light, silver, or blanco, these rums are clear to pale gold in color, light-bodied, and lightly sweet in flavor, with a dry aroma. The molasses is briefly fermented, usually distilled in a continuous still, and, after distillation, charcoal filtered and them aged in stainless steel tanks, yielding a liquid with little or no color. Some rums are aged for no longer than one year, in charred white oak, to add smoothness. Light rums range in flavor from floral and fruity (Cuban Havana Club) to neutral and crisp (Puerto Rican Bacardi) to soft and mellow with light coconut tones (Jamaican Appleton Estate White). With its delicate flavor, white rum is a versatile one to have on hand, an excellent choice for most mixed drinks, from tall rum coolers to Daiquiris.

GOLD RUMS

Labeled gold (oro) or amber (ambre), these medium-bodied, smooth rums are basically white rums that have become golden or light brown from aging. They are typically aged for one to three years (and even up to twelve years) in oak barrels, some of which have previously been used to age bourbon, to impart spicy notes. Occasionally they are enhanced by additional caramel coloring. These rums are used in many cocktails that call for white rum, to add a slightly more intense flavor. One of the oldest producers, Mount Gay, puts out a fine gold rum from Barbados; Jamaica's Appleton Special is another good choice.

DARK RUMS

Dark rums (deep gold or dark brown in color) are robust rums made in traditional pot stills and further refined through blending with a lighter, continuous-still spirit. They are then aged for anywhere from three to twelve years (but most for five to seven years) in well-charred oak barrels. These dark, full-bodied rums, such as Myers's Original Dark from Jamaica or Martinique rums (usually bottled in France), add aggressive flavor to cocktails and are best used to enhance the lighter rums in the more potent drinks. A splash of dark rum can give a rich molasses flavor to tall, fruity cocktails. For real dark rum fans, the traditional Jamaican cocktail Dark and Stormy is made with ginger beer. Excellent sippable dark rums include the deluxe Jamaican dark from Appleton Estate and Rhum Barbancourt from Haiti. If you find yourself in Martinique, the Saint James is sublime.

AGED, VIEUX, OR AÑEJO RUMS

Similar to the quality of a good brandy or bourbon, these vintage brown rums are aged for at least six years and are to be enjoyed like a Cognac. Unlike most dark rums, which are heavily flavored, these draw their intensity from a longer aging period. Sometimes blended to ensure continuity, they are always more expensive than younger rums. For rum connoisseurs, there are also single mark rums, which are unblended—that is, they are drawn from a single batch. These are rare and very expensive.

There are a few aged blends worth trying in your next (very dry) Rum Martini. Bacardi 8 is an eight-year-old blend, with intonations of orange blossom, pears, apples, and caramel. From Costa Rica there is Gran Blasón Añejo Especial, which has a slightly smoky flavor and a coffeelike bitterness. Myers's Legend is a dark reserve blend with cloves and cardamom, molasses, and coffee flavors. Martinique also produces high-quality *rhum vieux*.

SPICED OR FLAVORED RUMS

Growing in popularity, spiced or flavored rums can be made from a base of white, gold, or dark rum, infused with citrus flavors, vanilla, coconut, pineapple, and various other fruits. They are sold as rum liqueurs, bottled rum punches, and rum infusions and bring a new dimension of flavor to the classic rum drinks, such as Daiquiris and Mojitos. Of course, the traditional favorite is Captain Morgan Spiced Rum, great for hot rum drinks and spiced-up rum punch. Malibu rum, a popular, good-quality coconut-flavored rum, is worth using in your next Piña Colada.

OVERPROOF RUMS

The overproof rums, like Bacardi 151, are harsh, potent, and flammable, and not for drinking straight by any means. They are notoriously used to raise the alcohol content of "one-per-customer" Zombie-like concoctions. They are also used as the theatrical element in flaming drinks and desserts.

RUMS FROM AROUND THE WORLD

Although only a few Island rums are imported to the States (all the more reason to travel to the Islands for rum-tasting explorations), there remains quite a selection from which to choose.

------- CUBAN RUMS -------

Havana Club is the Cuban national brand, making high-quality rums that are light-bodied, clean, and crisp. It is the only internationally available Cuban rum, and was purportedly Hemingway's rum of choice while living in Havana. From their Silver Dry to their aged Añejo 7 Años, these rums are meant to be enjoyed with a good Havana cigar. They are, regrettably, not available in the United States, and so are worth checking out when traveling in other countries.

Brazil produces cachaça, a colorless spirit made from the juice of the first press of unrefined sugarcane (and sometimes from a combination of both molasses and sugarcane juice). This spicy rum is made in pot stills and not aged. It has a fiery tone, harsher than rum, with a bite similar to brandy. This is Brazil's national liquor, with 4,000 different brands from which to choose. Luckily, a few, such as Cachaça 51 and Toucano by Ypioca, have made their way into the United States. Cachaça is also known as *aguardiente de caña.*

------- **RUMS FROM BARBADOS** -------

Barbadian rums are typically light-bodied and sweet, produced using both the pot and column-still method. Local distiller Mount Gay is the oldest operating producer of rum (since 1663) and offers both mixing- and sipping-quality rums.

------- **HAITIAN RUMS** -------

Producing medium-bodied rums made from sugarcane juice rather than molasses, the Haitians follow the French traditional method of double distilling in small pot stills and aging them for long periods in oak casks. The results are full-flavored and smooth, exemplified by the extremely popular Rhum Barbancourt (founded in 1862), one of the finest rums not only of Haiti but of the world.

------- **JAMAICAN RUMS** -------

These are dark, aromatic, full-bodied, sweet rums that reflect their complex process, involving a long fermentation of molasses, double distillation by the old pot-still method, and aging in white oak barrels for at least five years.

------- **RUMS FROM GUYANA** -------

The rich and extremely popular Demerara rums come from Guyana. Produced in both pot and column stills and aged for long periods (some available on the market are twenty-five years old), they are typically blended with lighter rums. Similar rums come from French Guiana.

------- **RUMS FROM MARTINIQUE** -------

This French island is a busy producer of rum, with many distilleries producing both *rhum agricole* (from sugarcane juice) and *rhum industriel* (from molasses), using both pot and column stills. The rum is frequently aged for a minimum of three years, in barrels previously used for aging brandy.

------- **RUMS FROM TRINIDAD** -------

Light-bodied rums produced in column stills.

------- **RUMS FROM THE DOMINICAN REPUBLIC** -------

Full-bodied, aged rums produced in column stills, such as Brugal.

------- **PUERTO RICAN RUMS** -------

Typically known for its light-bodied rums, Puerto Rico produces many brands, such as Ronrico and Don Q and the most popular, Bacardi, which was originally made in Cuba. Bacardi makes a peppery rum—its light Superior rum—but it also produces aged rums, and the high-proof Bacardi 151 used to "float" and/or flame in cocktails. Captain Morgan Spiced Rum is another well-known Puerto Rican brand.

------- **VIRGIN ISLAND RUMS** -------

Similar to the light-bodied rums of Puerto Rico, these are medium-bodied and tend to have a more distinct molasses flavor.

Batavia Arak is a light-bodied and pungently aromatic rum made from cakes of Javanese red rice and molasses, first fermented and aged on the island of Java, then sent to age further in Holland for six years.

SERVING AND SIPPING RUM

Fine sipping rums have richly nuanced flavors that vary depending on the island they hail from, ranging from honey to vanilla, tropical fruits or spices to chocolate, caramel, or tobacco. These dark, aged, and spicy rums are best enjoyed at room temperature and treated like a fine Cognac, served in either sherry *copita* glasses or brandy snifters. Here are a few suggestions: Gran Blasón from Costa Rica, a great honey-flavored rum with a rich, warm body, and Gosling's Black Seal, with molasses tones. For a lovely aged rum, Myers's Legend (ten years), or Ron Añejo Aniversario, from Venezuela. In the Caribbean, the natural pairing of fine cigars and rum is enjoyed and further expressed in the ritual of dipping the end of the cigar into the rum. Whether enjoyed simply over ice or in your favorite Daiquiri, rum is the quintessential element for a tropical flavor experience.

RUM DRINKS

Acapulco

1½ ounces light rum
½ ounce Cointreau
½ ounce fresh lime juice
1 egg white (optional)
½ ounce simple syrup
Fresh mint sprig

Shake the liquid ingredients vigorously with ice. Strain into a chilled cocktail glass or over ice in an old-fashioned glass. Garnish with the mint sprig.

Ambassador

1 ounce light rum
⅓ ounce apple schnapps
2 dashes passion fruit liqueur
1 ounce cranberry juice

Shake the ingredients vigorously with ice. Strain into a chilled cocktail glass.

Atlantic Breeze

1½ ounces light rum
½ ounce apricot liqueur
2½ ounces pineapple juice
½ ounce fresh lemon juice
¼ ounce Galliano
Orange slice

Pour all the liquid ingredients except the Galliano into an ice-filled highball glass. Stir briefly. Float the Galliano on top of the drink. Garnish with the orange slice.

Bacardi Cocktail *A classic, this is the only cocktail protected by a court ruling. In 1936, a New York court ruled that this cocktail must be made with Bacardi rum. It is basically a Daiquiri made with grenadine in place of simple syrup.*

2 ounces Bacardi light or gold rum
1 ounce fresh lime juice
½ ounce grenadine
Maraschino cherry

Shake the liquid ingredients vigorously with ice. Strain into a chilled cocktail glass. Garnish with the cherry.

Bahama Mama

1 ounce dark rum
½ ounce coconut rum
½ ounce coffee liqueur
4 ounces pineapple juice
1½ ounces fresh lemon juice
1 tablespoon 151-proof Demerara rum
Pineapple wedge
Maraschino cherry

Shake all liquid ingredients but the 151 rum vigorously with ice. Strain into a chilled cocktail glass. Float the 151 on top of the drink. Garnish with the pineapple wedge and cherry.

Banshee

1 ounce rum
⅔ ounce crème de cacao
½ ounce crème de banane
2 ounces heavy cream
1 ripe banana, peeled and sliced

Combine the ingredients in a blender with ½ cup ice. Pour into a chilled balloon wineglass.

Barracuda

1½ ounces gold rum
1 ounce Galliano
3 ounces pineapple juice
½ ounce fresh lime juice
Lime wedge

Shake the liquid ingredients vigorously with ice. Strain into an ice-filled highball glass and stir gently. Garnish with the lime wedge.

VARIATION: **For an Atlantic Breeze,** substitute lime juice for the lemon juice, and add ½ ounce apricot liqueur.

Bay Breeze

2 ounces light rum
3 ounces cranberry juice
1 ounce pineapple juice

Pour the ingredients into an ice-filled highball glass and stir.

Beachcomber

Lime wedge
Superfine sugar
2 ounces gold rum
½ ounce Cointreau
¼ ounce maraschino liqueur
¼ ounce cherry brandy
½ ounce fresh lime juice
Lime slice

Rub the rim of a chilled wineglass with the lime wedge and rim with sugar. Shake the liquid ingredients vigorously with ice. Strain into the prepared glass. Garnish with the lime slice.

Between the Sheets *This is the decadent rum version of the classic cocktail, frequently made with just the Cognac.*

Lemon wedge
Superfine sugar
¾ ounce Demerera or spiced rum
¾ ounce Cognac (or brandy)
¾ ounce Grand Marnier
½ ounce fresh lemon juice
Lemon twist

Rub the rim of a chilled cocktail glass with the lemon wedge and rim with sugar. Shake the liquid ingredients vigorously with ice. Strain into the prepared glass. Garnish with the lemon twist.

Black Devil *Basically a rum Martini.*

2 ounces good-quality light rum
¼ ounce dry vermouth
Black olive

Stir the rum and vermouth in a mixing glass with ice. Strain into a chilled cocktail glass. Garnish with the black olive.

Black Widow

1 ounce gold rum
¼ ounce Southern Comfort
1 teaspoon sugar
1 ½ ounces fresh lime juice

Shake the ingredients vigorously with ice. Strain into a chilled sour glass.

Blue Hawaiian

1 ounce light rum
1 ounce blue curaçao
1 ounce cream of coconut
2 ounces pineapple juice
Pineapple wedge
Maraschino cherry

Shake the liquid ingredients vigorously with ice. Strain into an ice-filled highball glass. Garnish with the pineapple and cherry.

VARIATION: Combine all ingredients but the garnish in a blender with ½ cup ice. Blend until smooth.

Blue Marlin

Lemon wedge
Sugar
2 ounces citron rum
½ ounce blue curaçao
½ ounce sweet-and-sour
Orange blossom

Rub the rim of a chilled cocktail glass with the lemon wedge and rim with sugar. Shake the liquid ingredients vigorously with ice. Strain into the prepared glass. Float the orange blossom on top of the drink.

Bolero   *This is one of those drinks that have two very different versions known by the same name.*

BOLERO #1

1½ ounces light rum
¾ ounce Calvados (or applejack)
½ teaspoon sweet vermouth

Stir the ingredients in a mixing glass with ice. Strain into a chilled cocktail glass.

BOLERO #2   *The fruity version.*

2 ounces dark rum
½ ounce brandy
½ ounce fresh lime juice
½ ounce fresh orange juice
½ ounce simple syrup

Shake the ingredients vigorously with ice. Strain into a chilled cocktail glass.

Bossa Nova   *A Brazilian-inspired cocktail made with the favorite national spirit—cachaça.*

1½ ounces cachaça (or light rum)

1 ounce Frangelico

½ ounce Cointreau

¾ ounce fresh lime juice

¾ ounce cranberry juice

1 tablespoon honey

2 cranberries

Lime wedge

Combine the liquid ingredients in a blender with ½ cup ice. Blend until smooth. Pour into a chilled cocktail glass. Garnish with the cranberries and lime wedge, and serve with a straw.

Caribbean Millionaire

1 ounce gold or dark rum

1 ounce crème de banane

½ ounce apricot brandy

½ ounce fresh lemon juice

Dash of sloe gin

Banana slice

Shake the liquid ingredients vigorously with ice. Strain into an ice-filled collins glass. Garnish with the banana slice.

Caipirinha   *The name of this Brazilian classic loosely translates as "country bumpkin" or "little peasant girl," referring to its "uncivilized" preparation in the same glass from which it will be sipped. As you muddle the limes against the granulated sugar in the bottom of the heavy glass, the fragrant oils from the crushed lime peels are released. Traditionally made with cachaça, the fiery Brazilian spirit with the reputation of actually powering up a Ford Fairlane, this drink has a distinctive bite.*

4 or 5 lime wedges

2 teaspoons sugar or turbinado sugar

2 ounces cachaça

Muddle the sugar and lime wedges together in an old-fashioned glass until the sugar is dissolved and the lime juice is released. Fill the glass with ice and pour in the cachaça. Stir briefly.

VARIATIONS: Add a few pieces of fruit, such as raspberries, blueberries, or strawberries, to muddle with the lime wedges.

HERE ARE A FEW NEW FAVORITE CACHAÇA COCKTAILS FROM BRAZILIAN HOT SPOTS:

Spiced Mandarin Caipirinha: Muddle fresh lime and mandarin, cinnamon and sugar, fill with ice, and stir in aged cachaça and Mandarine Napoléon liqueur.

Caipitetra: Made with orange juice, honey, mint, and cachaça.

Granada Brasileira: Made with passion fruit juice, cream, sugar, and cachaça.

Caipirissima: Made with rum instead of cachaça.

Casablanca

2½ ounces light rum
½ ounce Cointreau
½ ounce maraschino liqueur
½ ounce fresh lime juice

Shake the ingredients vigorously with ice. Strain into a chilled cocktail glass.

Castro Cooler

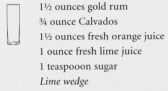

1½ ounces gold rum
¾ ounce Calvados
1½ ounces fresh orange juice
1 ounce fresh lime juice
1 teaspooon sugar
Lime wedge

Shake the liquid ingredients and sugar vigorously with ice. Strain into an ice-filled collins glass. Squeeze the lime wedge over the drink, and drop it in.

Centenario

1½ ounces gold rum
¾ ounce white rum
¼ ounce Tia Maria
¼ ounce triple sec
1½ ounces fresh lime juice
Dash of grenadine
Fresh mint sprig

Shake the liquid ingredients vigorously with ice. Strain into an ice-filled collins glass. Garnish with the mint sprig.

Citrus Aphrodisiac

1 lime, quartered
1 tablespoon honey
1 ounce Damiana liqueur
1½ ounces Rhum Barbancourt
3 ounces fresh tangerine juice

Squeeze the lime wedges over a chilled double old-fashioned glass, and then drop them in. Add the honey and Damiana, and muddle with the limes. Fill the glass with ice, and pour in the rum and tangerine juice. Stir briefly.

Cocoanut Groove   *Inspired by the famous 1950s hot spot, Cocoanut Grove.*

1½ ounces Malibu coconut rum
½ cup coconut sorbet or gelato
1 ounce fresh lime juice
1 ounce coconut milk
1 ounce pineapple juice
Pineapple wedge
Dusting of ground nutmeg

Combine all ingredients but the garnishes in a blender with ½ cup ice. Blend until smooth. Pour into a chilled cocktail glass. Garnish with the pineapple, and sprinkle the top with nutmeg.

Cuba Libre *Although this classic has a bit of a reputation as a sweet, youth-oriented drink, when made correctly, with lots of fresh lime juice, the sweetness of the cola is refreshingly counterbalanced. Cuba libre means "free Cuba" and, as cocktail lore tells it, the name was coined by an American soldier stationed in Cuba during the Spanish-American War, assisting in the liberation from Spain.*

½ lime
2 ounces light rum
4 to 6 ounces chilled cola
Lime wedge

Squeeze the lime half over an ice-filled highball glass, and drop it in. Add the rum, top with cola, and stir. Garnish with the lime wedge.

Cuban Sidecar

1 ounce light rum
1 ounce Cointreau
1 ounce fresh lime juice
Lime twist

Shake the liquid ingredients vigorously with ice. Strain into a chilled cocktail glass. Twist the lime peel over the drink, and drop it in.

VARIATION: **For a Cuban Special,** add ½ ounce pineapple juice, and garnish with a pineapple wedge.

Dark and Stormy *This classic Bermuda favorite is a sparkling refresher known to combat the heat as well as soothe the stomach. Jamaican ginger beer is enhanced with a kick of fresh ginger to really spice it up.*

1 to 2 slices fresh ginger (optional)
2 ounces dark rum
½ tablespoon ginger syrup or simple syrup
3 to 4 ounces chilled ginger beer
2 lime wedges

Fill an old-fashioned glass with ice and add the fresh ginger. Add the rum and ginger syrup, and stir. Top with ginger beer. Squeeze the lime wedges over the drink and drop them in.

VARIATION: **For a Caribbean Ginger Zing,** substitute 2 lemon wedges for the lime wedges.

Daiquiri ------

ACCORDING TO LEGEND, AROUND THE LATE 1890S, in Cuba's Daiquirí mountains, an American engineer came up with this now-famous rum-based concoction in an attempt to please his guests once the gin had disappeared. Given rum's status as the highly esteemed "milk of Cuba," however, it's likely that this combination had been enjoyed before. Soon Havana became the Daiquiri mecca, especially the El Floridita Bar, where legendary bartender Constantino Ribalaigua introduced the frozen version and elevated the Daiquiri to perfection. By straining the drink after blending it with crushed ice, he avoided further dilution while retaining the frosty character.

In its pure form, the Daiquiri is simple yet sublime, blending the delicate sweetness of rum with sugar and the juice of one lime. The secret of a perfect one is not just in the balance of ingredients, but in squeezing the lime with your fingers to allow the oils from the rind to mingle with the juice, creating the Daiquiri's signature intensity and flavor. Always use fresh lime juice; to use Rose's lime juice in a Daiquiri would be an unthinkable travesty.

Classic Daiquiri

2 ounces light rum
1 ounce fresh lime juice
½ ounce simple syrup
Lime slice

Shake the liquid ingredients vigorously with ice. Strain into a chilled cocktail glass. Garnish with the lime slice.

Frozen Daiquiri

2 ounces white rum
¾ ounce fresh lime juice
½ ounce simple syrup
Dash of maraschino liqueur

Combine the ingredients in a blender with ½ cup ice. Blend until smooth. Pour into a chilled cocktail glass, and serve with a straw.

Frozen Fruit Daiquiri   *Make a Frozen Daiquiri, with one of the following additions. Garnish with the appropriate fruit. Many prefer to add a dash or two of dark rum to their fruit Daiquiris.*

For a Daiquiri de Piña, add ½ cup cubed pineapple.

For a Peach Daiquiri, add ½ cup fresh peach slices and ½ ounce peach brandy.

For a Strawberry Daiquiri, add ½ cup sliced strawberries and ¼ ounce crème de framboise.

For a Banana Daiquiri, add ½ cup sliced ripe banana and ¼ ounce crème de banane (or other banana liqueur).

Frozen Watermelon Daiquiri

1 cup seeded, cubed watermelon
1½ ounces white rum
¾ ounce fresh lime juice
¼ cup lime sorbet
Lime wheel

In a blender, purée the watermelon until completely smooth. Add the rum, lime juice, lime sorbet, and ½ cup ice. Blend until smooth. Pour into a chilled cocktail glass. Garnish with the lime wheel.

Guavalicious Daiquiri   *An exotic spin on the Daiquiri.*

2 ounces Rhum Barbancourt
2 ounces guava nectar
¾ ounce fresh lime juice
1 teaspoon superfine sugar
Lime peel spiral

Shake the liquid ingredients and sugar vigorously with ice. Strain into a chilled cocktail glass. Garnish with the lime peel spiral.

Papa Hemingway's Daiquiri   *Also known by various aliases, including Papa Doble or Ernest Hemingway Special, this distinctly different Daiquiri was created for Hemingway by Constantino Ribalaigua, the famed Cuban bartender at El Floridita in Havana. Living in Cuba during Prohibition, Hemingway could indulge in Havana Club Silver Dry rum, and preferred his Daiquiris without sugar, cold and sour, and with a bit more rum than the traditional Daiquiri. If you prefer a lighter, sweeter version, use 2 ounces of rum and add a teaspoon of sugar.*

3 ounces blanco rum
½ ounce maraschino liqueur
1½ ounces fresh grapefruit juice
¾ ounce fresh lime juice
Lime wedge

Combine all ingredients but the garnish in a blender with ½ cup ice. Blend until smooth. Pour into a chilled cocktail glass. Squeeze the lime wedge over the drink, and drop it in.

VARIATION: **LA FLORIDITA DAIQUIRI**

2 ounces light rum
¼ ounce maraschino liqueur
1½ ounces fresh lime juice
1 teaspoon sugar

Prepare in the same manner as Papa Hemingway's Daiquiri.

Copabanana Daiquiri *Inspired by the legendary 1940s Copacabana nightclub.*

2 ounces Captain Morgan Spiced Rum
½ banana, peeled and sliced
¼ cup fresh or frozen raspberries
¾ ounce fresh lime juice
½ ounce simple syrup
2 fresh raspberries
1 lime wheel

Combine all ingredients but the garnishes in a blender with ½ cup ice.
Blend until smooth. Pour into a chilled cocktail glass. Garnish with the
raspberries and lime wheel.

Florida Special

1½ ounces gold rum
¼ ounce triple sec
¼ ounce maraschino liqueur
¾ ounce fresh orange juice

Shake the ingredients vigorously with ice. Strain into a chilled cocktail glass.

Golden Lillet Martini
Lillet is a delightful aperitif wine that imparts subtle flavors of honey, orange, lime, and mint. The fragrant tones of Lillet are an especially fine enhancement to warm, buttery Haitian rum, with a touch of limoncello liqueur.

2 ounces Rhum Barbancourt
1½ ounces Lillet
½ ounce limoncello liqueur
Lemon twist

Shake the liquid ingredients vigorously with ice. Strain into a chilled cocktail glass. Twist the lemon peel over the top of the drink, and drop it in.

Gorilla Tit

¾ ounce dark rum
¾ ounce bourbon
¾ ounce coffee liqueur

Shake the ingredients vigorously with ice. Strain into an ice-filled old-fashioned glass.

Green Flash
As South Pacific legend has it, there is a visually epic moment just as the sun goes down called the green flash, *in which a green glow appears for 2 or 3 seconds along the horizon line.*

1½ ounces silver rum
¾ ounce green Chartreuse
¾ ounce fresh lime juice

1 tablespoon superfine sugar
2 to 3 ounces chilled club soda
Lime wedge

Shake the rum, chartreuse, lime juice, and sugar vigorously with ice. Strain into an ice-filled highball glass. Top with club soda and stir gently. Squeeze the lime wedge over the drink, and drop it in.

Haitian Cooler

1 lemon wedge
2 lime wedges
2 tangerine (or orange) wedges
1 tablespoon sugar
2 ounces Rhum Barbancourt
3 to 4 ounces chilled ginger beer (or ginger ale)

Muddle the lemon, lime, and orange wedges with the sugar in the bottom of an old-fashioned glass. Fill the glass with ice, pour in the rum, and top with ginger beer.

Havana Sidecar

1½ ounces gold rum
¾ ounce Cointreau
¾ ounce fresh lemon juice

Shake the ingredients vigorously with ice. Strain into a chilled cocktail glass.

Heatwave

1 ounce dark rum
½ ounce peach schnapps
4 to 5 ounces pineapple juice
¼ ounce grenadine

Pour the rum and peach schnapps into an ice-filled highball glass. Top with pineapple juice, add the grenadine, and stir.

Honolulu Lulu

1½ ounces Myers's dark rum
1 ounce light rum
1 ounce Frangelico
½ ounce Kahlúa
3 ounces pineapple juice
1 ounce fresh lime juice
1 tablespoon simple syrup
Lime wedge

Shake the liquid ingredients vigorously with ice. Strain into a chilled large collins glass. Squeeze the lime wedge over the drink, and drop it in.

Hurricane   *The original Hurricane drink was superpotent, with double the rum, and was served over ice in a hurricane glass. If you wish to attempt the classic formula, do so at your own risk.*

1½ ounces dark rum
1 ounce light rum
½ ounce passion fruit juice
1½ ounces fresh orange juice
1 ounce fresh lime juice
1 ounce pineapple juice
Dash of Angostura bitters
Lime wedge
Pineapple wedge

Shake the liquid ingredients vigorously with ice. Strain into an ice-filled wineglass. Garnish with the lime and pineapple wedges.

I Dream of Jeanie Martini   *From The Beauty Bar, an East Village hot spot in New York City, this drink was created by its master mixologist, Lara Turchinsky.*

1½ ounces Malibu rum
1 ounce Stolichnaya lemon vodka (or other lemon-flavored vodka)
1 ounce Cointreau

1½ ounces cranberry juice
½ ounce fresh lime juice
Lemon twist

Shake the liquid ingredients vigorously with ice. Strain into a chilled cocktail glass. Twist the lemon peel over the drink, and drop it in.

Jade

1½ ounces light rum
½ teaspoon Cointreau
½ teaspoon green crème de menthe
¾ ounce fresh lime juice
1 teaspoon sugar
Thinly cut lime slice

Shake the liquid ingredients and sugar vigorously with ice. Strain into a chilled cocktail glass. Garnish by floating the lime slice on top of the drink.

Jamaican Martini

2 ounces dark Jamaican rum
½ ounce Tia Maria

Stir the ingredients in a mixing glass with ice. Strain into a chilled cocktail glass.

VARIATION: **For a Kingston Cocktail,** add ¼ ounce fresh lime juice.

La Floridita Cocktail

1½ ounces light rum
¾ ounce sweet vermouth
¼ ounce crème de cacao
1 ounce fresh lime juice
Dash of grenadine

Shake the ingredients vigorously with ice. Strain into a chilled cocktail glass.

Long Island Iced Tea   *Some purists claim you should never mix vodka and gin together, but this potent classic defies many taboos, and indeed tastes dangerously like iced tea.*

¾ ounce white rum

¾ ounce gin

¾ ounce vodka

¾ ounce tequila

¾ ounce Cointreau or triple sec

1 ounce fresh lime juice

¾ ounce fresh orange juice

2 to 3 ounces chilled cola

Lemon wedge

Pour all the liquid ingredients except the cola into an ice-filled collins glass. Top with cola and stir gently. Squeeze the lemon wedge over the drink, and drop it in.

VARIATIONS: **For a Miami Iced Tea,** substitute blue curaçao for the Cointreau (or triple sec).

For a New England Iced Tea, add 1 ounce simple syrup and substitute cranberry juice for the cola.

Mai Tai   *One of the true classics in the tropical drink genre, this original Trader Vic's recipe from 1944 lives up to its archetypal roots. When made with the classic ingredients, the Mai Tai deserves its Tahitian title, which means "out of this world." Martinique rum is the ideal component in this drink, but given its elusive availability in the States, any aged añejo rum will work just as well.*

1½ ounces Myers's dark or other dark Jamaican rum

1 ounce Martinique rhum vieux or other aged rum

½ ounce orange curaçao

¼ ounce simple syrup

½ ounce orgeat or almond-flavored syrup

1¼ ounces fresh lime juice

½ ounce fresh orange juice

1 orange blossom (or tiny purple orchid)

1 orange peel spiral

Shake the liquid ingredients with ice. Strain into an ice-filled collins glass or large wineglass. Garnish with the orange blossom and orange spiral.

Mandarin Passion

2 ounces white rum
1 ounce Mandarine Napoléon liqueur
1 ounce Monin passion fruit syrup (or other passion fruit syrup)
4 ounces pineapple juice
Pineapple wedge
Tangerine slice

Shake the liquid ingredients vigorously with ice. Strain into an ice-filled collins glass. Garnish with the pineapple wedge and tangerine slice.

Mojito   *Havana's refreshing answer to the Mint Julep has become a new classic in many American hot spots. Yet another of Hemingway's favorite Cuban cocktails, Mojitos are traditionally made by muddling together the mint, lime, and sugar, ideally with a white rum, with some versions adding a splash of club soda.*

Here are two different ways to prepare the Mojito. One is the traditional method; the other is a quicker version that takes the "shaken not stirred" route to Havana. Both get you to the same place.

1 ounce fresh lime juice
1 tablespoon superfine sugar
6 to 8 fresh mint leaves
2 ounces light rum
3 to 4 ounces chilled club soda
Fresh mint sprig

TRADITIONAL METHOD: In the bottom of a highball glass, muddle together the lime juice, sugar, and mint leaves until the sugar is dissolved. Add the rum. Fill the glass with ice and top with club soda. Garnish with the mint sprig.

SHAKEN METHOD: Shake the lime juice, sugar, mint leaves, and rum vigorously with ice. Without straining, pour the entire contents of the shaker into a highball glass, and top with club soda. Garnish with the mint sprig.

VARIATION: See the Old Cuban recipe on page 163 for a champagne variation on the Mojito from the Carlyle Hotel, Bemelmans Bar, in New York City.

My Mandarin from Havana *A frozen Daiquiri made with silver rum and a medley of citrus flavors, and strained the El Floridita way for a frosty cocktail.*

2 ounces silver rum
1 ounce Mandarine Napoléon liqueur
1 ounce fresh mandarin (or tangerine) juice
½ ounce fresh lime juice
1 teaspoon superfine sugar
1 thinly sliced lime wheel

Combine all ingredients but the garnish with ½ cup ice in a blender. Blend until slushy.

Using a fine-mesh metal strainer, slowly strain the mixture into a chilled cocktail glass. Float the lime wheel on top of the drink.

Nacional

1½ ounces gold rum
¾ ounce apricot brandy
¾ ounce pineapple juice
¼ ounce fresh lime juice

Shake the ingredients vigorously with ice. Strain into a chilled cocktail glass.

Navy Grog *This elaboration on the basic grog has come a long way from the rum, lime, and water beverage rationed out to 18th-century British sailors.*

1 ounce dark Demerara rum
1 ounce gold or Jamaican rum
1 ounce light rum
½ ounce fresh lime juice
½ ounce fresh orange juice
½ ounce passion fruit juice
½ ounce pineapple juice
½ ounce almond or orgeat syrup
Fresh mint sprig
Lime slice

Shake the liquid ingredients vigorously with ice. Strain into an ice-filled highball glass. Garnish with the mint sprig and lime slice.

VARIATION: Combine the liquid ingredients in a blender with 1/2 cup ice, and pour into a chilled wine goblet.

- -

Old San Juan

1½ ounces gold rum
½ ounce cranberry juice
1 ounce fresh lime juice
Lime wedge

Shake the liquid ingredients vigorously with ice. Strain into a chilled cocktail glass. Run the lime wedge around the rim, squeeze it over the drink, and drop it in.

- -

Pearl from Ipanema

Lime wedge
Superfine sugar
1½ ounces cachaça or light rum
2 ounces fresh grapefruit juice
1 ounce KeKe Beach lime liqueur
½ ounce fresh lemon juice
1 tablespoon pomegranate syrup (real grenadine)
Lime twist

Rub the rim of a chilled large cocktail glass with the lime wedge and rim with sugar. Shake the liquid ingredients vigorously with ice. Strain into the prepared glass. Twist the lime peel over the drink, and drop it in.

- -

Pedro Collins   *Also called a Ron Collins.*

2 ounces light rum
1 ounce fresh lime juice
1 tablespoon sugar
3 to 4 ounces chilled club soda
Lime slice
Maraschino cherry

Pour the rum, lime juice, and sugar into an ice-filled collins glass. Top with club soda and stir gently. Garnish with the lime slice and cherry.

Piña Colada   *This luscious Puerto Rican classic from the 1950s, purportedly invented by bartender Ramón "Monchito" Marrero at the Caribe Hilton in San Juan, made its way into the tropical repertoire of the Caribbean and gained further momentum with its extreme popularity in the 1970s. The key ingredient and inspiration comes in a can: the sweet, viscous coconut cream known as Coco López. It was created by Puerto Rican Ramón López Irizarry, also in the 1950s, and has become the quintessential tropical ingredient in many concoctions in the tropical drink genre. The phrase* piña colada *literally means "strained pineapple," and although the use of fresh juice is highly recommended in most cases, the prospect of extracting fresh pineapple juice, though commendable, is a bit daunting, so find a good-quality store-bought juice instead.*

Although many frozen and blended versions exist, the Piña Colada is traditionally shaken.

2 ounces Puerto Rican light rum
6 ounces pineapple juice
2 ounces coconut cream
Pineapple spear
Maraschino cherry

Shake the liquid ingredients vigorously with ice. Strain into a large ice-filled wineglass. Garnish with the pineapple spear and cherry.

Piña Colada Nueva   *A luxe variation on the Puerto Rican classic.*

2 ounces silver rum
1 ounce Alizé de France passion fruit liqueur
½ cup diced fresh pineapple
1½ ounces coconut cream
1½ ounces mango juice or nectar
½ ounce fresh lime juice
1 pineapple slice
1 mango slice
Shaved coconut

Combine all ingredients but the garnishes in a blender with 1 cup ice. Blend until smooth.

Pour into a chilled wineglass. Garnish with the pineapple and mango slices, and sprinkle the coconut on top.

Pinerito

1½ ounces light rum
2 ounces fresh grapefruit juice
1 ounce fresh lime juice
1 teaspoon sugar
Dash of grenadine

Pour the ingredients into an ice-filled highball glass, and stir.

Planter's Punch   *The origins of this tropical concoction range from the Myers rum company in Jamaica to an antebellum bartender at the Planter's House Hotel in St. Louis. With plenty of versions claiming to be the original, this is a great one. For a bit of effervescence, you may wish to add a splash of club soda.*

2 ounces dark rum
Dash of Cointreau
1½ ounces fresh orange juice
1½ ounces pineapple juice
½ ounces fresh lime juice
½ ounce simple syrup
Dash of grenadine
Orange slice
Maraschino cherry

Shake the liquid ingredients vigorously with ice. Strain into an ice-filled highball glass. Garnish with the orange slice and cherry.

Presidente

1½ ounces light rum
½ ounce dry vermouth
½ ounce sweet vermouth
¼ ounce triple sec
Orange twist

Stir the liquid ingredients in a mixing glass with ice. Strain into a chilled cocktail glass. Run the orange peel around the rim, twist it over the drink, and drop it in.

VARIATION: **For an El Presidente,** add ¼ ounce fresh lemon juice and a dash of grenadine.

Royal Palm Cocktail

1 tablespoon 99 Bananas liqueur (or crème de banane)
2 ounces vanilla-infused rum (see page 247)
Half a vanilla bean

Coat the inside of a chilled cocktail glass with the banana liqueur, and discard any remaining liqueur. Stir the vanilla-infused rum in a mixing glass with ice. Strain into the prepared glass and garnish with the vanilla bean.

Rum and Tonic

2 ounces dark rum
3 to 4 ounces chilled tonic water
Lime wedge

Pour the liquid ingredients into an ice-filled highball glass. Stir well. Run the lime wedge around the rim, squeeze it over the drink, and drop it in.

Rum Cooler

2½ ounces dark rum
6 ounces chilled ginger ale
Lemon twist

Stir the rum in a mixing glass with ice. Strain into an ice-filled collins glass. Top with ginger ale. Twist the lemon peel over the drink, and drop it in.

VARIATION: **For a Rum Buck,** substitute light rum for the dark.

Rum Sangaree

2 ounces dark rum
½ ounce Cointreau
½ ounce ruby port
Freshly grated or ground nutmeg

Stir the liquid ingredients in a mixing glass with ice. Strain into an ice-filled wineglass. Sprinkle the top with nutmeg.

Rum Swizzle   *The original swizzle, a Caribbean classic. See the description of the swizzle on page 45.*

2 ounces dark rum
½ ounce fresh lemon juice
½ ounce triple sec
5 to 6 ounces chilled ginger ale
Lemon wheel

Shake the rum, lemon juice, and triple sec vigorously with ice. Strain into an ice-filled collins glass. Top with ginger ale. Garnish with the lemon wheel.

Scorpion   *This potent concoction is another faux Polynesian classic from the South Seas–infatuated 1950s, hailing from the father of tiki mixology, Don the Beachcomber. A close cousin to the potent Mai Tai and Zombie, it was frequently served in a huge communal tiki bowl, enough for four patrons, and bedecked with gardenias and long straws. This recipe conveniently serves one, gardenias optional.*

2 ounces light or gold rum
½ ounce brandy
½ ounce dry vermouth
1½ ounces fresh orange juice
1½ ounces fresh lemon juice
½ ounce orgeat syrup
Pineapple spear
Maraschino cherry
Edible flower (such as orange blossom, gardenia, or nasturtium)

Shake the liquid ingredients vigorously with ice. Strain into a large ice-filled wineglass. Garnish with the skewered pineapple and cherry, and float the flower on top.

Spiced Rum Coco Martini

2 ounces spiced rum (such as Captain Morgan)
½ ounce chocolate liqueur (such as Godiva)
Orange twist
Maraschino cherry

Stir the liquid ingredients in a mixing glass with ice. Strain into a chilled cocktail glass. Run the orange peel around the rim, twist it over the drink, and drop it in, along with the cherry.

Tidal Wave

1½ ounces Malibu rum (or other coconut-flavored rum)
1 ounce blue curaçao
¾ ounce fresh lime juice
½ ounce amaretto
1 tablespoon coconut cream
1 teaspoon superfine sugar
Lime slice
Small orchid

Shake the liquid ingredients and sugar vigorously with ice. Strain into a chilled cocktail glass. Garnish with the lime slice and orchid.

Tiger's Milk

1 ounce dark rum
1 ounce brandy
4 ounces half-and-half
2 teaspoons sugar
Freshly grated or ground nutmeg

Shake the rum, brandy, half-and-half, and sugar vigorously with ice. Strain into a chilled wineglass. Sprinkle the top with nutmeg.

Tikitini

1½ ounces pineapple-infused rum (see page 247)
½ ounce maraschino liqueur
½ ounce Thai coconut milk
2 ounces mango juice

Shake the ingredients vigorously with ice. Strain into a chilled cocktail glass.

Tobago Coconut Flip

1½ ounces Malibu rum
1 ounce Thai coconut milk
¼ ounce Goldschläger cinnamon schnapps

Ground cinnamon
Orange blossom

Shake the liquid ingredients vigorously with ice. Strain into a chilled cocktail glass. Sprinkle a dusting of cinnamon over the top, and float the orange blossom on top.

VARIATION: For those who are fond of cinnamon, add an additional ¼ ounce of the cinnamon schnapps.

Velvet Voodoo

1½ ounces Rhum Barbancourt
½ ounce Pernod (or other absinthe substitute)
½ ounce amaretto
¼ cup softened vanilla ice cream
Freshly grated or ground nutmeg
Chocolate shavings

Combine all the ingredients but the garnishes in a blender with ½ cup ice. Blend until smooth. Pour into a chilled cocktail glass. Dust the top with the nutmeg and sprinkle with a few chocolate shavings.

West Indian Punch

2 ounces dark rum
¾ ounce banana liqueur
1 ounce fresh orange juice
1 ounce fresh lime juice
1 ounce pineapple juice
Freshly grated or ground nutmeg

Shake the liquid ingredients vigorously with ice. Strain into a chilled collins glass. Dust the top with nutmeg.

Yellow Bird   *A Caribbean favorite.*

1 ounce dark rum
1 ounce light rum
¼ ounce Tia Maria
1¼ ounces fresh orange juice

~ CONTINUED

1 ounce fresh lime juice
Fresh mint sprig
Maraschino cherry

Shake the liquid ingredients vigorously with ice. Strain into a chilled highball glass. Garnish with the mint sprig and cherry.

VARIATION: Substitute ½ ounce Galliano and ½ ounce Cointreau for the Tia Maria and orange juice.

Zombie *Don the Beachcomber's mind-altering concoction has always posed a challenge for creative mixologists and has been subject to variation since its conception in 1934. Not surprisingly, given the euphoric reaction of a country just coming out of Prohibition, the Beachcomber's Zombie combined three types of rum—light, gold, and dark—with a blend of fresh fruit juices. The classic finishing touch of a float of 151-proof rum on top made it a high-octane concoction indeed. A deceptively smooth glass of velvet dynamite, it well deserves Don's house rule of "only two per customer."*

1 ounce light Puerto Rican rum
1 ounce gold (añejo) rum
1 ounce dark Jamaican rum
½ ounce apricot brandy
1 ounce crème de banane
1 ounce pineapple juice
1 ounce fresh lemon juice
1 ounce fresh lime juice
¼ ounce grenadine
1 tablespoon brown sugar
½ ounce 151-proof Demerara rum
Pineapple wedge
Lime wheel
Fresh mint sprig
Green orchid
Maraschino cherry

Shake all liquid ingredients but the 151 vigorously with ice. Strain into an ice-filled 16-ounce chilled zombie glass (or large chilled wineglass). Float the 151 rum on top. Garnish with a skewer of fresh fruit and edible flowers.

Tequila

THIS MEXICAN SPIRIT HAS COME A LONG WAY from its Aztec origins, becoming increasingly sophisticated—some even reaching a refined snifter-quality smoothness—but it still retains the mystique inherited from *pulque,* that ancient agave spirit thought to be a gift from the gods.

Tequila is a distillate of the blue agave, a succulent plant that grows wild all over Mexico, and it is socially and economically the national drink. A precursor to tequila, *pulque* is made from fresh, fermented agave juice and was once imbibed in religious ceremonies by the Aztec people. The Spanish conquistadors brought the distillation process to the region, and in 1795, Don José María Guadalupe Cuervo set up a distillery in Tequila, Mexico, to produce from cultivated agave what is now known as tequila. Technically speaking, tequila is a mescal that by law is produced in designated regions, mainly in the state of Jalisco, Mexico. Within these specifically designated areas, the huge heart, or *piña,* of the mature blue agave plant is harvested and cooked, producing the fresh agave juice for the fermentation process, to then be distilled, refined, and regulated, producing many distinctive styles.

The best-quality tequilas state their 100 percent blue *Agave tequilana Weber* status on the label, signifying that they have superior flavor, were bottled in Mexico, and are guaranteed by law to be produced with sugar that was strictly from the blue agave plant. The lesser-quality tequilas, basically tequila blends, are made with a blend of different sugars, including juice from sugarcane, with a minimum of 51 percent blue agave; these are known as *mixto* tequilas. The moderately priced *mixto* brands are a fine choice for mixed drinks and when blending pitchers of frozen Margaritas for a crowd, but to make the best-quality cocktails, 100 percent agave tequila is well worth the added expense.

TYPES OF TEQUILA

Unlike vodka, which filters out all flavor, the best tequilas reflect the flavor of the agave plant and the soil in which it grew, bringing herbaceous, earthy flavors and notes anywhere from vanilla to mushrooms, mint, or pepper. Tequilas have varying degrees of quality and flavor, from the harsh, rough mescal blends to the deluxe tequilas of smooth, aged añejos. This guide will help you decipher the labels on the many tequilas that are on the market.

------- **BLANCO OR PLATA** (WHITE OR SILVER) -------

The blanco ("white") or plata ("silver") tequilas are not aged but are freshly distilled and bottled within 60 days. Double distilled to produce clear white tequila, this spirit has a fiery quality that is a bit harsher than the aged tequilas, but it has the full-on agave flavor that is preferred by many tequila aficionados and is perfect for fruity Margaritas, spicy concoctions, and tequila infusions. These tequilas are available in both 100 percent agave and *mixto*.

------- **JOVEN ABOCADO** (GOLD) -------

Tequilas labeled joven abocado ("young and smooth") are usually referred to as gold or dorado, referring to the caramel color. These are not aged tequilas but merely silver tequilas with added coloring and flavoring that slightly mellows them out. They are almost always *mixtos,* fine for using with mixes and juices and well suited for multilayered shooters.

------- **REPOSADO** -------

A reposado ("rested") tequila has been mellowed and improved by aging for two months to a year in oak barrels and is very smooth. The pale gold to deeper gold hues come from aging, although sometimes additional coloring has been added as well. Known to bring traces of honey and vanilla tones, these tequilas add a rich, warm dimension to Margaritas. Reposados are also deserving of straight sipping. Available in 100 percent agave or *mixto*.

------- **AÑEJO** -------

Meaning "aged," the name says it all. These deluxe tequilas are aged for at least one year, and no more than five, in wood barrels. Typically made with 100 percent agave, they are highly regulated for quality and are label-dated. Some coloring and flavoring are permitted. The best añejos are a perfect taste balance of tequila and wood, versus those that weigh in with a predomi-nantly heavy wood flavor. These aged tequilas are the sippable equivalent of a good Cognac.

------- **MEZCAL** (THE ONE WITH THE WORM) -------

Although an agave-based spirit, mezcal does not come specifically from the designated tequila area, and it is made from a variety of agaves, rather than just the blue agave. Mezcals tend to have a smokier flavor than tequila due to the roasting of the agave (agave for tequila is oven-baked) and are distilled only once, therefore tending to be unregulated and decidedly harsher. There are, however, a few small-batch "single-village" producers from the area of Oaxaca that put out quality mezcals. The infamous worm is actually the larva of an insect that lives in the agave plant. It serves as a sign of authenticity and bestows luck and strength upon the one who swallows it. Although mezcal is made in many areas of Mexico, Oaxaca is the main exporter of mezcal to the United States.

A product from Mexico that originated with the Aztecs, this freshly fermented juice is made from various species of agave. A mildly alcoholic, milky white spirit that is not the smoothest of beverages, it is often made more palatable with the addition of various ingredients such as nuts, spices, chiles, fruits, or herbs. The Spanish conquistadors, arriving in Mexico in 1519, took this fermented brew, the precursor to tequila, and distilled it, making a tequila closer to mezcal.

MIXING AND SIPPING TEQUILA

The tequilas typically suitable for mixed drinks are the silver (blanco) or gold tequilas, usually a *mixto,* but a moderately priced reposado is a luxe alternative, bringing a warm, rich complexity to many drinks.

The best tequilas for sipping will be 100 percent agave and should be treated like a fine single-malt scotch or Cognac, enjoyed either at room temperature, especially the añejos, or, as many prefer, chilled in the freezer or refrigerator. Serve it neat in brandy snifters or sherry *copita* glasses, or in a shot glass for the classic tequila shot, in which case a premium silver is appropriate, complete with lime wedge and salt.

------- **A FEW SUGGESTIONS FOR SIPPABLE TEQUILAS** -------

- El Tesoro de Don Felipe Silver: strong agave, citrus, and peppery notes.

- Patrón Silver: citrus and vanilla notes.

- Don Julio Añejo: a moderately priced aged tequila with a fruity, brandylike quality.

- Chinaco Añejo: an aged high-end tequila with flavors reminiscent of pine needles.

- Sauza Hornitos Reposado: a moderately priced tequila, herbaceous and earthy.

- Patrón Reposado: vanilla notes.

- Alcatraz Reposado: gin notes.

- El Conquistador Reposado: pear notes.

TEQUILA DRINKS

Acapulco

1 ounce gold tequila
1 ounce gold rum
2 ounces fresh grapefruit juice
3 ounces pineapple juice

Shake the ingredients vigorously with ice. Strain into an ice-filled highball glass.

Bird of Paradise

¾ ounce tequila
¾ ounce white crème de cacao
¼ ounce amaretto
1½ ounces heavy cream

Shake the ingredients vigorously with ice. Strain into a chilled cocktail glass.

Bite of the Iguana   *A spicy Bloody Maryesque Margarita, made with tequila infused with hot and spicy pepper.*

2 lime wedges
Salt
1½ ounces pepper-infused tequila (see page 71)
¾ ounce triple sec or other orange liqueur
1½ ounces sweet-and-sour
½ cup washed, stemmed, halved orange cherry tomatoes
1 clove garlic, finely minced
1 chopped green onion
2 to 3 dashes Worcestershire sauce
2 orange cherry tomatoes

~ CONTINUED

Rub the rim of a chilled margarita glass with a lime wedge and rim with salt. Blend all ingredients except the garnish with 3 to 4 ice cubes until puréed and smooth. Pour the blended mixture into the prepared glass. Garnish with the remaining lime wedge, skewered between the two tomatoes.

Black Sombrero

1 ounce tequila
1 ounce vodka
2 ounces Kahlúa

Shake the ingredients vigorously with ice. Strain into a chilled cocktail glass.

Bloody Maria   *A tequila-based Bloody Mary, also known as a Tequila Maria.*

2 ounces silver tequila
1½ ounces fresh lime juice
1 clove garlic, finely minced
¼ cup chopped cucumber
2 to 3 dashes Worcestershire sauce
2 to 3 dashes Tabasco sauce or other hot sauce
4 to 5 ounces tomato or V8 juice
Lime wedge
Celery stalk

Combine the tequila, lime juice, garlic, cucumber, Worcestershire, and Tabasco in a blender, and blend until smooth. Pour into an ice-filled highball glass, and top with the tomato juice. Stir well. Squeeze the lime wedge over the drink, and drop it in. Garnish with the celery stalk.

VARIATION: **For a Tequila Clam Digger,** substitute Clamato juice for the tomato juice.

Blue Moon

¾ ounce tequila
¼ ounce blue curaçao
2 to 3 dashes Galliano
1½ ounces heavy cream

Shake the ingredients vigorously with ice. Strain into a chilled cocktail glass.

Blue Shark

1½ ounces tequila
1½ ounces vodka
½ ounce blue curaçao

Shake the ingredients vigorously with ice. Strain into a chilled cocktail glass, or into an ice-filled old-fashioned glass.

Bonsai Margarita

Lime wedge
Salt
1½ ounces silver tequila
1 ounce Midori liqueur
½ ounce Harlequin orange liqueur
½ ounce fresh lime juice
1 tablespoon superfine sugar
Lemon twist

Rub the rim of a chilled margarita glass with the lime wedge and rim with salt. Fill the prepared glass with ice. Shake the tequila, Midori, orange liqueur, lime juice, and sugar vigorously with ice. Strain into the prepared glass. Garnish with the lemon twist.

Brave Bull   *A tequila variation on the Black Russian.*

1½ ounces gold tequila
1 ounce Kahlúa (or Tia Maria)
Whipped cream topper (optional)

Shake the tequila and Kahlúa vigorously with ice. Strain into an ice-filled old-fashioned glass. Top with whipped cream, if desired.

VARIATION: **For a Southern Bull,** add 1 ounce Southern Comfort.

Chapala

1½ ounces silver tequila
½ teaspoon Cointreau (or triple sec)
1 ounce fresh orange juice
½ ounce fresh lemon juice
¼ ounce grenadine
Orange slice

Shake the liquid ingredients vigorously with ice. Strain into an ice-filled double old-fashioned glass. Garnish with the orange slice.

Cherry Picker

1 ounce gold tequila
1 ounce cherry brandy
½ ounce fresh lime juice
1 ounce apple juice
Lime twist

Shake the liquid ingredients vigorously with ice. Strain into a chilled cocktail glass. Twist the lime peel over the drink, and drop it in.

Classic Tequila Shot

1½ ounces silver tequila
Lime wedge
Kosher salt

Pour the tequila into a chilled shot glass. Rub the area between the thumb and forefinger with the lime wedge to moisten the skin. Sprinkle salt on the moistened area. Lick the salt, then quickly gulp the tequila, and bite into the lime wedge.

Compadre

2 ounces reposado tequila
2 ounces fresh grapefruit juice
½ ounce Campari

2 to 3 ounces chilled club soda
Orange twist

Shake the tequila, grapefruit juice, and Campari vigorously with ice.
Strain into an ice-filled highball glass. Top with club soda and stir gently.
Twist the orange peel over the drink, and drop it in.

El Diablo

½ lime
1½ ounces tequila
½ ounce crème de cassis
3 to 4 ounces chilled ginger ale

Squeeze the lime half into an ice-filled old-fashioned glass. Pour in the
tequila and crème de cassis, top with ginger ale, and stir.

Freddy Fudpucker   *The tequila version of the Harvey Wallbanger—also known as a Tequila Wallbanger.*

1½ ounces silver tequila
4 to 5 ounces fresh orange juice
½ ounce Galliano

Pour the tequila and orange juice into an ice-filled highball glass. Stir.
Float the Galliano on top.

Frostbite

1½ ounces tequila
¾ ounce blue curaçao
½ ounce crème de cacao
¼ ounce crème de menthe
2 ounces heavy cream

Shake the ingredients vigorously with ice. Strain into a chilled cocktail
glass.

Hot Pants

Lemon wedge
Kosher salt
1½ ounces tequila
¾ ounce peppermint schnapps
¾ ounce fresh grapefruit juice
1 teaspoon powdered sugar

Rub the rim of a chilled old-fashioned glass with the lemon wedge and rim with salt. Shake the tequila, peppermint schnapps, grapefruit juice, and sugar vigorously with ice. Strain into the prepared glass.

La Bomba

1 ounce gold tequila
½ ounce Cointreau
½ ounce pineapple juice
½ ounce fresh orange juice
2 dashes grenadine

Shake the tequila, Cointreau, pineapple juice, and orange juice vigorously with ice. Strain into a chilled cocktail glass. Float the grenadine on top.

La Conga

2 ounces silver tequila
¼ ounce pineapple juice
3 dashes Angostura bitters
3 to 4 ounces chilled club soda
Lemon slice

Pour the tequila, pineapple juice, and bitters into an ice-filled old-fashioned glass. Top with club soda and stir. Garnish with the lemon slice.

Loco Padre

2 ounces reposado tequila
1½ ounces fresh orange juice
½ ounce maraschino liqueur
¼ ounce Frangelico
Orange slice

Shake the liquid ingredients vigorously with ice. Strain into an ice-filled old-fashioned glass. Garnish with the orange slice.

Madagascar Mood Shifter

1½ ounces vanilla-infused tequila (see page 71)
¾ ounce Citrónge (or other orange liqueur)
2 ounces fresh tangerine juice
1 ounce sweet-and-sour
3 or 4 fresh mint leaves
Tangerine wheel
Mint sprig

Shake the liquid ingredients and mint leaves vigorously with ice. Strain into a chilled cocktail glass. Garnish with the tangerine wheel and mint sprig.

Matador   *Here are two versions: on the rocks, and frozen.*

1½ ounces gold tequila
3 ounces pineapple juice
½ ounce fresh lime juice

Shake the ingredients vigorously with ice. Strain into an ice-filled old-fashioned glass.

VARIATION: **FROZEN MATADOR**

2 ounces gold tequila
¼ ounce triple sec
¼ cup fresh pineapple chunks
½ ounce fresh lime juice

Combine the ingredients in a blender with ½ cup crushed ice, and blend until smooth. Pour into a chilled highball glass.

The Classic Margarita

LEGENDS SURROUNDING THE CREATION of the Margarita are numerous, with locations ranging from California to Mexico, but a few tales have remained steadfast. Setting the stage for creativity, the cultural climate of 1940s America had become enthralled with all things Latin, and bartenders were excitedly shaking up cocktails to promote this mysterious and fiery new spirit from Mexico. There was some speculation over one particularly brilliant bartender in California, who, in order to push the new fiery liquor, switched out the brandy and lemon juice for tequila and lime juice, turning the classic and wildly popular Sidecar made with triple sec into the now-classic Margarita cocktail.

Another legendary story gives an American socialite credit. Margaret Sames reportedly served a drink containing tequila, lime juice, and her favorite orange liqueur, Cointreau, at a party down in Acapulco in around 1948, in salt-rimmed glasses etched with the Mexican version of her name—and purportedly the "Margarita" was born.

However this great tequila cocktail came about, one thing remains true: the key to the best Margarita is to adhere to the basic recipe, using freshly squeezed lime juice combined with 100 percent agave tequila and a premium orange liqueur. The classic approach involves pouring the shaken mixture into a margarita glass with a salted rim, but muddling the ingredients in the bottom of an old-fashioned glass with wedges of fresh lime and serving it on the rocks is equally acceptable. A Margarita made with Rose's lime juice or a bottled margarita mix is not recommended. A desirable alternative to freshly squeezed lime juice is frozen limeade, which makes a great shortcut, with the added bonus of sweetness. The simplicity of the Margarita makes it an ideal vehicle for frozen and blended variations made with fresh fruits.

Classic Margarita   *The beauty here is in the balance of tequila, lime juice, and orange liqueur, making this a versatile base for many creative variations such as the Cucumber Margarita (page 293), or frozen Strawberry Margarita (below). If you prefer your Margarita a bit sweeter, add 1 tablespoon of sugar; if you like it tart, add another squeeze of lime.*

2 lime wedges
Kosher salt
1½ ounces premium silver tequila
1½ ounces fresh lime juice
1 ounce Cointreau

Rub a wedge of lime around the rim of a chilled margarita glass, and salt the rim. Fill the prepared glass with ice. Shake the liquid ingredients vigorously with ice. Strain into the prepared glass. Squeeze the remaining lime wedge over the drink, and drop it in.

Strawberry Margarita

2 ounces tequila
½ ounce Cointreau
½ ounce strawberry liqueur
½ ounce fresh lime juice
2 to 3 sliced, hulled fresh strawberries
1 strawberry
1 lime wheel

Blend all ingredients except the garnish with 1 cup crushed ice until smooth. Pour into a chilled margarita glass. Garnish with the strawberry and lime wheel.

VARIATIONS: **For a Peach Margarita,** substitute 1 peach, peeled and diced, and peach schnapps for the strawberries and strawberry liqueur.

For a Mango Margarita, substitute ½ mango, diced, for the strawberries and strawberry liqueur, and substitute Tuaca for the Cointreau.

For a Melon Margarita, substitute ½ cup cubed honeydew melon and ½ ounce melon liqueur for the strawberries and strawberry liqueur.

Avocado Margarita

1½ ounces silver tequila
½ ounce Cointreau
1 ounce fresh lime juice
½ ounce fresh lemon juice
¼ cup diced ripe avocado
1 ounce half-and-half
1 teaspoon sugar
Lime wedge
Avocado slice

Combine all ingredients but the garnishes in a blender with ½ cup ice. Blend until smooth. Pour into a chilled cocktail glass. Garnish with the lime and avocado.

Cadillac Margarita   *Also known as a Golden Margarita.*

2 ounces good-quality reposado tequila
1 ounce Grand Marnier
1 ounce fresh lime juice
Lime peel spiral

Shake the liquid ingredients vigorously with ice. Strain into a chilled cocktail glass. Garnish with the lime spiral.

Chocolate Margarita

1½ ounces gold tequila
¾ ounce Godiva liqueur
½ ounce Cointreau
1 ounce sweet-and-sour
¼ ounce fresh orange juice
Chocolate shavings (optional)

Shake the liquid ingredients vigorously with ice. Strain into a chilled cocktail glass. Shave chocolate over the top, if desired.

Cucumber Margarita   *A fresh and innovative twist on the Margarita.*

1 tablespoon superfine sugar
1 ounce fresh lime juice
¼ cup thinly sliced English cucumber
1½ ounces silver tequila
1 ounce Cointreau

Put the sugar and lime juice in the bottom of an old-fashioned glass. Add the cucumber and muddle. Add the tequila and Cointreau. Fill the glass with ice and stir.

Blue Margarita

Lime wedge
Kosher salt
2 ounces tequila
1 ounce blue curaçao
1 ounce Cointreau (or triple sec)
1 ounce fresh lime juice

Rub the rim of a chilled cocktail glass with the lime wedge and rim with salt. Shake the liquid ingredients vigorously with ice. Strain into the prepared glass.

Papaya Margarita   *This refreshing pitcher of puréed Papaya Margarita serves four. It replaces the usual triple sec with Damiana liqueur.*

MAKES 4 SERVINGS
2 cups cubed ripe papaya
6 ounces fresh sweet-and-sour
6 ounces silver tequila
2 ounces Damiana liqueur
4 lime wedges
4 small pink orchids (optional)

Chill 4 margarita glasses. Set aside. In a blender, mix the papaya, sweet-and-sour, tequila, and Damiana until thoroughly puréed. Add 2 cups ice and blend until the mixture is smooth. Divide the mixture evenly among the prepared glasses. Garnish each with a skewered lime wedge and orchid.

Mexican Madras

1 ounce gold tequila
3 ounces cranberry juice
½ ounce fresh orange juice
¼ ounce fresh lime juice
Orange slice

Shake the liquid ingredients vigorously with ice. Strain into an ice-filled old-fashioned glass. Garnish with the orange slice.

Mexican Mule

2 ounces gold tequila
1 ounce fresh lime juice
1 teaspoon simple syrup
3 to 4 ounces chilled ginger ale

Shake all ingredients but the ginger ale vigorously with ice. Strain into an ice-filled highball glass, and top with ginger ale.

Mexicola   *A tequila twist on the Cuba Libre.*

2 ounces tequila
½ ounce fresh lime juice
2 to 3 ounces chilled cola
Lime wedge

Pour the tequila and lime juice into an ice-filled collins glass. Top with cola and stir. Squeeze the lime wedge over the drink, and drop it in.

Multiple Orgasm

½ ounce amaretto
½ ounce Kahlúa
½ ounce Irish cream liqueur
1 ounce heavy cream
1 ounce gold tequila

Shake the amaretto, Kahlúa, Irish cream, and heavy cream vigorously with ice. Strain into an ice-filled highball glass. Float the tequila on top.

Nectarine Dream

1 ripe nectarine, pitted and sliced
2 ounces reposado tequila
1 ounce Mandarine Napoléon liqueur
1½ ounces fresh lime juice
½ ounce fresh orange juice
1 tablespoon superfine sugar
Nectarine slice

Combine all ingredients but the garnish in a blender with 1 cup cracked ice. Blend until smooth. Pour into a chilled wineglass. Garnish with the nectarine slice.

Prickly Agave   *Look for prickly pear juice in specialty and natural food markets.*

Lime wedge
Sugar and salt
1½ ounces silver tequila
1 ounce Tuaca
1 ounce prickly pear juice
1 ounce fresh lime juice
Lime peel spiral

Rub the rim of a chilled margarita or large cocktail glass with the lime wedge and rim with sugar and salt. Shake the liquid ingredients vigorously with ice. Strain into the prepared glass, and garnish with the lime peel spiral.

Rosita   *Also called a Rosalita, this is the tequila version of the gin-based Negroni.*

1 ounce tequila
½ ounce Campari
½ ounce dry vermouth
½ ounce sweet vermouth
Lemon twist

Stir the liquid ingredients in a mixing glass with ice. Strain into a chilled cocktail glass, or pour into an ice-filled old-fashioned glass. Garnish with the lemon twist.

Rude Cosmopolitan   *This new classic substitutes tequila for the traditional vodka.*

2 ounces gold tequila
1½ ounces cranberry juice
1 ounce triple sec or Cointreau
½ ounce fresh lime juice

Shake the ingredients vigorously with ice. Strain into a chilled cocktail glass.

Salty Chihuahua   *The tequila version of the Salty Dog.*

Lemon wedge
Kosher salt
2 ounces silver tequila
5 to 6 ounces fresh grapefruit juice

Rub the rim of a chilled highball glass with the lemon wedge and rim with salt. Fill the prepared glass with ice cubes, and pour in the tequila and grapefruit juice. Stir.

Shady Lady

1 ounce tequila
1 ounce melon liqueur
4 ounces fresh grapefruit juice

Pour the ingredients into an ice-filled highball glass. Stir.

Short Fuse

2 ounces gold tequila
½ ounce apricot brandy
1½ ounces fresh lime juice
3 ounces fresh grapefruit juice
¼ ounce maraschino cherry juice (from a jar of cherries)
Lime wedge

Shake the liquid ingredients vigorously with ice. Strain into an ice-filled highball glass. Squeeze the lime wedge over the drink, and drop it in.

Silk Stocking

1½ ounces tequila
1½ ounces white crème de cacao
1 ounce heavy cream
¼ ounce Chambord
Pinch of cinnamon

Shake the liquid ingredients vigorously with ice. Strain into a chilled cocktail glass, and sprinkle cinnamon over the top.

Sloe Tequila

1 ounce tequila
½ ounce sloe gin
½ ounce fresh lime juice
Cucumber peel strip

Combine the liquid ingredients in a blender with ½ cup crushed ice. Blend until smooth. Pour into a chilled old-fashioned glass. Garnish with the cucumber peel.

South of the Border

½ lime
1 ounce tequila
¾ ounce Kahlúa (or Tia Maria)

Squeeze the lime half over a chilled highball glass, and drop it in. Fill with ice and pour in the tequila and Kahlúa. Stir.

Tequila Cocktail   *This 1930s concoction was the inspiration for the Tequila Sunrise. It is elegantly shaken or blended with ice, and served up in a cocktail glass.*

2 ounces silver tequila
1 ounce fresh lime juice
Dash of grenadine
Dash of orange flower water

Shake the ingredients vigorously with ice. Strain into a chilled cocktail glass.

Tequila Colada

1½ ounces tequila
¼ ounce Kahlúa
2 ounces pineapple juice
¾ ounce heavy cream
¼ ounce coconut cream

Shake the ingredients vigorously with ice. Strain into an ice-filled highball glass.

Tequila Fizz

2 ounces silver tequila
1 ounce fresh lime juice
1 teaspoon sugar
2 to 3 ounces chilled club soda

Shake the tequila, lime juice, and sugar vigorously with ice. Strain into an ice-filled highball glass, and top with club soda. Stir.

Tequila Ghost

2 ounces silver tequila
1 ounce Pernod
½ ounce fresh lemon juice

Shake the ingredients vigorously with ice. Strain into an ice-filled old-fashioned glass.

Tequila Mockingbird

2 ounces silver tequila
½ ounce white crème de menthe
1 ounce fresh lime juice
Thinly sliced lime wheel

Shake the liquid ingredients vigorously with ice. Strain into a chilled cocktail glass. Garnish by floating the lime wheel on top.

Tequila Sour

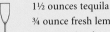

1½ ounces tequila
¾ ounce fresh lemon juice
½ ounce simple syrup
Maraschino cherry

Shake the liquid ingredients vigorously with ice. Strain into a chilled sour glass. Garnish with the cherry.

Tequila Sunrise   *There are two ways to serve this concoction, made popular in the 1970s—the traditional method, served over ice in a highball glass, or shaken and served up in a cocktail glass. Either will achieve the "sunrise" effect.*

1½ ounces silver tequila
6 ounces fresh orange juice
½ ounce grenadine (or Chambord)
2 to 3 ounces chilled club soda (optional)

STIRRED OVER ICE: Pour the tequila and orange juice into an ice-filled highball glass, and stir. Float the grenadine on top, and let it slowly descend through the drink. Top with club soda, if desired.

SHAKEN: Pour the grenadine in the bottom of a chilled cocktail glass. Shake the tequila and orange juice vigorously with ice, and strain into the glass.

Tequilatini   *A signature drink from the Four Seasons Martini Bar in New York.*

1½ ounces José Cuervo Especial tequila
½ ounce Grand Marnier
½ ounce Cointreau
Orange slice

Shake the liquid ingredients vigorously with ice. Strain into a chilled cocktail glass. Garnish with the orange slice.

Tequini   *A tequila Martini.*

2 ounces good-quality silver tequila
2 to 3 dashes dry vermouth
Dash of Angostura bitters
Lemon twist

Stir the liquid ingredients with ice in a mixing glass. Strain into a chilled cocktail glass. Run the lemon peel around the rim, twist it over the drink, and drop it in.

Tijuana Speedball   *Created by master mixologist Felicia Sledge, bartender from Blue Hour, a Portland, Oregon, hot spot.*

1 ounce reposado tequila
½ ounce Kahlúa
½ ounce Baileys Irish cream
1½ ounces cold espresso
Pinch of ground cinnamon

Shake the liquid ingredients vigorously with ice. Strain into a chilled cocktail glass. Sprinkle the cinnamon on top.

Tijuana Taxi   *A tequila take on the Sidecar.*

Lemon wedge
Sugar
2 ounces reposado tequila
1 ounce fresh lemon juice
1 ounce fresh orange juice
1 ounce Cointreau
½ ounce simple syrup
Lemon twist

Rub the rim of a chilled cocktail glass with the lemon wedge and rim with sugar. Shake the liquid ingredients vigorously with ice. Strain into the prepared glass. Garnish with the lemon twist.

Toreador

1½ ounces silver tequila
½ ounce white crème de cacao
Whipped cream
Unsweetened cocoa powder

Shake the tequila and crème de cacao vigorously with ice. Strain into a chilled cocktail glass. Float a dollop of whipped cream on top, and sprinkle with cocoa powder.

The Jake *A signature drink from Seattle's Mayflower Park Hotel.*

¼ ounce cabernet sauvignon
1½ ounces premium silver tequila
Lime peel spiral

Rinse a chilled cocktail glass with the cabernet sauvignon, and discard any remaining wine. Stir the tequila with ice in a mixing glass. Strain into the prepared glass, and garnish with the lime peel spiral.

Vampiro *This tequila classic is a hot and fiery hybrid between the Sangrita and the Bloody Maria.*

1½ ounces silver tequila
2 ounces tomato juice
1 ounce fresh orange juice
1 teaspoon honey
½ ounce fresh lime juice
1 tablespoon diced onion
1 teaspoon diced jalapeño chile
2 to 3 dashes Worcestershire sauce
Lime wedge
Jalapeño chile slice

Shake all ingredients but the garnishes vigorously with ice. Strain into a highball glass filled with ice, and garnish with the lime wedge and chile slice.

MEZCAL DRINKS

Mezcal Buck

2 ounces mezcal
1 ounce fresh lime juice
1 teaspoon simple syrup
3 to 4 ounces chilled ginger beer

Shake all ingredients but the ginger beer vigorously with ice. Strain into an ice-filled highball glass, and top with ginger beer.

Pan-Am

1 ounce mezcal
1 ounce bourbon
Dash of Angostura bitters
Dash of simple syrup

Pour the ingredients into an ice-filled old-fashioned glass, and stir.

Spanish Fly

2 ounces mezcal
1 ounce Grand Marnier
Pinch of instant coffee

Pour the mezcal and Grand Marnier into an ice-filled old-fashioned glass. Sprinkle instant coffee on top.

Vodka

VODKA—A WORD MEANING "LITTLE WATER" IN RUSSIAN—certainly characterizes this clean and most neutral of all spirits. As opposed to other clear spirits, such as *akvavit* and gin (clean base spirits that are redistilled with caraway and juniper, respectively), vodka's main objective is to have as clean a spirit as possible, without any discernible flavor or aroma.

Although vodka is synonymous with the chilly northeastern European cultures of Scandinavia, Russia, Poland, and Ukraine, all of which vie for the credit of inventing it, they were more accurately preceded by the Italians, who brought the art of distillation to the area. These cultures can, however, take credit for mastering the art of distilling it to perfection, and they have been consuming it like—well—water, ever since, as a bracer not only against the northern winters but also through a frequently oppressive existence.

VODKA HITS AMERICA

Until the late 1940s, vodka was virtually unknown outside Russia, Poland, and Scandinavia. In the West, America's enthusiasm for whiskey and gin overshadowed any interest in vodka, which was known simply as a spirit vaguely linked to dark Chekhov plays and Tolstoy novels. That all changed, however, due in no small part to a Russian refugee named Vladimir Smirnoff, whose family previously ran the Moscow distillery that was the official purveyor of vodka to the czar. Smirnoff's family, having escaped to America after the Bolshevik revolution, eventually sold the production rights to vodka, which were later acquired by the Heublein Company. By 1946, vodka had begun to make a discernible ripple in the American cocktail culture, when a Smirnoff representative named John Martin began promoting vodka as the perfect base ingredient for cocktails. In collaboration with Jack Morgan, owner of the Cock 'n' Bull Restaurant in Hollywood, he came up with a drink that propelled vodka into the mainstream. The Moscow Mule, as the drink was known, made with Smirnoff's foreign-tasting vodka, lime, and ginger beer served in a copper mug, soon tripled Smirnoff's sales. By the 1960s, along with the Moscow Mule, Screwdriver, and Bloody Mary, the producers of Smirnoff further popularized vodka by promoting it in conjunction with the James Bond movies, capitalizing on the connection between the highly glamorized machismo of Bond and his signature Vodka Martini.

Vodka has become the top-selling spirit in American bars. With its distinctively neutral taste, it not only lends itself to a wide variety of cocktails but is also favored over gin in a Martini. Although the differences between vodkas available from various countries are practically indiscernible, the Eastern Europeans continue to produce the most highly esteemed vodkas.

THE DISTILLATION PROCESS

This colorless spirit is historically made with potatoes but today is more often made from grain, such as rye, wheat, corn, or barley. It can even be made from molasses, sugar beets, maize, millet, or whey. Most of the better imported vodkas are made from either grain or potato, and all vodkas distilled in the United States are made from grain, usually filtered through activated charcoal, to obtain the required neutral spirits, with no distinctive character, aroma, taste, or color. Potato characteristically produces vodka with a creamy quality, whereas rye-based vodkas have a bite and wheat gives a more subtle delicacy.

The majority of vodkas are made in continuous stills, distilled at a high proof (95 percent pure alcohol), with a rectification column to remove unwanted trace elements, such as congeners and botanicals that would otherwise lend flavor and aroma. When made in old-fashioned pot stills, vodka needs to be distilled two or more times to reach the right level of alcohol content.

FILTRATION

Once it has been distilled and redistilled to a high alcohol content, the spirit is filtered through activated charcoal to remove any remaining impurities and harsh edges, resulting in vodka's neutral, clean taste. Unlike other spirits, with the exception of a few Polish and Russian vodkas aged in oak, it achieves its mild smoothness through multiple filtrations rather than through aging.

The highest-quality vodkas are filtered many times, and some methods can be more complex and exotic than others. For example, Smirnoff will send its spirit through seven columns packed with charcoal, Stolichnaya and Altai use silver-birch charcoal and pure quartz sand for multiple filtrations, and Suhoi is purportedly filtered through diamonds.

VODKA STYLES

The essentially neutral character of vodka makes it the most versatile of all spirits, ideal for mixing in a wide variety of cocktails. Among the premium vodkas, there are distinctly different aromatic whispers and nuances, which are best discerned and enjoyed in a Vodka Martini. Given the virtual absence of flavor, the most distinctive feature of vodka is its "mouthfeel," or how it feels in the mouth on the palate—whether it's oily or soft, viscous or buttery. When it comes to vodka styles, they can generally be categorized by the country of origin. Western vodkas are, for the most part, tasteless and well suited for cocktail mixing, whereas Eastern European vodkas tend to have more discernible subtle flavors.

Smirnoff is a good example of the American style—very clean, with absolutely no trace of character. There are, however, a few premium American vodkas that have slightly detectable nuances, such as the crisp and nutlike Skyy and the delicately softer Rain.

Poland's vodka is indelibly linked to the potato, though it was originally made from grain. By the early 1800s, the country's predominant crop was being used primarily for distillation. The spirit not only played an integral part in daily life but was actually a commodity, used as a form of currency to barter with. Since the 1500s, when the spirit's original use was as an aftershave or after-bath rubbing toner scented with herbs and spices, the Poles have perfected the distillation of vodka. By the eighteenth century, the Russians and Swedes were using the Poles' advanced charcoal-filtration techniques, which produced a clean, quality spirit while still retaining a whisper of the characteristic elements.

Today, most of the estimated 1,000 brands of Polish vodka available are made from grain, but a few potato-based vodkas of quality are still made. Luksusowa is one of the best examples of these, with a verdant aroma and viscous sweetness. Quotes is a great aromatic example of a luxe triple-distilled potato vodka, and Chopin vodka is a rich, buttery quadruple-distilled luxury potato vodka. Wyborowa, made from rye, has more of a lime-zest quality and is one of the best overall examples of Polish vodka, with Belvedere also a popular choice for those who prefer a vaguely astringent and peppery vodka.

Russian culture is practically synonymous with vodka—from Smirnoff to Stolichnaya, Dostoyevsky to Chekhov, it has played an integral role in Russian society, providing the compensatory balm to bolster the spirits of the masses. The Russians began implementing methods of distillation in around 1430, after an enlightening trip to Italian monasteries, which were making aqua vitae at the time. By 1861, their distillation and filtration methods had evolved to produce a clean, quality spirit, and Piotr Smirnov began making a vodka that was perfected enough for the czar of Russia. Although Russian vodka has had its share of low-quality moments throughout its history, with overly oily home-distilled bathtub spirits made in a desperate reaction to government sanctions, the Russians' reputation for making elegant, clean spirits still holds today.

Smirnoff's Russian producers have returned to the classic pot-still method, making Black Label a fine vodka, crisp and clean, with citrus and floral notes.

One of the most popular Russian vodkas is Stolichnaya, called "Stoli" by aficionados. Made from wheat, it is oily in body and silky smooth, with a slightly fragrant, peppery palate. They also make a variety of flavored vodkas, one of the best of which is Stoli Ohranj.

Holland puts out one of the most elegant-tasting vodkas in the premium vodka market. Ketel One is made from wheat, using the pot-still method for a very smooth, elegant vodka described as having big body and a rich, powerful flavor, reminiscent of fresh sea spray and spice.

They say that the farther north the vodka hails from, the better it is, but there are always exceptions. As a case in point, France has brought its refined palate into the vodka market with a few remarkable premium vodkas, such as the wheat-based Citadelle, described as having distinctively anise and black-currant aromas, and Grey Goose, a very aromatic vodka with faint aromas impressionably encompassing everything from vanilla to pine to pear and chocolate.

The Scandinavians hold their own, with a reputation for making vodkas that have the perfect balance of pure, clean neutrality with a smooth texture or "mouthfeel" and finish. Sweden produces one of the most popular brands of vodka in the world—Absolut, whose original name, *Absolut Rent Brannvin,* translates as "absolutely pure vodka" and epitomizes its lineage as the first refined filtered spirit to be distilled in Sweden, by Lars Olsson Smith in 1879. Absolut's taste has been described as clean and light with a whisper of lemon and pine notes. Of its many popular flavored vodkas, their mandarin-flavored vodka stands out, with a flavor described as reminiscent of Creamsicles.

Scandinavia is better known for its *akvavit,* or aquavit, an ancestor of the flavored vodkas. Similar to the brandy eaux-de-vie, the vodka is redistilled with botanicals, rather than being infused with the flavor later. Typically, aquavits are flavored with dill and caraway. Denmark and Germany both make fine aquavits, known there as schnapps. Aquavits are traditionally served ice-cold and are drunk down in one gulp.

Hailing from Finland, the land of state-of-the-art distilleries, is the aptly named Finlandia vodka, made from wheat and barley to produce a pure light, citrusy spirit. The company also makes an exceptional cranberry-flavored vodka popularly used in Cosmos.

FLAVORED VODKAS

Although it may seem like a trendy contemporary concept, adding flavor to vodka is really an ancient technique dating as far back as the eleventh and twelfth centuries. The use of herbs, spices, and fruits to flavor spirits soon evolved into a common practice in Polish and Russian households to help mask the harsh taste of rudimentary distillates.

This popular trend in flavored vodkas opens up a whole new world of creative cocktail options, with an ever-widening variety of choices. Beyond the usual lemon or orange, flavors such as grapefruit, peach, and chocolate have joined the flavored-vodka realm, along with black currant, apple, pepper, cranberry, mandarin orange, and vanilla. Here are a few tasty examples of the vodka exotica available: Zubrowka Bison Grass vodka has complex aromas of herbs, lavender, and sweet tobacco; Smirnoff Vanilla Twist is a rich, warm option; and Kremlyovskaya makes a chocolate vodka with a great cocoa flavor, as well as Limonnaya, black currant, and pepper vodkas.

WHAT MAKES THE "BEST" VODKA?

While many vodka connoisseurs concur that there are very distinct differences in the spectrum of vodkas, others insist that these nuances are practically indiscernible for all practical purposes, and that just about any type of vodka, once chilled in the freezer, will make a fine Vodka Martini. Ultimately, it all becomes rather subjective, with flowery adjectives used to describe the various flavors and aromas that are projected onto this clear spirit, and the choice is best left up to personal preference.

THE ART OF SIPPING VODKA

Although Americans tend to mix their vodka in a variety of cocktails, with the exception of an elite group of Vodka Martini fans, the Russians, Poles, Swedes, and Western Europeans still enjoy their vodka neat, either as an aperitif with appetizers before a meal or sipped as an after-dinner drink.

When it comes to sipping vodka straight or in a Martini, the superpremium brands, such as Grey Goose and Pravda, are really the only choice. Even the regular premium vodkas tend to have a somewhat harsh finish, so unless you wish to evoke a Dostoyevskian moment, they are really suitable only as mixers.

The practice of chilling vodka in the freezer serves the very important purpose not only of enhancing the flavor but also of promoting its characteristic viscosity. The traditional ritual of serving vodka straight from the freezer, neat in a small glass, is the best way to enjoy a premium vodka. Some may even enjoy their premium vodkas over ice, a practice that many purists find sacrilegious, as the vodka becomes too diluted.

Especially crucial to enjoying your vodka neat or shaken in a Martini is well-washed glassware, which should be hand washed with unscented dish soap, or you will taste it in your drink. The best glassware for sipping is either a cocktail glass, a thick 3- to 4-ounce glass, or a 1-ounce cut-crystal shot glass.

When it comes to the multitude of vodka-based cocktails, a moderately priced vodka is fine. A premium vodka will just get lost in all the other flavors, and is not worth the expense. Save your high-end vodkas for icy shots, Martinis, and Vodka Tonics.

Food is always recommended to be served with spirits, and chilled shots of premium vodka are best chased with mineral water and then bread and caviar, of course, along with finger food such as dark rye bread, dill pickles, and whitefish (herring) or oysters.

And by all means, clink glasses and toast before sipping.

VODKA DRINKS

Agent Orange

1½ ounces vodka
¾ ounce Grand Marnier
¼ ounce Cointreau
½ ounce fresh orange juice
Orange twist

Shake the liquid ingredients vigorously with ice. Strain into a chilled cocktail glass. Run the orange peel around the rim, twist it over the drink, and drop it in.

Apple Martini   *Technically not a Martini at all, of course, but a currently popular cocktail concoction nonetheless.*

1½ ounces vodka (regular or apple flavored)
½ ounce green apple schnapps
1 ounce apple purée (or apple juice)
¼ ounce fresh lemon juice
1 or 2 thin slices of apple

Shake the liquid ingredients vigorously with ice. Strain into a chilled cocktail glass. Garnish with the apple slices.

VARIATION: **SPICED APPLE MARTINI**

1½ ounces Zubrowka Bison Grass vodka
½ ounce green apple liqueur
¼ ounce butterscotch schnapps
¼ ounce fresh lemon juice

Shake the ingredients vigorously with ice. Strain into a chilled cocktail glass.

Ballet Russe

1 ounce vodka
¾ ounce crème de cassis
1½ ounces fresh lime juice
½ ounce fresh lemon juice
1 ounce simple syrup

Shake the ingredients vigorously with ice. Strain into a chilled cocktail glass.

VARIATION: **For a Russian Fizz,** add 3 to 5 ounces ginger ale and stir. Serve over ice in a highball glass.

Bay Breeze

1½ ounces vodka
1 ounce cranberry juice
4 ounces pineapple juice

Pour the ingredients into an ice-filled highball glass, and stir.

Belmont Stakes   *A cocktail served at the Belmont Stakes horse race.*

1½ ounces vodka
½ ounce gold rum
½ ounce strawberry liqueur
½ ounce fresh lime juice
Dash of grenadine
Orange slice

Shake the liquid ingredients vigorously with ice. Strain into a chilled cocktail glass. Garnish with the orange slice.

Black Russian

1½ ounces vodka
¾ ounce Kahlúa (or Tia Maria)
Lemon twist

Shake the liquid ingredients vigorously with ice. Strain into an ice-filled old-fashioned glass. Twist the lemon peel over the drink, and drop it in.

VARIATIONS: **For a Black Magic,** add a dash of fresh lemon juice.

For a White Russian, float ½ ounce heavy cream on top.

Brass Monkey

1 ounce vodka
¾ ounce light rum
4 ounces fresh orange juice
½ ounce Galliano

Pour the vodka, rum, and orange juice into an ice-filled highball glass. Stir well. Float the Galliano on top.

Caipiroska   *A Caipirinha made with vodka instead of the traditional cachaça.*

1 lime, cut into 8 wedges
1 tablespoon sugar
2 ounces vodka

Muddle the lime wedges with the sugar in the bottom of an old-fashioned glass. Fill the glass with crushed ice, add the vodka, and stir well.

VARIATION: **For an Orange Caipiroska,** substitute orange (or mandarin) vodka for the regular vodka, and a few orange and lemon wedges for the lime.

Bloody Mary

THIS CLASSIC, WHICH HIT THE CONTINENT in about the mid-1930s, became America's favorite drink and the quintessential brunch cocktail. It is purportedly named after the infamous Mary Tudor, daughter of Henry VII, who, after becoming queen of England in 1553, was notorious for persecuting Protestants, and thus had bestowed upon her the nickname Bloody Mary.

The original cocktail was a much simpler, and blander, blend of vodka and tomato juice, with various lore surrounding its conception. As one story tells it, Fernand "Pete" Petiot, a bartender from Harry's New York Bar in Paris, created the Bloody Mary in 1930. He landed in Manhattan in 1934 to tend bar at the King Cole Bar at the St. Regis Hotel, where he served his specialty up to his American patrons, changing the name briefly to the less-offensive Red Snapper. Evidently New Yorkers found the drink rather dull and requested a spicier version. Other accounts have given Hemingway credit for inventing the spiced-up version we know today.

2 ounces vodka
4 ounces tomato juice
½ ounce fresh lemon juice
¼ teaspoon horseradish (freshly grated, if possible)
2 to 3 dashes Tabasco sauce
2 to 3 dashes Worcestershire sauce
Lemon wedge
Celery stick

Shake the liquid ingredients vigorously with ice. Strain into an ice-filled highball glass. Squeeze the lemon wedge over the drink, and drop it in. Garnish with the celery stick.

VARIATIONS: **For a Caesar** (also known as Bloody Caesar or Clamdigger), substitute Clamato juice for the tomato juice.

For a Bloody Marie, add ¹/2 teaspoon anisette.

For a Virgin Mary, omit the vodka.

- -

Tokyo Mary   *An extra-spicy Bloody Mary with an Asian twist.*

Lime wedge
¼ teaspoon grated fresh ginger
½ teaspoon wasabi (or prepared horseradish)
½ teaspoon minced garlic
4 dashes soy sauce
½ ounce fresh lemon juice
Pinch of freshly cracked pepper
2 ounces vodka (or pepper-flavored vodka)
3 ounces chilled tomato juice
Lemongrass stalk

Rub the rim of a chilled highball glass with the lime wedge. Combine the ginger, wasabi, garlic, soy sauce, lemon juice, and pepper in the bottom of the glass. Fill the glass with ice, add the vodka and tomato juice, and stir. Squeeze the lime wedge over the drink, and drop it in. Garnish with the lemongrass stalk for a stir stick.

Cape Codder

2 ounces vodka
4 to 5 ounces cranberry juice
½ ounce fresh lime juice
Lime wedge

Shake the liquid ingredients vigorously with ice. Strain into an ice-filled highball glass. Squeeze the lime wedge over the drink, and drop it in.

VARIATIONS: Add a splash of club soda.

For a classic Madras, add 2 ounces fresh orange juice and top with the cranberry juice, slowly blending; do not stir.

Chocolate Mandarin Martini

Orange wedge
1 tablespoon sweetened cocoa powder
1½ ounces vodka
1 ounce Godiva chocolate liqueur
¼ ounce Mandarine Napoléon liqueur
Bittersweet chocolate shavings

Rub the rim of a chilled cocktail glass with the orange wedge and rim with cocoa powder. Shake the liquid ingredients vigorously with ice. Strain into the prepared glass. Sprinkle the top of the drink with bittersweet chocolate shavings.

Chocolate Martini
Also known as a Chocotini, the ultimate Chocolate Martini is made with Godiva chocolate liqueur, giving the drink a light-brown hue. Many chocoholics enjoy a cocoa powder rim as well.

1½ ounces vodka (or vanilla-flavored vodka)
¼ ounce Godiva chocolate liqueur (or dark crème de cacao)
¼ ounce white crème de cacao
Bittersweet chocolate shavings

Shake the liquid ingredients vigorously with ice. Strain into a chilled cocktail glass. Sprinkle bittersweet chocolate shavings over the top.

VARIATIONS: **For a Clear Chocolate Martini,** substitute white crème de cacao for the Godiva.

For a White Chocolate Martini, rim the glass with powdered sugar, substitute Godiva white chocolate liqueur for the Godiva, and add 1/4 ounce crème de banane. Garnish with white chocolate truffle shavings.

Cosmopolitan *Called the "Cosmo" by aficionados, this extremely popular cocktail has become a classic. The original was a tart concoction of citron vodka, lime juice, Cointreau to sweeten, and cranberry juice, used merely to add a slight blush of color. You will find that most recipes have evolved into deep-pink variations emphasizing the cranberry juice.*

ORIGINAL COSMOPOLITAN

1½ ounces citron vodka
1½ ounces Cointreau
1 ounce fresh lime juice
1 to 2 dashes cranberry juice
Lemon twist

Shake the liquid ingredients vigorously with ice. Strain into a chilled cocktail glass. Garnish with the lemon twist.

CRANBERRY-ESQUE COSMOPOLITAN

2 ounces citron vodka
¾ ounce Cointreau
1 ounce cranberry juice
1 ounce fresh lime juice
Lemon twist

Shake the liquid ingredients vigorously with ice. Strain into a chilled cocktail glass. Garnish with the lemon twist.

VARIATIONS: **For a Ginger Cosmo,** add a few thin slices of fresh ginger and shake with the liquid ingredients.

For a Crantini, substitute cranberry-flavored vodka for the citron vodka, add another ounce of cranberry juice, and reduce the lime juice to 1/2 ounce.

Electric Leninade

1½ ounces vodka
½ ounce blue curaçao
2 ounces sweet-and-sour
3 to 4 ounces chilled 7-Up
Lemon wedge

Pour all the liquid ingredients but the 7-Up into an ice-filled highball glass. Stir well. Top with 7-Up. Squeeze the lemon wedge over the drink, and drop it in.

Espresso Martini

1½ ounces vodka (or vanilla-flavored vodka)
½ ounce espresso or strong coffee
½ ounce Kahlúa
½ ounce crème de cacao
3 espresso beans

Stir the liquid ingredients in a mixing glass with ice. Strain into a chilled cocktail glass. Garnish with the espresso beans.

VARIATION: **For a Javanese Martini** (a dark, and aromatic version for coffee-lovers), rim the glass with turbinado sugar, substitute 1 ounce Tia Maria for the Kahlúa, leave out the crème de cacao, and garnish with a lemon twist.

Fig Leaf Fizz

1½ ounces vodka
½ ounce Tuaca
½ ounce white crème de cacao
2 to 3 ounces sparkling tangerine or orange beverage
Orange slice
Fresh mint sprig

Shake the vodka, Tuaca, and crème de cacao vigorously with ice. Strain into an ice-filled highball glass. Top with the sparkling tangerine beverage. Garnish with the orange slice and mint sprig.

French Martini

1½ ounces vodka
½ ounce Chambord
1 ounce pineapple juice
Lemon twist

Shake the liquid ingredients vigorously with ice. Strain into a chilled cocktail glass. Twist the lemon peel over the drink, and drop it in.

Goldfinger

1½ ounces vodka
1 ounce pineapple juice
¾ ounce Galliano

Shake the ingredients vigorously with ice. Strain into a chilled cocktail glass.

Greyhound   *A variation on the Screwdriver, best made with fresh grapefruit juice.*

2 ounces vodka
5 to 6 ounces fresh grapefruit juice

Pour the ingredients into an ice-filled highball glass and stir.

Harvey Wallbanger   *This classic 1970s concoction evolved from a float of Galliano added to a Screwdriver. Despite the name, it is a fine cocktail.*

1½ ounces vodka
4 to 5 ounces fresh orange juice
½ ounce Galliano

Shake the vodka and orange juice with ice, and strain into an ice-filled highball glass. Float the Galliano on top of the drink.

Kamikaze Cocktail   *A cocktail version of the shooter.*

2 ounces vodka
½ ounce Cointreau (or triple sec)
¼ ounce fresh lime juice

Shake the ingredients with ice, and strain into a chilled cocktail glass.

Lemon Drop *A new classic, this cocktail has the perfect balance of sweet and tart. It is further improved if the vodka is put in the freezer for a couple of hours, until icy cold.*

Lemon wedge
Superfine sugar
1½ ounces lemon-flavored vodka
1 ounce Grand Marnier (or Cointreau)
1½ ounces fresh lemon juice
½ ounce fresh orange juice
Lemon peel spiral

Rub the rim of a chilled large cocktail glass with the lemon wedge and rim with sugar. Shake the liquid ingredients vigorously with ice. Strain into the prepared glass. Garnish with the lemon peel spiral.

VARIATION: **For a Bullfrog,** shake the ingredients and pour into an ice-filled highball glass. Top with chilled club soda. Squeeze a wedge of lemon over the drink, and drop it in.

Love Potion

1½ ounces lemon-flavored vodka
¾ ounce Chambord
¾ ounce cranberry juice

Shake the ingredients vigorously with ice. Strain into a chilled cocktail glass.

Melon Ball

1 ounce vodka
1 ounce Midori or other melon liqueur
4 ounces fresh orange juice
Orange slice
Watermelon wedge

Shake the liquid ingredients vigorously with ice. Strain into an ice-filled wineglass. Garnish with the orange slice and watermelon wedge.

Metropolitan   *A variation on the Cosmo. Many enjoy the burnt-orange flavor of a flamed orange peel for garnish.*

2 ounces black currant vodka
¾ ounce Cointreau
¾ ounce cranberry juice
¾ ounce fresh lime juice
Thinly sliced lime wheel or flamed orange twist

Shake the liquid ingredients vigorously with ice, and strain into a chilled cocktail glass. Float the lime wheel on top of the drink, or garnish with a flamed orange peel.

Moscow Mule   *This was the libation that propelled vodka into popularity in 1940s America. Inspired by the need to move the not-yet-popular Smirnoff vodka, along with a surplus of ginger beer, John Martin of the Heublein import company collaborated with Jack Morgan, owner of the Cock 'n' Bull Restaurant in Hollywood, and with the addition of a squeeze of lime, the Moscow Mule was created.*

The proper vessel for a Moscow Mule is a copper mug (the original mugs actually came complete with engraved kicking mules), but a collins glass is fine.

2 ounces vodka
½ ounce fresh lime juice
4 ounces ginger beer (or ginger ale)
Lime wedge

Pour the vodka and lime juice into an ice-filled highball glass. Top with ginger beer and stir. Squeeze the lime wedge over the drink, and drop it in.

Mudslide

1 ounce vodka
1 ounce Kahlúa
1 ounce Baileys Irish Cream
1 ounce heavy cream
Unsweetened cocoa powder (or chocolate shavings)

Shake the liquid ingredients vigorously with ice. Strain into a chilled cocktail glass. Sprinkle the top with cocoa powder or chocolate shavings.

VARIATION: **For a Frozen Mudslide,** combine the ingredients in a blender with ½ cup crushed ice. Blend until smooth. Pour into a chilled wineglass.

Nutty Martini

2½ ounces vodka
½ ounce Frangelico
Orange twist

Stir the liquid ingredients in a mixing glass with ice. Strain into a chilled cocktail glass. Twist the orange peel over the drink, and drop it in.

Orange Martini

Orange wedge
Superfine sugar
3 ounces orange-flavored vodka
¼ ounce Lillet Blanc
Drop of orange flower water
Orange peel spiral

Rub the rim of a chilled cocktail glass with the orange wedge and rim with sugar. Stir the liquid ingredients with ice in a mixing glass. Strain into the prepared glass. Garnish with the orange peel spiral.

Papaya Citron Cocktail

1½ ounces citron vodka
4 ounces passion fruit nectar
1 ounce fresh lime juice
1½ cups seeded, peeled, cubed papaya
8 fresh mint leaves
Lime wheel
Papaya slice
Fresh mint sprig

Combine all ingredients but the garnishes in a blender. Blend until smooth. Pour into an ice-filled highball glass. Garnish with a skewer of lime wheel, papaya slice, and mint sprig.

VARIATION: **For a great nonalcoholic smoothie,** simply omit the vodka.

Pearl Diver Martini   *A pan-Asian pearl of a cocktail, made with ginger-infused vodka and a float of sake. Momokawa Pearl sake is the recommended choice for this drink.*

2 ounces ginger-infused vodka (see page 70)
½ ounce chilled premium sake
Orange twist or thin slice of candied ginger

Stir the vodka in a mixing glass with ice. Strain into a chilled cocktail glass. Slowly pour the sake to float on the top of the drink. Garnish with the orange twist or candied ginger.

Pearl Harbor

1½ ounces vodka
¾ ounce melon liqueur
1 ounce pineapple juice

Shake the ingredients vigorously with ice. Strain into a chilled cocktail glass.

Pink Fetish

1 ounce vodka
1 ounce peach schnapps
2 ounces cranberry juice
2 ounces fresh orange juice
Lime wedge

Shake the liquid ingredients vigorously with ice. Strain into an ice-filled old-fashioned glass. Squeeze the lime wedge over the drink, and drop it in.

Pink Lemonade

1½ ounces vodka
½ ounce triple sec
1 ounce cranberry juice
½ ounce fresh lemon juice
½ ounce fresh lime juice
4 to 5 ounces chilled 7-Up
Lemon wedge

Shake all liquid ingredients except the 7-Up vigorously with ice. Strain into an ice-filled collins glass. Top with 7-Up and stir gently. Squeeze the lemon wedge over the drink, and drop it in.

Purple Passion

2 ounces vodka
3 ounces fresh grapefruit juice
3 ounces chilled purple grape juice

Pour the ingredients over ice in a chilled collins glass and stir.

Raspberry Mint Martini

¼ cup fresh raspberries
6 mint leaves
2 ounces vodka
1 ounce crème de framboise

Muddle the raspberries and mint together in a cocktail shaker. Add ice and the liquid ingredients, and shake well. Strain into a cocktail glass.

Ruby Martini

1½ ounces vodka
½ ounce cranberry juice
½ ounce blue curaçao
Lemon twist

Stir the liquid ingredients in a mixing glass with ice. Strain into a chilled cocktail glass. Run the lemon peel around the rim, twist it over the drink, and drop it in.

Russian Bear   *Also called a Velvet Hammer.*

1 ounce vodka
¼ ounce brown crème de cacao
1½ ounces heavy cream
1 teaspoon sugar

Shake the ingredients vigorously with ice. Strain into a chilled cocktail glass.

VARIATION: **For a Polar Bear,** substitute ¾ ounce white crème de cacao for the brown.

Russian Cadillac

1 ounce vodka
¾ ounce Galliano
¼ ounce white crème de cacao
1 ounce heavy cream

Shake the ingredients vigorously with ice. Strain into a chilled cocktail glass.

Russian Quaalude

¾ ounce Frangelico
¾ ounce Irish cream liqueur
¾ ounce vodka

Shake the ingredients vigorously with ice. Strain into a chilled cocktail glass, or into an ice-filled old-fashioned glass.

VARIATION: Serve layered as a pousse-café drink, carefully pouring in the ingredients in the order given.

Sake Martini

2 ounces vodka
½ ounce dry sake
1 teaspoon plum wine

Stir the vodka and sake in a mixing glass with ice. Strain into a chilled cocktail glass. Float the plum wine on top of the drink.

Salty Dog *A variation on the Greyhound, with the addition of a salt rim. This drink is best made with freshly squeezed grapefruit juice.*

Lemon wedge

Salt

2 ounces vodka

4 to 6 ounces fresh grapefruit juice

Rub the rim of a chilled highball glass with the lemon wedge and rim with salt. Fill the glass with ice, pour in the vodka and grapefruit juice, and stir. Squeeze the lemon wedge over the drink, and drop it in.

VARIATIONS: To serve in a cocktail glass, use 2 ounces vodka and 2 ounces fresh grapefruit juice. Shake and strain into a chilled cocktail glass.

For a Lemon Dog, use citron vodka in place of the regular vodka.

Screwdriver *As legend tells it, back in the 1950s, American oilmen working on an oil rig in Iran used screwdrivers to stir their vodka and orange juice. The drink and the name caught on to become the classic highball served as a Sunday brunch libation. This is best enjoyed when made with fresh orange juice.*

2 ounces vodka

4 to 6 ounces fresh orange juice

Orange slice

Pour the vodka and orange juice into an ice-filled highball glass, and stir. Garnish with the orange slice.

VARIATIONS: **For a Slow Comfortable Screw,** add 1/2 ounce sloe gin and 1/2 ounce Southern Comfort.

For a Cordless Screwdriver (a shooter-style version), see page 421.

Sea Breeze *Another classic summer highball.*

1½ ounces vodka

3 ounces fresh grapefruit juice

2 ounces cranberry juice

Lime wedge

Pour the liquid ingredients into an ice-filled highball glass, and stir. Moisten the rim with the lime wedge, and then squeeze it over the drink and drop it in.

Sex on the Beach   *There are many different versions of this new classic highball, including a shooter (see page 427).*

SEX ON THE BEACH #1   *An elaboration on the Sea Breeze.*

1 ounce vodka
1 ounce peach schnapps
3 ounces fresh grapefruit juice
3 ounces cranberry juice
Maraschino cherry

Pour all the liquid ingredients into an ice-filled highball glass. Stir and garnish with the cherry.

SEX ON THE BEACH #2

Add 3 ounces fresh orange juice to the previous recipe.

SEX ON THE BEACH #3

1 ounce vodka
½ ounce Chambord
½ ounce melon liqueur
1 ounce pineapple juice
¼ ounce cranberry juice

Shake all ingredients except the cranberry juice vigorously with ice. Strain into a chilled cocktail glass (or, if you prefer, over ice in a highball glass). Float the cranberry juice on top of the drink.

Suntory Cocktail   *Named after the Japanese distillery that produces Midori, the popular melon-flavored liqueur.*

1½ ounces lemon-flavored vodka
1 ounce Midori (or other melon-flavored liqueur)
1 ounce fresh grapefruit juice

Shake the ingredients vigorously with ice. Strain into a chilled cocktail glass.

Vespa

2 ounces vodka

1 ounce banana liqueur

3 to 5 ounces chilled ginger ale

Pour the ingredients into an ice-filled collins glass, and stir.

Vodka Gimlet   *The vodka version of the classic gin-based Gimlet uses the signature gimlet ingredient—Rose's lime juice.*

1½ ounces vodka

1½ ounces Rose's lime juice

Stir the ingredients in a mixing glass with ice. Strain into a chilled cocktail glass.

Vodka Tonic   *Those who prefer a Vodka Martini over a Gin Martini will also undoubtedly enjoy this over the classic Gin and Tonic, with a few extra squeezes of lime suggested for additional refreshing lime flavor.*

1 to 3 lime wedges

2 ounces vodka

3 to 5 ounces chilled tonic water

Rim a chilled highball glass with a lime wedge, and drop it in. Fill the glass with ice, pour in the vodka, and top with tonic water. Squeeze the remaining lime wedges over the drink, and drop them in.

Walnut Martini

1½ ounces vodka

¾ ounce Tuaca

¼ ounce walnut liqueur

Orange twist

Shake the liquid ingredients vigorously with ice. Strain into a chilled cocktail glass. Twist the orange peel over the drink, and drop it in.

Vodka Martini

OTHERWISE KNOWN AS THE VODKATINI, this clear, clean-tasting cocktail eclipsed the traditional Gin Martini in popularity by the late 1950s, due in no small part to James Bond and Smirnoff simultaneously promoting a stylish preference for Russian vodka into the mainstream of popular culture.

Shaking your Vodka Martini: Whereas Gin Martini drinkers prefer theirs stirred (so as not to bruise the gin), Vodka Martini drinkers tend to agree with James Bond, preferring theirs shaken. Fill a three-part stainless steel shaker with cracked ice (or fresh ice cubes made with filtered water). Before the ice starts melting, pour the ingredients into the shaker, and shake vigorously until the shaker becomes frosty, about 12 to 15 revolutions. Quickly strain the Martini into a chilled cocktail glass (pulled out of the freezer).

THESE ARE THE CLASSIC PROPORTIONS FOR A VODKA MARTINI:

2 ounces vodka
½ ounce dry vermouth
Lemon twist (or green cocktail olive)

Stir the liquid ingredients in a mixing glass with ice. Strain into a chilled cocktail glass. Run the lemon peel around the rim, twist it over the drink, and drop it in (or garnish with an olive).

VARIATIONS: **For a Kangaroo** (less dry than the classic Vodka Martini), use 1½ ounces vodka and ¾ ounce dry vermouth.

For a Dirty Vodka Martini, add a dash of juice from a jar of green olives.

For a "bone-dry" Vodka Martini, simply sip chilled vodka neat.

Watermelon

1 ounce vodka
1 ounce melon liqueur
2 ounces cranberry juice
Dash of grenadine

Shake the ingredients vigorously with ice. Strain into an ice-filled collins glass.

White Cloud

1½ ounces vodka
¾ ounce crème de cacao
2 ounces pineapple juice
¾ ounce heavy cream

Shake the ingredients vigorously with ice. Strain into an ice-filled highball glass.

White Russian   *There are three ways to enjoy this classic: served over ice, elegantly up, or the frothy blended version.*

2 ounces vodka
1 ounce Kahlúa
1 ounce heavy cream

OVER ICE: Pour the vodka and Kahlúa into an ice-filled old-fashioned glass, and stir. Float the cream on top.

UP: Stir the vodka and Kahlúa in a mixing glass with ice. Strain into a chilled sherry glass. Float the cream on top.

BLENDED (KNOWN AS A RUSSIAN COFFEE): Combine the ingredients in a blender with ½ cup crushed ice. Blend until smooth. Serve in a chilled cocktail glass.

White Spider   *The quintessential nightcap, this is one of many vodka Stinger versions. Peppermint schnapps is preferred over the usual crème de menthe, and while some prefer this drink up, others enjoy it over crushed ice.*

2 ounces vodka
¾ ounce peppermint schnapps (or white crème de menthe)
Fresh mint sprig

Shake the liquid ingredients vigorously with ice. Strain into an ice-filled old-fashioned glass or chilled cocktail glass. Garnish with the mint sprig.

VARIATIONS: **For a Mint Martini,** increase the peppermint schnapps to 1¼ ounces, and serve in a chilled cocktail glass.

For a Green Spider, substitute ¾ ounce peppermint syrup for the peppermint schnapps, and add tonic water.

For a Green Russian, substitute green crème de menthe for the peppermint schnapps.

Woo Woo   *See also the Woo Woo Shooter on page 429.*

1¼ ounces vodka
¾ ounce peach schnapps
3 ounces cranberry juice

Shake the ingredients vigorously with ice. Strain into an ice-filled highball glass.

Yellow Fever

1½ ounces vodka
½ ounce Galliano
½ ounce fresh lime juice
1 ounce pineapple juice

Shake the ingredients vigorously with ice. Strain into a chilled cocktail glass.

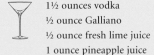

Whisk(e)y

CONJURING IMAGES OF ROLLING GREEN HILLS, Irish mist, Scottish peat bogs, and the Kentucky Derby, whiskey has a multifaceted and rich lineage, all infused in a glass of amber liquid imparting its characteristic glowing warmth.

The ancient roots of whiskey can be traced back to the Irish Emerald Isles around the twelfth century (some even say as far back as the sixth century), where the Celtic people made the first whiskey. Their term for the spirit, *uisge beatha* or *uisce beatha,* is Gaelic for "water of life" (the word "whiskey" derives from *uisce,* pronounced "ish-kee"). The spelling changes with the region from which it comes. The Irish and Americans spell it "whiskey," whereas the Scots and Canadians follow the British spelling, omitting the "e."

Whiskey is made from a fermented grain mash of corn, rye, oats, wheat, or barley. The type of grain used determines the taste and type of the resulting whiskey. Methods of production vary, from traditional pot stills to more modern column stills, but all are aged in barrels (or casks). The type of wood, size of barrel, and length of time aged are all factors in its distinctive color, aroma, and taste.

Generally speaking, whiskey produced in Scotland or Ireland is made from malted barley, while American whiskey is typically distilled from rye, maize, or wheat, as well as from corn, which produces a sweeter whiskey, such as bourbon and Tennessee whiskey. The nuanced differences among blended and straight whiskeys are many, but the descriptions here clarify the basic differences in the styles and give an understanding of the appropriate whiskeys for sipping and mixing.

STRAIGHT WHISKEY

By U.S. standards, straight whiskey must be made with at least 51 percent of a single kind of grain, aged no less than two years in oak, and combined only if from the same distilling period from the same distiller. Bourbon, Tennessee whiskey, and rye are straight whiskey.

Unblended scotch is called *single-malt* scotch; *single-malt* Irish whiskey is also unblended.

Unblended bourbon is called *single-barrel* bourbon; it is aged and bottled from the same cask and never blended with other bourbons. Equally refined are the premium unblended *small-batch* bourbons, which are a combination of a few superior barrels from one distillery.

BLENDED WHISKEY

Whiskey made from a blend of grains is known as blended whiskey. These versatile and popular whiskeys are lighter-bodied and smoother than straight whiskey and range from the cheaper styles, made with a blend of straight whiskey and a neutral grain spirit, to the sippable high-end blends, which combine a variety of superior straight whiskeys.

Blended whiskey, such as Barton Reserve and Dewar's, is the main ingredient for the classic Manhattan cocktail, and can also be enjoyed neat. Seagram's 7 Crown and Jim Beam are perfect for mixed drinks calling for whiskey.

IRISH WHISKEY

As any Irishman will tell you, Ireland is the birthplace of whiskey distillation. Irish monks are said to have been distilling *uisce beatha* as far back as the 6th century A.D. It is made from a blend of fermented grain, both unmalted and malted barley, which is sent through pot stills three times for purification before finally being stored in wooden casks for at least three years. As opposed to scotch whisky, for which the malt is dried over burning peat to impart smoky notes, Irish whiskey is made from barley roasted over coal or gas in closed kilns to give a clear barley flavor and a smoothness described as a pleasant maltiness reminiscent of honeyed biscuits.

Blended Irish whiskey, which is made from three styles of whiskey—pot still, grain, and malt whiskey—makes up most of the bottlings produced in Ireland, but a few single-malt Irish whiskeys are available, such as Tullamore Dew and Bushmills, and have gained in popularity.

Here are a few examples of premium single-malt Irish whiskeys:

- Jameson 1780 Reserve (twelve years): spices and rich, woody sweetness.
- Midleton Very Rare Redbreast (twelve years): burned-apricot and spice notes.
- Tullamore Dew: aged in bourbon, port, and sherry casks for four to seven years for a smooth and sophisticated taste.
- Bushmills (purportedly the oldest distillery in Ireland, founded in 1608): the twenty-one-year-old is the best—light-bodied, with a palate reminiscent of dried tropical fruits, tangy salt, and minerals.
- Connemara: similar to scotch whisky, with a smoky, peaty palate like the softer Islay malts and honey-roasted aromas of nuts and dried fruits.

SCOTCH WHISKY

⌒ THERE ARE TWO THINGS A HIGHLANDER LIKES NAKED, AND ONE OF THEM IS MALT WHISKY. —SCOTTISH PROVERB

Scotch is a malt whisky, made from malted barley. Before the malted barley is mashed, fermented, and distilled, it is dried over peat fires, giving it the characteristically smoky flavor scotch whisky is known for. The distillate is then barrel aged (anywhere from ten to eighteen years—or longer for premium scotch), where it picks up additional flavor nuance from the wood, as well as from the outside air of the region. As the whisky ages, it evaporates over time, creating an empty gap at the top of the barrel, which is called the "angel's portion." Some distilleries will occasionally add artificial caramel colors, which add a touch of sweetness.

------- SINGLE-MALTS VERSUS BLENDS -------

When you savor a sip of scotch, you are experiencing all the characteristics of that particular area of Scotland. From the heathered Highlands to the salty sea-sprayed Scottish island of Islay, single-malts are all distinctly different, taking your palate on a virtual tour of the many regions that produce scotch whisky.

Blended scotch whiskies, on the other hand, are a combination of grain whiskies from many different distilleries, from various areas of Scotland. There is an art to blended scotch. The best are complex and smooth, with a mellowness so popular that they make up 90 percent of the market. A few highly regarded blended scotch brands are Johnny Walker Black Label, Dewar's, and Chivas Regal.

Whisky connoisseurs, however, prefer single-malts for their distinctive style, believing that the blends are too homogenized in flavor. There is a burgeoning market for single-malts, reflecting a trend as popular as microbrews, in search of the finest, most refined spirits.

The following is a description of the differing single-malt styles from traditionally designated areas, but the best way to find your personal favorite is simply to taste for yourself.

------- **THE HIGHLANDS** -------

Located in northern Scotland, this area produces scotches that are heathery, flowery, and fresh, distinctively different in flavor from the more briny tones from the sea air of Islay. A good example is Glenmorangie, a popular Highland whisky, with gentle, flowery, woody notes. Highland Park (twelve years), produced in the Orkneys north of Scotland, as far north a Highland whisky as you can get, is peaty, with sherry sweetness.

Part of the Highland region, the Speyside area holds its own, with a saturation of 50-plus distilleries producing a wide variety of well-known whiskies, including Knockando, Balvenie, Glenfiddich, and Glenlivet.

------- **THE LOWLANDS** -------

Scotches produced in southern Scotland are light-bodied, pale, cleaner, and fragrant, with little to no peating. Brands include Oban and Johnny Walker.

------- **ISLAY AND THE SCOTTISH ISLES** -------

Characterized by peat bogs and sea spray, the whiskies of Islay are the quintessential island style, producing scotches described as smoky, peaty, seaweedy, and briny.

Islay, pronounced "Eye-luh," is an island off Scotland's southwest coast, home to Laphroaig, Langalvulin, and Ardbeg, distilleries on the south shore. Bowmore, from the center of the island, has more clovey, spicy notes.

Farther north, from the Isle of Skye, is the Talisker distillery, producing Robert Louis Stevenson's favorite whisky, with smoky, seaweedy, and peppery notes.

Here are a few single-malt scotch whiskies that are excellent for sipping:

Aberlour (ten years), Balvenie (fifteen years), Benriach, Bowmore, Cardhu, Cragganmore (twelve years), Glendronach (twelve years), Glenfiddich, Glenkinchie, Glenlivet (twelve years), and Glenmorangie.

AMERICAN WHISKEY

------- BOURBON -------

Our American romance with Mint Juleps and the Derby is immutably linked to the all-American whiskey named after the area in which it was first made, in Bourbon County, Kentucky. For a whiskey to be called bourbon, it must come from Kentucky and must be made from at least 51 percent corn. The whiskey must age for four years in charred American white oak barrels, and must never be blended with neutral grain spirits.

You will find that the best-tasting bourbons typically come from producers of "single-barrel" or "small-batch" bourbons, such as Knob Creek. These are meant to have the traditional look, feel, taste, and even high 100 proof of the pre-Prohibition good-quality bourbons. Small-batch and single-barrel bourbons may be milder than scotch, but they are just as highly regarded by whiskey connoisseurs.

Great sipping bourbons include the premium-quality small-batch bourbons such as Knob Creek (nine years), with maple-sugar aromas and tones of toasted nuts, orange peel, spice, and vanilla; Woodford Reserve, with notes of orange and honey; and Maker's Mark, a moderately priced premium-quality bourbon with cinnamon tones; and the single-barrel bourbons such as Elijah Craig (eighteen years), with nutty vanilla overtones; and Blanton's. Fine for use in mixed drinks are the moderate to cheaper-priced bourbons such as Jim Beam.

RYE WHISKEY

Similar to bourbon, but not as refined, this original American whiskey is made mostly with rye and is mixed with other neutral spirits, producing a heavier-bodied whiskey that has a spicy, bittersweet character. Rye whiskey must be made from at least 51 percent rye and aged in oak barrels for at least two years. It is often confused with Canadian whisky, which also uses rye in its blends.

Well-known brands include Old Overholt 4 Year Old Straight Rye, Wild Turkey, and Mount Vernon.

TENNESSEE WHISKEY

Sometimes called Tennessee bourbon or sour-mash whiskey, this straight whiskey is also similar to bourbon but is sweeter due to the process of slowly filtering it through vats of sugar-maple charcoal, and it has a smooth, mild flavor. It is made from a soured yeast mash containing at least 51 percent of a single grain, typically corn, and aged for at least two years in oak barrels. Well-known brands are Jack Daniel's (and its premium brand, Gentleman Jack) and George Dickel.

CANADIAN WHISKY

Whiskies from Canada are typically a blend of rye whiskey with other bourbonlike whiskies made from corn, and a neutral spirit. The best Canadian whiskies are reminiscent of the spicy, bittersweet flavor of a rye whiskey, together with a bourbony vanilla sweetness. They are sometimes offered when you order a rye whiskey, but should not be confused with the straight rye whiskey from America.

The blends, using on average anywhere from 15 to 20 different whiskies, produce a whisky that is light in body and delicate, without any overpowering flavors.

Seagram, for example, makes complex blends (from corn, rye, wheat, and barley) of 50 different straight whiskies for blending. Other Canadian whiskies include Canadian Club and Crown Royal.

JAPANESE WHISKEY

From Osaka, Japan, Suntory Japanese whiskey has gained in popularity in the United States with its fine sipping whiskeys such as Suntory Yamazaki single-malt and pure malt whiskey (twelve years), a mellow whiskey with wood, sweet fruit, and spices; Suntory Hakushu; and blended Suntory Hibiki, smooth without the sweetness.

WHISKEY-BASED LIQUEURS

Rock and Rye (see page 241 in the liqueurs section): a citrus-flavored rye-whiskey-based liqueur. There is a piece of rock candy in each bottle.

------- **SOUTHERN COMFORT** -------

Although technically a liqueur, this very popular whiskey-based American spirit has inspired so many cocktails that drinks made with it belong in the whiskey section. Made with American whiskey, specifically bourbon, Southern Comfort is sweet and smooth and flavored with peaches and oranges. As the oldest American liqueur, it evolved from a traditional cocktail served in New Orleans of whiskey mixed with peach juice, a natural combination given the abundance of peaches growing in Southern states. Originally produced in New Orleans, it is now produced by the same company that makes Jack Daniel's Tennessee blended whiskey.

Other whiskey-based liqueurs include Drambuie (page 236), Glayva (page 236), Irish Mist (page 237), and Wild Turkey Liqueur.

SERVING AND MIXING WHISKEYS

With a few exceptions, the best whiskeys for mixed drinks are the blended whiskeys. Good-quality blends such as Johnny Walker Red Label, Famous Grouse, Dewar's, and White Horse, as well as Irish whiskeys and Canadian whiskies, such as Canadian Club, are suitable to use with mixers, such as citrus juices, syrups, or grenadine. Also fine for mixed drinks are the distinctively strong straight whiskeys such as rye and Tennessee whiskey.

Except for a few cocktails that are immensely improved upon with premium bourbons and scotches, using a refined single-malt scotch or high-end small-batch bourbon in a mixed drink is absolutely pointless, not to mention sacrilegious. For example, it is perfectly appropriate to enjoy a good-quality blended scotch, such as Johnny Walker Gold, over ice with a splash of club soda, or in a Manhattan, and a moderately priced small-batch bourbon is the perfect choice for a Mint Julep or Sazerac—but save your good single-malt scotches, such as Bowmore 17, for sipping neat.

Serve single-malt scotch whiskies and small-batch bourbons meant for sipping neat in a tulip-shaped sherry *copita* glass (to capture the aromas) at room temperature. Many connoisseurs suggest that you can taste the whiskey better if you gently add a couple of drops of spring water, which will open up the nose and taste. Another way to release the aroma is to cup the bottom of the glass with your hand, which warms the whiskey slightly.

The type of whiskey called for in many of these drinks is based on the classic recipe, whether it be an Irish whiskey for a Blarney Stone, a blended whiskey for a Manhattan, or a bourbon for a Mint Julep. It is not the classic drink if made with some other whiskey.

However, given the wide variety of whiskeys available, whiskey-based drinks have a versatile nature, and even those in the classic category have been subject to change at one time or another, according to personal preference. You may like your Whiskey Sour made with bourbon, rye, or even scotch, and although the classic Old-Fashioned was originally made with bourbon, most recipes these days call for blended Canadian whisky.

WHISKEY DRINKS

Alabama Slammer

1 ounce Southern Comfort
1 ounce amaretto
½ ounce sloe gin
1 ounce fresh orange juice

Shake the ingredients vigorously with ice. Strain into an ice-filled highball glass, or into a tall shot glass without ice.

Algonquin   *Named for the Algonquin Hotel in New York, the famed 1920s meeting place for the infamous literary "round table" group of writers, critics, and poets, including Dorothy Parker, Edna Ferber, and Robert Sherwood, who referred to themselves as "the vicious circle."*

2 ounces rye (or blended whiskey)
½ ounce dry vermouth
1 ounce pineapple juice

Stir the ingredients in a mixing glass with ice. Strain into a chilled cocktail glass.

Amalfi Cocktail

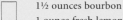

1½ ounces bourbon
1 ounce fresh lemon juice
½ ounce Galliano
1 teaspoon orgeat syrup
3 to 5 ounces chilled club soda

Shake all ingredients except the club soda vigorously with ice. Strain into an ice-filled highball glass. Top with club soda and stir gently.

Belmont Breeze *The new official drink of the Belmont Stakes, created by Dale DeGroff, master mixologist from New York City.*

1½ ounces blended American whiskey
¾ ounce Harveys Bristol Cream Sherry
½ ounce fresh lemon juice
1 ounce simple syrup
1½ ounces fresh orange juice
1½ ounces cranberry juice
1 ounce chilled 7-Up
1 ounce chilled club soda
Whole strawberry
Lemon slice
Mint sprig

Shake all liquid ingredients except the 7-Up and club soda vigorously with ice. Strain into an ice-filled highball glass. Top with the 7-Up and club soda and stir. Garnish with the strawberry, lemon slice, and mint sprig.

Bent Nail *Also called a Mammamattawa.*

1½ ounces Canadian blended whisky
½ ounce Drambuie
¼ ounce kirsch

Shake the ingredients vigorously with ice. Strain into a chilled cocktail glass.

Blarney Stone

2 ounces Irish whiskey
¼ ounce Cointreau
¼ ounce absinthe substitute (Pernod or anisette)
Dash of maraschino liqueur
Dash of Angostura bitters
Lemon twist

Stir the liquid ingredients in a mixing glass with ice. Strain into a chilled cocktail glass. Run the lemon peel around the rim, twist it over the drink, and drop it in.

Blizzard

3 ounces bourbon (or blended whiskey)
1 ounce cranberry juice
½ ounce fresh lemon juice
1 ounce simple syrup
Lemon slice

Shake the liquid ingredients vigorously with ice. Strain into an ice-filled old-fashioned glass. Garnish with the lemon slice.

VARIATION: Combine the liquid ingredients in a blender with ½ cup ice. Blend for a few seconds, and pour into a chilled wineglass.

Bobby Burns   *A variation on the Rob Roy, this Scottish classic is named after the poet who wrote "Auld Lang Syne" and "Comin' Through the Rye."*

1½ ounces scotch
1½ ounces sweet vermouth
¼ ounce Bénédictine
Lemon twist

Shake the liquid ingredients vigorously with ice. Strain into a chilled cocktail glass. Twist the lemon peel over the drink, and drop it in.

VARIATION: **For a Brainstorm Cocktail,** substitute Irish whiskey for the scotch, and use ¼ ounce dry vermouth in place of the sweet vermouth.

Boilermaker   *The quintessential pairing of the whiskey shot with a beer chaser. Some prefer the ritual of dropping the shot glass into the mug of beer.*

1½ ounces blended whiskey
8- to 12-ounce mug of beer

Pour the whiskey into a shot glass. Quickly gulp down the shot. Serve the beer in a chilled beer mug as a chaser.

Bourbon à la Crème

2 ounces bourbon
1 ounce dark crème de cacao
1 to 2 vanilla beans or ½ teaspoon vanilla extract

Combine the ingredients in a shaker. Refrigerate for 1 hour. Add ice, shake vigorously, and strain into a chilled cocktail glass.

Bourbon Buck

Lemon wedge
2 ounces bourbon
5 ounces chilled ginger ale

Squeeze the lemon wedge into an ice-filled highball glass. Add the bourbon, top with ginger ale, and stir gently.

VARIATIONS: **For a Scotch Buck,** substitute scotch for the bourbon.

For an Irish Buck, substitute Irish whiskey for the bourbon.

For a Horse's Neck, add a dash of Angostura bitters, and coil a lemon peel spiral in the highball glass.

For a Presbyterian, reduce the ginger ale to 2 ounces, add 2 ounces chilled club soda, and garnish with a lemon twist, omitting the lemon wedge.

344

Bourbon Crusta   *Characterized by the signature sugared rim and the lemon peel spiral, the Bourbon Crusta can be made with either Cointreau or maraschino liqueur, according to personal preference.*

Lemon wedge
Sugar
Lemon peel spiral
2 ounces bourbon
½ ounce Cointreau (or maraschino liqueur)
½ ounce fresh lemon juice

Rub the rim of a chilled sour glass with the lemon wedge and rim with sugar. Uncoil the lemon peel spiral in the prepared glass. Shake the liquid ingredients vigorously with ice. Strain into the prepared glass.

VARIATION: **For a Scotch Crusta,** substitute scotch for the bourbon and maraschino liqueur for the Cointreau.

Bourbon Milk Punch   *A classic New Orleans favorite.*

2 ounces bourbon
½ ounce dark crème de cacao
4 ounces milk (or 3 ounces half-and-half)
Dash of vanilla extract
¼ teaspoon ground cinnamon
Freshly grated or ground nutmeg

Shake the liquid ingredients and cinnamon vigorously with ice. Strain into an ice-filled old-fashioned glass. Sprinkle the top with nutmeg.

Bourbon Sling

2½ ounces bourbon
½ ounce Southern Comfort
½ ounce fresh lemon juice
5 to 6 ounces chilled club soda
Lemon wedge

Shake all liquid ingredients except the club soda vigorously with ice. Strain into an ice-filled highball glass. Top with club soda and stir gently. Squeeze the lemon wedge over the drink, and drop it in.

Bourbon Swizzle

2 ounces bourbon
½ ounce apricot brandy
½ ounce fresh lemon juice
5 to 6 ounces chilled ginger ale
Lemon wheel

Shake all liquid ingredients except the ginger ale vigorously with ice. Strain into an ice-filled collins glass. Top with ginger ale. Garnish with the lemon wheel, and add a swizzle stick.

VARIATION: **For a Scotch Swizzle,** substitute scotch for the bourbon, triple sec for the apricot brandy, and lime juice for the lemon juice.

Blue Grass Cocktail

1½ ounces bourbon
1 ounce pineapple juice
1 ounce fresh lemon juice
¼ ounce maraschino liqueur

Shake the ingredients vigorously with ice. Strain into a chilled cocktail glass.

Brooklyn Cocktail   *One of the few drinks that still calls for rye, this variation on the Manhattan has a bit more intensity than the classic version.*

1½ ounces rye
¾ ounce sweet vermouth
Dash of maraschino liqueur
Lemon twist

Stir the liquid ingredients in a mixing glass with ice. Strain into a chilled cocktail glass. Run the lemon peel around the rim, twist it over the drink, and drop it in.

VARIATION: Use Canadian whisky, dry vermouth, and a dash each of Amer Picon and maraschino liqueur.

Canadian Cocktail

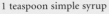

2 ounces Canadian blended whisky
½ ounce Cointreau
1 teaspoon simple syrup
2 dashes Angostura bitters

Shake the ingredients vigorously with ice. Strain into an ice-filled old-fashioned glass or a chilled cocktail glass.

Casanova

1½ ounces bourbon
¾ ounce sweet Marsala
¾ ounce Kahlúa
1 ounce heavy cream

Shake the ingredients vigorously with ice. Strain into a chilled cocktail glass.

Churchill Downs Cooler

1½ ounces bourbon
1 ounce brandy
½ ounce triple sec
4 ounces chilled ginger ale

Pour all ingredients but the ginger ale into an ice-filled highball glass.
Top with the ginger ale and stir gently.

Commodore Cocktail

1½ ounces bourbon
¾ ounce crème de cacao
½ ounce fresh lemon juice

Shake the ingredients vigorously with ice. Strain into a chilled cocktail
glass.

Commonwealth   *Also called a Chapel Hill.*

1½ ounces Canadian whisky
½ ounce Grand Marnier
¼ ounce fresh lemon juice
Orange twist

Shake the liquid ingredients vigorously with ice. Strain into a chilled
cocktail glass. Twist the orange peel over the drink, and drop it in.

Dancing Leprechaun

1½ ounces Irish whiskey
¾ ounce Drambuie
¾ ounce fresh lemon juice
3 to 4 ounces chilled ginger ale
Lemon twist

Shake all liquid ingredients except the ginger ale vigorously with ice.
Strain into an ice-filled highball glass. Top with ginger ale and stir gently.
Twist the lemon peel over the drink, and drop it in.

Debonair Cocktail   *This cocktail calls specifically for a single-malt scotch—the flavor of the drink will vary depending on the scotch you use. For a lighter, fragrant drink, use a Highland scotch; for a more robust drink, try it with a scotch from Islay.*

2 ounces single-malt scotch
1 ounce Canton ginger liqueur
Lemon twist

Shake the liquid ingredients vigorously with ice. Strain into a chilled cocktail glass. Twist the lemon peel over the drink, and drop it in.

- -

Delta

1½ ounces blended whiskey
½ ounce Southern Comfort
½ ounce fresh lime juice
1 teaspoon sugar
Orange slice
Peach slice

Shake the liquid ingredients and sugar vigorously with ice. Strain into an ice-filled old-fashioned glass. Garnish with the orange and peach slices.

VARIATION: **For a Little Colonel,** substitute bourbon for the blended whiskey, increase the Southern Comfort to 1 ounce, and omit the sugar.

- -

Derby

1½ ounces blended whiskey
½ ounce sweet vermouth
½ ounce Cointreau
½ ounce fresh lime juice
Mint sprig

Shake the liquid ingredients vigorously with ice. Strain into an ice-filled old-fashioned glass. Garnish with the mint sprig.

VARIATION: **For an Oriental Cocktail,** substitute bourbon for the blended whiskey, and omit the mint sprig.

Everybody's Irish

2 ounces Irish whiskey
¼ ounce green Chartreuse
¼ ounce green crème de menthe
Green cocktail olive

Stir the liquid ingredients in a mixing glass with ice. Strain into a chilled cocktail glass. Garnish with the green olive.

Fine and Dandy

2 ounces Canadian blended whisky
½ ounce Cointreau
½ ounce Dubonnet Rouge
Lemon twist

Stir the liquid ingredients in a mixing glass with ice. Strain into a chilled cocktail glass. Run the lemon peel around the rim, twist it over the drink, and drop it in.

VARIATIONS: **For a Trois Rivières** (French for "three rivers"), reduce the Cointreau to ¼ ounce, and use an orange twist instead of lemon.

For a Temptation Cocktail, add a dash of Pernod.

French Twist

1½ ounces bourbon
1½ ounces brandy
½ ounce Grand Marnier
¼ ounce fresh lemon juice

Shake the ingredients vigorously with ice. Strain into a chilled cocktail glass.

Godfather *A popular drink from the 1970s.*

2 ounces scotch or bourbon
1 ounce amaretto

Shake the ingredients vigorously with ice. Strain into an ice-filled old-fashioned glass.

SPIRITS & DRINKS

C.05

349

Horse's Neck *Similar to a buck, the signature element separating the two is the citrus spiral. Like many whiskey drinks, this versatile drink can be made with a favorite whiskey of choice, whether it be bourbon, scotch, or rye, in place of the blended whiskey.*

Lemon peel spiral
2½ ounces blended whiskey
3 to 5 ounces chilled ginger ale

Place the lemon peel spiral in a chilled highball glass. Fill with ice, pour in the whiskey, and top with ginger ale. Stir briefly.

VARIATION: **For an elaboration on this recipe,** see the Horse's Neck in the Hangover Remedies section, page 453.

For a Klondike Cooler, substitute rye for the blended whiskey, add 1 teaspoon sugar, and use an orange peel spiral instead of lemon.

Iced Irish Coffee

1½ ounces Irish whiskey
1 teaspoon brown sugar
4 ounces cold coffee
1 to 2 ounces heavy cream

Pour the whiskey and sugar into a chilled old-fashioned glass. Stir to combine. Fill with ice, add the coffee and cream, and stir.

Irish Shillelagh *This potent drink is named for the Irish policemen's nightstick.*

1½ ounces Irish whiskey
½ ounce light rum
½ ounce sloe gin
1 ounce fresh lemon juice
1 teaspoon sugar
Peach slice
Orange slice
2 to 3 raspberries
Maraschino cherry

Shake all the ingredients except for the fruit vigorously with ice. Strain into an ice-filled old-fashioned glass. Garnish with the fruit.

Japanese Fizz

2 ounces blended whiskey
½ ounce ruby port
2 teaspoons fresh lemon juice
1 teaspoon sugar
3 to 5 ounces chilled club soda
Pineapple wedge
Orange slice

Shake the whiskey, port, lemon juice, and sugar vigorously with ice.
Strain into an ice-filled collins glass. Top with club soda and stir gently.
Garnish with the pineapple wedge and orange slice.

John Collins *A variation on the gin-based Tom Collins, the John Collins was originally made with Holland gin, but in America you will find it made with either bourbon or Canadian blended whisky. To confuse the situation even further, it is frequently found under different names as well. For example, the Colonel Collins is made with bourbon, and the Captain Collins, also known as the Bourbon Collins, uses Canadian blended whisky.*

2 ounces bourbon (or blended Canadian whisky)
1 ounce fresh lemon juice
½ ounce simple syrup
5 to 6 ounces chilled club soda
Orange slice
Lemon slice
Maraschino cherry

Shake the bourbon, lemon juice, and simple syrup vigorously with ice.
Strain into an ice-filled collins glass. Top with club soda and stir gently.
Garnish with the orange and lemon slices and the cherry.

VARIATIONS: **For a Sandy Collins,** also called a Jock Collins, use scotch.

For a Mike Collins, use Irish whiskey.

Kentucky Colonel

2½ ounces bourbon
½ ounce Bénédictine
Lemon twist

Stir the liquid ingredients in a mixing glass with ice. Strain into a chilled cocktail glass. Run the lemon peel around the rim, twist it over the drink, and drop it in.

VARIATION: **For an S.S. Manhattan,** add 2 ounces fresh orange juice.

Kentucky Sidecar

This refreshing variation on the Sidecar retains the classic tartness by using tangerine juice, although orange juice is an equally suitable alternative. A good-quality moderately priced small-batch bourbon, such as Maker's Mark, will add a rich, warm complexity to the drink.

Lemon or tangerine wedge
Sugar
1½ ounces small-batch bourbon
¾ ounce Cointreau
1 ounce fresh tangerine juice
½ ounce fresh lemon juice
Mint sprig

Rub the rim of a chilled cocktail glass with the lemon or tangerine wedge and rim with sugar. Shake the liquid ingredients vigorously with ice. Strain into the prepared glass. Garnish with the mint sprig.

VARIATIONS: **For a superminty version,** add 4 or 5 fresh mint leaves to the cocktail shaker, and shake with the liquid ingredients.

For a Kentucky Fizz, serve over ice in an old-fashioned glass with a splash of club soda.

For a Kentucky Orange Blossom, increase the tangerine juice to 1½ ounces, and omit the lemon juice. Add a dash of orange flower water, and serve over ice in an old-fashioned glass.

Manhattan

AS LEGEND HAS IT, THE MANHATTAN was created in honor of Lady Randolph Churchill (Sir Winston's mother) in 1874 at the Manhattan Club in New York, served during a celebration dinner for Governor Samuel J. Tilden. Originally made with rye, this classic American aperitif is a perfect example of the fine balance between the ratio of whiskey to vermouth to the essential bitters, all coming together for optimum smoothness. The type of whiskey used is crucial to the taste and ultimately becomes a personal preference. Many prefer bourbon, such as Knob Creek or Maker's Mark, bringing a sweetness complementary to the vermouth, over the classic rye, which for today's tastes is a bit harsh. Others adamantly prefer a much mellower Manhattan using blended Canadian whisky, the bourbon or rye imparting too much intensity. Whichever way you swing, a premium whiskey will always give the best results. Traditionally, a Manhattan is served up in a cocktail glass, but many prefer it over ice in an old-fashioned glass, which gives it a bit of dilution and chill. Although it is classically garnished with a cherry, a lemon twist is an acceptable option.

Variations on the Manhattan include everything from the addition of various bitters, such as Peychaud's or orange, to dashes of other ingredients such as maraschino cherry syrup from the jar, Dubonnet Rouge, green Chartreuse, kirschwasser, blue curaçao, and other liqueurs.

Classic Manhattan

2 ounces rye, bourbon, or blended Canadian whisky
¾ ounce sweet vermouth
2 to 3 dashes Angostura bitters
Maraschino cherry

Stir the liquid ingredients in a mixing glass with ice. Strain into a chilled cocktail glass. Garnish with the cherry.

Perfect Manhattan

2½ ounces rye, bourbon, or blended Canadian whisky
½ ounce sweet vermouth
½ ounce dry vermouth
2 to 3 dashes Angostura bitters
Lemon twist

Stir the liquid ingredients in a mixing glass with ice. Strain into a chilled cocktail glass. Run the lemon peel around the rim, twist it over the drink, and drop it in.

Sweet Manhattan

2 ounces rye, bourbon, or blended Canadian whisky
1 ounce sweet vermouth
2 to 3 dashes Angostura bitters
Lemon twist

Stir the liquid ingredients in a mixing glass with ice. Strain into a chilled cocktail glass. Run the lemon peel around the rim, twist it over the drink, and drop it in.

Dry Manhattan *Some consider this version an oxymoron, as the quintessential Manhattan is by definition a sweet vermouth-based drink.*

2 ounces rye, bourbon, or blended Canadian whisky
¾ ounce dry vermouth
2 to 3 dashes Angostura bitters
Lemon twist

Stir the liquid ingredients in a mixing glass with ice. Strain into a chilled cocktail glass. Run the lemon peel around the rim, twist it over the drink, and drop it in.

VARIATIONS: **For a Scotch Manhattan,** see the Rob Roy (page 364).

For an Irish Manhattan (also known as a Paddy Cocktail or Paddy Wagon), use Irish whiskey in the Classic Manhattan recipe.

For a Canadian Manhattan, make a Classic Manhattan with Canadian whisky.

For a Southern Comfort Manhattan (a very sweet version), use Southern Comfort in place of the whiskey in the Classic Manhattan recipe.

For an Eastern Manhattan, use 2 ½ ounces Suntory Japanese whiskey, ¼ ounce Ricard, and ½ ounce sweet vermouth.

For an Old-Fashioned Manhattan, use 1 ½ ounces each blended whiskey and sweet vermouth.

For a Dubonnet Manhattan, make a classic Manhattan with bourbon, and substitute ½ ounce Dubonnet for the sweet vermouth.

Kentucky Stinger

1½ ounces bourbon
¼ ounce Southern Comfort
¼ ounce white crème de menthe

Shake the ingredients vigorously with ice. Strain into an ice-filled wineglass.

Louisville Stinger

1 ounce bourbon
1 ounce light rum
½ ounce white crème de cacao
¼ ounce crème de menthe

Shake the ingredients vigorously with ice. Strain into a chilled cocktail glass.

Mamie Taylor

2 ounces blended scotch
½ ounce fresh lime juice
3 to 5 ounces chilled ginger ale
Lemon slice

Pour the scotch and lime juice into an ice-filled highball glass. Top with ginger ale and stir gently. Garnish with the lemon slice.

Mint Condition

¾ ounce bourbon
¾ ounce peppermint schnapps
¾ ounce vodka
½ ounce Kahlúa

Shake the ingredients vigorously with ice. Strain into a chilled sour glass.

Mint Julep

A KENTUCKY TRADITION THAT HAS BEEN AROUND since the late 1800s, the refreshing and quintessentially Southern frosted julep is traditionally enjoyed as a celebratory libation to usher in the spring on May Day and, more importantly, is the official signature drink at the Kentucky Derby on the first Saturday in May. Traced back to the 15th century, Juleps were originally medicinal concoctions blending herbs, sugar, and water. They later evolved into drinks combining mint with brandy, peach brandy, or Cognac, until around 1875, when fine Kentucky bourbon became the spirit of choice.

Traditionally, the mint's only function was as an aromatic flourish at the edge of the drink, but inevitably, as variations ensued, controversy arose over the correct methodology, which Southerners still debate today. Some say that the key is in the placement of the mint, which should be extended above the rim to allow one to inhale the aroma while sipping the bourbon. Some, however, prefer to muddle the mint first to infuse the bourbon with its aromatic fragrance. Extreme mint aficionados will go so far as to infuse a bottle of bourbon with a few cups of mint leaves, a method that is quite efficient when one is hosting a crowd, as it can be refrigerated for up to a week.

In keeping with tradition, the julep is classically served in a silver julep cup, the perfect vessel to achieve that signature frost as the bourbon and crushed ice are stirred until the condensation turns icy. It is perfectly suitable to serve a julep in either a collins, highball, or old-fashioned glass, although the type of glassware is less important than the type of bourbon used—a premium bourbon such as Maker's Mark, Knob Creek, or Woodford Reserve is essential to a sublime julep.

Traditional Southern-Style Mint Julep

4 ounces Kentucky bourbon
1 teaspoon simple syrup
4 to 6 mint sprigs

Pour the liquid ingredients into a julep cup or collins glass filled with crushed ice. Stir well until the glass is frosty. Garnish with the mint sprigs, extending them above the rim, and serve with a straw.

VARIATION: Add a splash of club soda or water.

Muddled Mint Julep

12 to 14 fresh mint leaves
1 teaspoon simple syrup
4 ounces Kentucky bourbon
2 to 3 mint sprigs
Lemon twist (optional)

Muddle the mint leaves and simple syrup in the bottom of a chilled julep cup or old-fashioned glass. Fill the glass with crushed ice, add the bourbon, and stir until the glass is frosty. Garnish with the mint sprigs, extending them above the rim, and a twist of lemon peel, if desired.

Frozen Mint Julep

6 small mint leaves
3 ounces Kentucky bourbon
1 ounce fresh lemon juice
1 ounce simple syrup
Mint sprig

Muddle the mint leaves with the bourbon, lemon juice, and simple syrup in the bottom of a small glass. Pour the mixture into a blender, add 1/2 cup crushed ice, and blend until slushy. Pour into a chilled old-fashioned glass. Garnish with the mint sprig.

Mint Juleps for a Crowd   *Great for entertaining because the mint flavor is infused into the bourbon ahead of time and ready to go. It can be refrigerated for up to one week, but no longer, as the mint will turn bitter. For those who prefer an exuberant amount of mint flavor, add another cup of mint.*

MAKES 6 SERVINGS

1 bottle (750 ml) Kentucky bourbon

2 cups fresh mint leaves (or 10 to 12 mint sprigs)

1 to 3 ounces simple syrup

12 to 18 fresh mint sprigs

6 lemon twists (optional)

Combine the bourbon and mint leaves in a large glass jar with a lid. Cover and refrigerate for a few hours or overnight. Strain the bourbon into a large glass pitcher, discarding the mint. Add simple syrup to taste, and stir.

For each serving, pour 4 ounces of the infused bourbon into a julep cup or collins glass filled with crushed ice. Add a few mint sprigs and a twist of lemon peel, if desired, to each drink, and serve with straws.

OTHER JULEP VARIATIONS: **For a Georgia Mint Julep**, use 1 teaspoon powdered sugar, 1 tablespoon water, 10 to 12 mint sprigs, 2 ounces Cognac, and 2 ounces peach brandy.

For a Manila Hotel Mint Julep (served in Luzon, the Philippines, since 1926), float 1/2 ounce rum on top of a Mint Julep, and garnish with fresh pineapple.

Mississippi Mist

1½ ounces bourbon
1½ ounces Southern Comfort

Pour the ingredients into an ice-filled old-fashioned glass. Stir well.

VARIATIONS: **For a Kentucky Cowhand,** add ¼ ounce light cream. Shake and serve up.

For a Little Colonel, add 1 ounce fresh lime juice. Shake and serve up.

Nevins

1½ ounces bourbon
½ ounce apricot brandy
1 ounce fresh grapefruit juice
½ ounce fresh lemon juice
Dash of Angostura bitters

Shake the ingredients vigorously with ice. Strain into a chilled cocktail glass.

New Yorker

1½ ounces bourbon (or rye)
¾ ounce fresh lime juice
1 teaspoon sugar
Dash of grenadine
Orange twist
Lemon twist

Pour the bourbon and lime juice into an ice-filled old-fashioned glass. Add the sugar and grenadine and stir well. Twist the lemon and orange peels over the drink, and drop them in.

VARIATION: **For a New York Cocktail,** substitute blended whiskey for the bourbon. Some recipes also substitute lemon juice for the lime juice.

Pink Almond

1 ounce blended whiskey
½ ounce crème de noyaux
½ ounce amaretto
½ ounce kirsch
½ ounce fresh lemon juice
Lemon slice

Shake the liquid ingredients vigorously with ice. Strain into a chilled cocktail glass. Garnish with the lemon slice.

Poire Williams Fizz

1½ ounces blended whiskey
½ ounce pear brandy
2½ ounces fresh grapefruit juice
3 to 4 ounces chilled club soda

Pour the whiskey, pear brandy, and grapefruit juice into an ice-filled highball glass. Top with club soda and stir gently.

Preakness Cocktail   *The official cocktail imbibed in honor of the Preakness Stakes, from the Pimlico racetrack in Baltimore, which hosts the second leg of the annual Triple Crown.*

Lemon twist
2 ounces Canadian blended whisky
½ ounce Bénédictine
½ ounce sweet vermouth
2 dashes Angostura bitters

Rub the lemon peel around the rim of a chilled cocktail glass. Shake the liquid ingredients vigorously with ice. Strain into the prepared glass. Twist the lemon peel over the drink, and drop it in.

Old-Fashioned

THIS IS YET ANOTHER CLASSIC AMERICAN COCKTAIL created in bourbon country around the late 1800s. As legend has it, a bartender at the Pendennis Club of Louisville, Kentucky, created this fruity elixir for a local bourbon distiller—Colonel James E. Pepper. Like most classic cocktails that have been around forever, this one has gone through many transmutations since then, including the main spirit. The most traditional liquor—given the locale from which it hails—would be Kentucky bourbon, although blended whiskey is the usual choice and scotch has its fans.

In the spirit of true design, in which form follows function, this drink inspired a sturdy, heavy-bottomed glass of the same name, specifically designed to accommodate the muddling of the ingredients. That is where the essential character of this drink lies, in the muddling of the fruit, sugar, and bitters, the resulting juices producing the quintessential Old-Fashioned. Many prefer to muddle the whiskey along with the fruit to further infuse fruitiness, and those who enjoy a little extra tartness use a wedge of lemon instead of a peel. Variations include wetting the sugar with a bit of water, club soda, or even an added dash of Cointreau—and when it comes to a final splash of club soda, the purists refuse.

1 sugar cube (or 2 teaspoons sugar)
3 dashes Angostura bitters
1 strip lemon zest
1 orange slice
1 maraschino cherry
2½ ounces bourbon (or blended whiskey)
2 to 3 ounces chilled club soda (optional)
Orange slice
Maraschino cherry

In the bottom of a chilled old-fashioned glass, saturate the sugar cube with the bitters. Add the lemon zest, orange slice, and cherry. Muddle together the sugar, bitters, and fruit. Fill the glass with ice, add the bourbon, and stir well. Top with club soda, if desired. Garnish with the orange slice and cherry.

VARIATIONS: **For an Eccentric Old-Fashioned,** place 1 complete lemon peel spiral in the glass. Shake 2 ounces blended whiskey, a dash of curaçao, and ¹/2 teaspoon sugar, and strain into the glass.

For a Canadian Old-Fashioned, substitute blended Canadian whisky for the bourbon, and add ¹/4 ounce Cointreau, and a dash of fresh lemon juice.

For a Scotch Old-Fashioned, substitute blended scotch for the bourbon.

For a Claremont (a fruitier version), muddle 2 maraschino cherries and 2 orange slices, and add ³/4 ounce orange curaçao.

Prince Edward

1½ ounces scotch
½ ounce Lillet Blanc
¼ ounce Drambuie
Orange slice

Shake the liquid ingredients vigorously with ice. Strain into an ice-filled old-fashioned glass. Garnish with the orange slice.

Rob Roy   *Named for the legendary 17th-century Scottish brigand Robert MacGregor (the Scottish Robin Hood), hero of Sir Walter Scott's novel from the early 1800s. This variation of the Manhattan has a distinctly different flavor. Made with scotch instead of rye or bourbon, it has more of a bite and can be served either up or over ice.*

CLASSIC ROB ROY

2½ ounces blended scotch
½ ounce sweet vermouth
Dash of Angostura bitters
Maraschino cherry

Stir the liquid ingredients in a mixing glass with ice. Strain into a chilled cocktail glass or into an ice-filled old-fashioned glass. Garnish with the cherry.

VARIATIONS: **For a Dry Rob Roy,** substitute dry vermouth for the sweet vermouth, and garnish with a lemon twist.

For a Perfect Rob Roy, use ¼ ounce dry vermouth and ¼ ounce sweet vermouth, and garnish with a lemon twist.

For an Affinity (a classic variation on the Perfect Rob Roy), use equal parts (1 ounce each) scotch, dry vermouth, and sweet vermouth.

For another version of an Affinity, use equal parts (1 ounce each) scotch, dry sherry, and ruby port. Garnish with a cherry.

For a Highland Fling (closer to a Manhattan), increase the sweet vermouth to ¾ ounce, and use orange bitters in place of the Angostura.

For a Thistle cocktail, use equal parts (1½ ounces each) scotch and sweet vermouth.

For a Flying Scotsman (a sweeter variation), add ¼ ounce simple syrup.

Rusty Nail *Fantastically popular with the 1960s swinging set, this drink has stood the test of time. If it's too sweet for your tastes, make a drier version by using only ¼ ounce of Drambuie.*

1½ ounces scotch
1 ounce Drambuie
Lemon twist

Pour the iquid ingredients into an ice-filled highball glass. Stir well. Twist the lemon peel over the drink, and drop it in.

Scarlett O'Hara *Another New Orleans classic named after the quintessential Southern belle.*

2 ounces Southern Comfort
2 ounces cranberry juice
½ ounce fresh lime juice
½ ounce fresh lemon juice
1 teaspoon sugar

Shake the ingredients vigorously with ice. Strain into a chilled cocktail glass.

Scotch Mist

2 ounces scotch
Lemon twist

Pour the scotch over crushed ice in an old-fashioned glass. Twist the lemon peel over the drink, and drop it in.

Scotch Sangaree

2 ounces scotch
½ ounce port
½ ounce Drambuie
Freshly grated or ground nutmeg

Stir the liquid ingredients in a mixing glass with ice. Strain into a chilled wineglass. Sprinkle the top with a dusting of nutmeg.

VARIATION: Add a teaspoon of heather honey (with a little bit of water) and top with club soda.

Sazerac

THIS NEW ORLEANS CLASSIC IS AS CHARMING as a soft Southern drawl. As cocktail legend has it, it was the first drink to be concocted and specifically called a cocktail. Around the 1830s, a Frenchman named Peychaud was behind the counter of his Pharmacie in New Orleans, serving up this elixir in a *cocquetier*, or egg cup. When mispronounced, according to the tale, *cocquetier* resulted in the term "cocktail." He came up with this drink, originally made with Cognac and his Peychaud's bitters, as a vehicle for his soothing digestive creation. By the 1850s, the cocktail had become enormously popular, and it had been given the name "Sazerac" after an imported French Cognac, Sazerac de Forge et Fils, that was used to make it. By 1870, the ingredients had changed, as drinking establishments opted for the cheaper American rye whiskey to replace Cognac and absinthe was introduced into the equation. Once absinthe became illegal, Pernod replaced it.

Traditionally made with good-quality Cognac, or its replacement of rye whiskey (such as Old Overholt), the Sazerac is now often preferred with a great bourbon such as Knob Creek or Maker's Mark. In New Orleans, Herbsaint, a local anise-flavored liqueur, is favored over Pernod.

Later recipes have added a sugar cube and water, but the following is the original method. The glass must be thoroughly chilled, and although Sazerac purists will tell you not to drop the lemon twist in the drink, a subtle spritz of lemon oil is quite a pleasant addition. Drop it in if you prefer.

Classic Sazerac

1 teaspoon Pernod (or Herbsaint)
2 ounces Cognac (or bourbon or rye)
3 to 4 dashes Peychaud's bitters
Lemon twist

Coat the inside of a chilled old-fashioned glass with the Pernod, discarding the excess. Shake the Cognac and bitters vigorously with ice. Strain into the prepared glass. Twist the lemon peel over the drink, and drop it in.

New Orleans Sazerac *Also called a New Orleans Cocktail, originally made with absinthe.*

1 sugar cube
Dash of Peychaud's or Angostura bitters
2 ounces bourbon
¼ ounce Herbsaint (or Pernod or Ricard)
½ ounce fresh lemon juice
Lemon twist

Place the sugar cube in the bottom of an old-fashioned glass, and saturate with the bitters. Add ice and pour in the bourbon, Herbsaint, and lemon juice. Stir well. Twist the lemon peel over the drink, and drop it in.

Seven and Seven

2½ ounces Seagram's 7 Crown whiskey
3 to 4 ounces chilled 7-Up
Lemon twist

Pour the liquid ingredients into an ice-filled highball glass. Stir well. Twist the lemon peel over the drink, and drop it in.

Shamrock

1½ ounces Irish whiskey
¾ ounce crème de menthe
2 ounces heavy cream
Maraschino cherry

Shake the liquid ingredients vigorously with ice. Strain into an ice-filled old-fashioned glass. Garnish with the cherry.

VARIATION: Add 4 ounces vanilla ice cream, combine in a blender, and blend until smooth. Serve in a chilled wineglass.

Soul Kiss

2 ounces blended Canadian whisky or bourbon
¼ ounce dry vermouth
¼ ounce Dubonnet Rouge
½ ounce fresh orange juice

Shake the ingredients vigorously with ice. Strain into a chilled cocktail glass.

VARIATION: **For a Rue de Rivoli,** use equal parts (1 ounce) of each liquor. Serve over ice in an old-fashioned glass.

Twin Hills

2 ounces rye
½ ounce Bénédictine
¼ ounce fresh lemon juice
¼ ounce fresh lime juice
¼ ounce simple syrup
Thin slice of lemon

Shake the liquid ingredients vigorously with ice. Strain into a chilled cocktail glass. Float the lemon slice on top of the drink.

Vieux Carré   *This classic cocktail from the 1930s hails from the Carousel Bar at the Monteleone Hotel, and is named for the French Quarter in New Orleans.*

½ teaspoon Bénédictine
Dash of Peychaud's bitters
Dash of Angostura bitters
½ ounce rye
½ ounce Cognac
½ ounce sweet vermouth
Lemon twist

Shake the liquid ingredients vigorously with ice. Strain into an ice-filled old-fashioned glass. Garnish with the lemon twist.

Waldorf Cocktail   *This classic is a variation on the Sazerac, with the addition of sweet vermouth.*

1½ ounces bourbon
¾ ounce Pernod
½ ounce sweet vermouth
Dash of Angostura bitters

Stir the liquid ingredients in a mixing glass with ice. Strain into a chilled cocktail glass.

Wally Wallbanger

1½ ounces bourbon
½ ounce Galliano
1 ounce fresh lemon juice
1 teaspoon sugar
Mint sprig

Shake all the ingredients except for the mint vigorously with ice. Strain into an ice-filled old-fashioned glass. Garnish with the mint sprig.

Ward Eight   *A classic from Boston, named for an election district, traditionally made with either bourbon or rye.*

2 ounces bourbon (or rye)
1 ounce fresh lemon juice
1 ounce fresh orange juice
Dash of grenadine
Maraschino cherry
Orange slice
Lemon slice

Shake the liquid ingredients vigorously with ice. Strain into an ice-filled old-fashioned glass or a chilled cocktail glass. Garnish with the cherry and orange and lemon slices.

Waterloo

1½ ounces blended whiskey
¾ ounce Mandarine Napoléon liqueur
¼ ounce fresh lemon juice
¼ ounce simple syrup
3 to 5 ounces chilled club soda
Orange slice

Shake the liquid ingredients vigorously with ice. Strain into an ice-filled old-fashioned glass. Top with club soda and stir gently. Garnish with the orange slice.

Whiskey Sour

THE QUINTESSENTIAL SOUR IS THE WHISKEY SOUR, a classic cocktail dating from the mid-1800s, inspiring many variations. The key to a sublime Whiskey Sour is freshly squeezed lemon juice, and although many prefer it with bourbon, a blended whiskey or other favorite whiskey of choice is suitable. Always shaken and traditionally served in a sour glass, it can also be served in a highball glass with ice. This refreshing drink was perfectly described by Esquire's 1945 *Handbook for Hosts*: "This is simply a species of fortified lemonade in concentrated form."

2 ounces bourbon (or blended whiskey)
¾ ounce fresh lemon juice
½ ounce simple syrup
Lemon or orange slice
Maraschino cherry

Shake the liquid ingredients vigorously with ice. Strain into a chilled sour glass. Garnish with the lemon slice and cherry.

VARIATIONS: **For a Boston Sour,** add an egg white and shake vigorously.

For a Double Standard Sour, use ³/₄ ounce each of whiskey and gin, and add a dash of grenadine.

For a Frisco Sour, add ¹/₄ ounce Bénédictine and ¹/₂ ounce fresh lime juice.

For a New York Sour, float ¹/₂ ounce dry red wine on top of a Whiskey Sour. Garnish with a lemon slice.

For a Park Lane, add ¹/₂ ounce sloe gin.

For a Southern Comfort Sour, substitute Southern Comfort for the bourbon, and add ¹/₄ ounce fresh orange juice.

For a Stinger Sour, add 1 teaspoon peppermint schnapps, garnish with a fresh mint sprig, and serve over ice in an old-fashioned glass.

Whiskey Fizz

2 ounces blended or other whiskey
1 ounce fresh lemon juice
½ ounce simple syrup
3 to 5 ounces chilled club soda
Lemon wedge

Shake the whiskey, lemon juice, and simple syrup vigorously with ice. Strain into an ice-filled highball glass. Top with club soda and stir gently. Squeeze the lemon wedge over the drink, and drop it in.

Whiskey Rickey

2 ounces blended or other whiskey
½ ounce fresh lime juice
¼ ounce simple syrup
3 to 5 ounces chilled club soda
Lime wedge

Shake the whiskey, lime juice, and simple syrup vigorously with ice. Strain into an ice-filled highball glass. Top with club soda and stir gently. Squeeze the lime wedge over the drink, and drop it in.

Woodward

1½ ounces blended scotch
½ ounce dry vermouth
½ ounce fresh grapefruit juice

Shake the ingredients vigorously with ice. Strain into a chilled cocktail glass.

VARIATION: **For a Brigadoon,** serve over ice in an old-fashioned glass.

Wine & Fortified Wines

~ *THE WINE URGES ME ON, THE BEWITCHING WINE, WHICH SETS EVEN A WISE MAN TO SINGING AND TO LAUGHING GENTLY AND ROUSES HIM UP TO DANCE AND BRINGS FORTH WORDS WHICH WERE BETTER LEFT UNSPOKEN.*

—HOMER (ca. 800 B.C. to 700 B.C.), in The Odyssey

WINE IS THE NECTAR OF THE GODS, a bacchanalian libation that has evolved along with civilization since about 1100 B.C., the era of the Phoenicians and Greeks, and it has been enjoyed the world over since then. The Romans extensively domesticated and cultivated what are now the most renowned and distinguished vineyards of the European world. The art of winemaking evolved along with the grapevine, and today fertile ground can be found producing fine grapes everywhere from Australia to America's West Coast, Africa, and South America.

Stated simply, wine is made from the naturally fermenting sugars in the juice of ripe grapes. The type of grape, along with the specific process used, dictates the type of wine produced. Wine grapes may produce red, white, or rosé wines, and come in a variety of styles, from dry to sweet. Wine is classified into four main categories: sparkling wine (such as champagne); still wine, which is without carbonation (such as red, white, or rosé); fortified wine, which is fortified with brandy (such as port or sherry); and aromatic wine, which is flavored with herbs and spices (such as vermouth or Lillet).

THE WINEMAKING PROCESS

Once the ripe grapes are harvested, they are crushed to release their juices, which are collected in a vat. The riper the grape, the stronger the wine will be. The type of grape determines how it is handled. For white wine, the grape stems are removed, and contact between the skins and juice is avoided when the grapes are pressed, so as not to produce an undesirable astringency. Red wine grapes are also stemmed, but some of the stems are thrown in to help produce desirable tannins. Dark skins, which give the wine its red hue, are deliberately retained for body, color, and tannins.

The grape juice is filtered to remove debris, then yeast is added to start the fermentation process, in which the yeast consumes the natural sugars and converts them to alcohol, turning sweet juice into a dry, complex wine.

The wine is then placed in vats to rest, where deposits of solids and sediment, or lees, settle to the bottom. The wine is moved to clean vats or barrels soon after fermentation, and many times thereafter, to separate it from the lees, and eventually it is moved to oak barrels for further aging. Once the wine has matured to the winemaker's specific criteria and satisfaction, the wine is filtered and clarified and then it is bottled. The wine is then stored for bottle aging.

SERVING AND ENJOYING WINE

〜 THIS WINE IS TOO GOOD FOR TOAST-DRINKING, MY DEAR. YOU DON'T
WANT TO MIX EMOTIONS UP WITH A WINE LIKE THAT. YOU LOSE THE TASTE.
—ERNEST HEMINGWAY

The best way to start is with a good, basic wineglass that holds at least 10 ounces, has a large bowl that tapers slightly smaller at the top, and has a long stem to hold, allowing the bowl to showcase the wine. The glassware should be clean and polished free of any detergent or cupboard smells. Wine should be poured into the glass to only half its capacity, leaving headspace for the act of swirling, which enables aeration and releases the bouquet.

Wines differ in a variety of subtle and not so subtle ways, from their color and complex aromas to their texture, strength, structure, and body. There are ways to navigate wine by using the smell, taste, and visual cues to appreciate the complex flavors.

The easiest way to discern and describe wine is the color. Visually, the age of a wine is easily discerned by tipping your glass of wine at an angle, giving the best view. You are looking for a ring of color at the edges or rim of the wine. For reds, generally, those that are deeper in hue (with a suggestion of purple-red around the edges) and still deeply opaque at the rim are younger or were made from grapes with thicker skin. As red wine ages, it becomes paler, less intense, less blue-purple, and more orange, with a much paler (more translucent) rim, and a more brownish brick-red color around the edges. White wine, on the other hand, gains rather than loses color, beginning as an almost clear water color, pale yellow, or pale green and acquiring a deeper, more brown tinge of color as it ages. As a rule, the more visible the gradations of shades in the color, the better the wine.

Describing our sense of smell and taste is a bit more difficult. Taste is connected to our sense of smell, which is great at detecting the subtle flavors as wine reaches those upper nasal areas by vapors inhaled through the nose as well as at the back of the mouth. Keep this in mind while swirling it around in the glass to release the aroma (or bouquet), and take in a deep sniff. As the strongest and most primitive of the senses, your sense of smell will quickly connect the wine's impressions to the memory banks of the brain, triggering an impression and evoking associations with other smells and tastes.

Your palate is the best way to gauge sweetness, acidity, bitterness, drying tannins, and texture, all important flavor triggers. Taking a good mouthful of wine will allow your taste buds to get a full impression of the wine on these fronts.

↜ A BOTTLE OF WINE CONTAINS MORE PHILOSOPHY THAN ALL THE BOOKS IN THE WORLD. —LOUIS PASTEUR

------- **WINE SERVING TEMPERATURES** -------

There are no absolutes when it comes to the correct temperatures, as personal tastes vary and will sway any rule. Generally speaking, though, fuller-bodied red and white wines (such as white Burgundy and chardonnay) are served at a cool room or cellar temperature (60°F to 68°F), whereas light reds such as lambrusco, gamay, and Beaujolais are best slightly chilled (50°F to 55°F). White wine is appropriately refreshing when chilled to 45°F, but no lower, as the flavors are not discernible when overchilled. The best way to remedy an overchilled wine is to simply cup your hand around the glass to warm it. Dry wines are better at room temperature than sweet wines.

------- DECANTING WINES -------

Decanters are a young wine's friend, because they help to oxygenate and open up their bouquet, which enhances the flavor. The best are openmouthed carafes, which allow the wine to breathe. They also help avoid the sediment deposited during aging in the bottom of the bottle. After the bottle has been standing upright long enough to allow the sediment to sink to the bottom, slowly pour the wine into the decanter, holding the bottle at an angle in front of a bright light to illuminate where the sediment is, and avoid pouring it out as you slowly reach the end.

When faced with the restaurant ritual of uncorking and tasting a small sample of the chosen wine that the waiter has poured for your inspection, you are checking to be sure that the wine is at the appropriate temperature, that it isn't faulty, and that the cork isn't moldy. Cloudiness or fizziness in a nonsparkling wine is an indication that it has gone musty or bad. The purpose of sampling a newly uncorked bottle of wine is never to send it back simply because you don't care for it.

Ultimately, the best wines are those that appeal to you and fit within your budget, but with the wide selection of amazing wines out there, experiencing something beyond the usual is always a pleasurable part of the wine experience.

GLOSSARY OF WINE-TASTING TERMS

ACIDITY

An integral component present in wine, from fruit acids that add a sharpness of flavor.

AROMA

The fragrance released by a wine, reflecting the grape, its fermentation process, and aging, all of which form a bouquet.

BALANCE

The harmony achieved between flavor components to make a quality wine.

BODY

The fullness of a wine due to alcohol strength, ranging from light to medium to full.

BOUQUET

The complex aroma of a mature wine, released when the wine is opened.

DRY

A wine with no sweetness; a dry champagne is known as *brut*.

FERMENTATION

The act of converting natural grape sugar to alcohol (and carbon dioxide), accomplished by adding yeast to crushed grapes.

FINISH

The aftertaste, which, if persistent, is the sign of a good-quality wine.

NOSE

A mix of aroma and bouquet.

TANNIN

A characteristic resulting from the deliberate addition of grape stems during the fermentation process, producing a noticeable astringency that sometimes leaves a slightly bitter aftertaste.

> ∾ *REMINDS ME OF MY SAFARI IN AFRICA. SOMEBODY FORGOT THE*
> *CORKSCREW AND FOR SEVERAL DAYS WE HAD TO LIVE ON NOTHING BUT*
> *FOOD AND WATER.   —W. C. FIELDS*

Apple Sangria Cooler

1 ounce Calvados
1 ounce peach brandy
3 ounces sweet-and-sour
2 ounces Beaujolais
Orange twist

Pour all liquid ingredients except the Beaujolais into an ice-filled wine-glass. Top with the Beaujolais—do not stir. Twist the orange peel over the drink, and drop it in.

Bâtonnet   *From the Ritz Hotel in Paris.*

½ ounce Cognac
3 ounces chilled white wine
4 ounces chilled tonic water
Cinnamon stick

Pour the Cognac and white wine into an ice-filled collins glass. Top with the tonic water and stir gently. Twist the lemon peel over the drink, and drop it in. Garnish with the cinnamon stick.

Bishop *This classic, dating back to the 18th century, was originally served as a warmed mulled wine drink and has evolved into this refreshing contemporary iced version. Cabernet sauvignon or merlot (a lighter version) is best suited for this drink, which was purportedly named for the color of the bishop's robes.*

1 ounce fresh lemon juice
1 ounce fresh orange juice
½ ounce simple syrup
4 ounces chilled light, dry red wine
Orange slice

Shake the citrus juices and simple syrup vigorously with ice. Strain into an ice-filled wineglass. Pour in the wine and stir. Garnish with the orange slice.

Classic Spanish Sangria *Sangria's roots can be traced back to 133 B.C., when the Romans residing in Andalusia quenched their thirst during the hot summer months with a mixture of fruit juices and the local rudimentary wine. Spanish Sangria began simply as a blend of the juice of fresh oranges with a light red wine, with a little sugar and lemon juice mixed in, and was served as a chilled punch. From there it evolved into the classic formula given here—juicy, fresh slices of citrus fruit, fortified with brandy for warmth and depth, and served chilled with the additional effervescence of club soda. Sangria's inherently versatile nature has inspired many variations on the classic, including versions made with white wine, champagne, and rosé, and with other liqueurs in place of the brandy, as well as a wide variety of other fruits.*

A light, fruity red wine, such as the traditional Spanish red Rioja, is best in the classic recipe. Some Sangrias may include slices of apples and ginger ale or even grapefruit soda, but the following is the quintessential traditional recipe, serving 4 to 6. It can be multiplied if needed and served in a punch bowl with a floating block of ice.

1 orange, sliced
1 lime, sliced
½ lemon, sliced
1½ ounces brandy
1½ ounces Cointreau
2 tablespoons sugar
One 750-ml bottle dry red wine, chilled
One 12-ounce bottle club soda, chilled
About 3 cups ice cubes

In a large (2-quart) glass pitcher, combine the orange, lime, and lemon slices. Add the brandy, Cointreau, and sugar, and stir to combine. Gently stir in the wine. Refrigerate for at least 2 hours or as long as overnight to chill.

When ready to serve, add the club soda, stirring gently. Pour into ice-filled wine goblets, letting some fruit fall into each drink.

VARIATIONS: **For Sangria Blanca,** a white wine version, use either a chilled sauvignon blanc, pinot grigio, or chardonnay in place of the red wine, and add red and green grapes, peach or apple slices, or strawberries and mint sprigs.

For Sparkling Sangria, use chilled dry champagne instead of the red wine, and add grapefruit or pineapple, and mango or raspberries. Add the champagne right before serving.

For a Rosado Sangria, use rosé wine instead of the red wine, and add raspberries and blackberries, or limes and peaches.

The Punches section also has several Sangria variations. See page 415.

Kir *This elegant aperitif was created in Burgundy and named after Canon Félix Kir, the famous French war hero, once the mayor of Dijon. The classic recipe calls for a dry, sharp white wine, such as a sauvignon blanc, and just a whisper of crème de cassis (any more than ¼ ounce of the syrupy sweet black currant liqueur will make it too sweet). Many prefer this drink over ice. A variation made with champagne is called a Kir Royale (page 160).*

½ teaspoon crème de cassis
6 ounces chilled dry white wine
Lemon twist

Pour the cassis and wine into a chilled wineglass. Stir well. Run the lemon peel around the rim, twist it over the drink, and drop it in.

Pineapple Cooler

2 ounces chilled dry white wine
   (such as chardonnay, pinot gris, or sauvignon blanc)
2 ounces pineapple juice
¼ ounce fresh lemon juice
½ teaspoon superfine sugar
2 to 3 ounces chilled club soda
Lemon twist

Shake the wine, pineapple juice, lemon juice, and sugar vigorously with ice. Strain into an ice-filled highball glass. Top with club soda and stir gently. Run the lemon peel around the rim, twist it over the drink, and drop it in.

Red Wine Cooler

6 ounces chilled dry red wine
4 ounces chilled lemon-lime soda
Lemon twist

Pour the wine and soda into an ice-filled highball glass. Stir well. Twist the lemon peel over the drink, and drop it in.

White Wine Spritzer   *A great summer refresher. Inexpensive dry white wine is ideal, such as a pinot grigio.*

6 ounces chilled dry white wine
2 to 3 ounces chilled club soda
Lemon twist

Pour the wine into an ice-filled wineglass. Top with club soda and stir gently. Twist the lemon peel over the drink, and drop it in.

FORTIFIED WINES

Fortified wines are wines to which a stronger spirit, usually a brandy, has been added to increase the alcohol content as well as serve as a preservative. Port, sherry, Madeira, Marsala, muscat, and moscatel are all fortified wines.

Madeira is a drier, lighter-bodied aperitif wine, fortified with brandy. Produced on the Portuguese island of Madeira off the coast of northwest Africa, it falls somewhere between the dryness of sherry and the richness of port, with burnt-orange and honey-sweet caramel flavors. Enjoyed both as an aperitif and as a dessert wine, it is best served slightly chilled.

Malaga is an Iberian fortified wine, a golden and sweet raisiny dessert wine from the southern Andalusian coast of Spain. A quality wine made with moscatel and pedro ximénez white grapes, its extreme sweetness has regrettably fallen out of popularity.

Marsala is a fuller-bodied fortified aperitif wine offered in both sweet and dry versions. It is made in Sicily from light-skinned grapes, falling somewhere between a sherry and a Madeira. These days, it is used mostly for cooking.

Muscat (moscato and moscatel) is a thick, sweetish wine produced in Australia, Italy, Spain, and Portugal, among other places.

------- PORT -------

This lovely fortified wine is produced from a specifically and legally designated area of northern Portugal, in the Douro River Valley, home to many vineyards and vintners producing port. A popular after-dinner and dessert wine, port gains its sweetness not only from the use of sweet grapes, but through the fermentation process, which is stopped by the addition of brandy to a portion of the wine before all the sugars are converted to alcohol. Relative dryness is reached through aging, usually in the cask. These are called "wood ports," with the different styles designated by how long they have matured (and where they were aged, in the case of vintage ports).

Ports are best served at room temperature, although many enjoy them chilled as well. The quintessential accompaniment is a fine English Stilton cheese.

Dry white port is a dry aperitif port, made from white grapes and aged for several years in wood casks. A local Douro favorite, it is imbibed chilled.

Ruby port is a sweet, basic red port, wood aged for three years and made up of a blend of vintages.

Tawny port has been aged in wood for at least five years, although the best are aged for 20 years and some have even been aged for up to 40 years, with the color getting continually paler as it ages. Young tawny ports are sweet, while the aged tawny ports are medium-dry and smooth. If there is no indication of age on the bottle, it usually is an inexpensive blend of ruby and white ports, and not technically a tawny.

Colheita port, although made from a single vintage year, is more of an aged tawny than a vintage port. It is a wood-aged port matured in the cask for at least seven years, and should be enjoyed soon after the bottling date on the label.

Vintage port, the finest of all ports, is made from one vintage (an exceptionally good year), unblended and matured in casks for only two years, and then bottle aged (anywhere from 20 to 40 years) to mature further to a medium-dry status. Because they age in the bottle, they collect deposits, and therefore it is imperative that they be decanted upon opening.

------- **SHERRY** -------

This famous fortified wine is produced only in a small, specifically designated area on the Mediterranean coast of Spain, which includes the Jerez de la Frontera, Sanlúcar de Barrameda, and Puerto de Santa María. Made from mostly palomino white grapes, with the addition of pedro ximénez and moscatel in sweeter sherries, sherry's distinction is due to its complex process. After fermentation, the wine is placed in oak casks, leaving enough room to allow a particular type of yeast, called *flor,* to develop on the surface, which protects it from oxidation and lends that distinct flavor sherry is famous for. The sherries have two basic categories, fino and oloroso, determined by the amount of *flor* developed. From these two categories come the various styles. *Solera* is a specific method of maturing sherries, in which different vintages and casks are blended and then aged.

∾ **FINO SHERRY**   The fino sherries are affected by *flor,* while olorosos have little to no *flor* development. Finos are best served slightly chilled.

Fino is the driest style, a pale, light-bodied sherry aged under flor.

Manzanilla is the lightest style of sherry; manzanilla pasada is an aged manzanilla.

Amontillado is a full-bodied style that has developed beyond the fino stage. It has a nutty flavor, depth, and amber color.

Pale cream is a fino-based sherry that has been sweetened.

∾ **OLOROSO SHERRY**   This style of sherry rarely develops *flor.* These sherries are usually heavy, fuller-bodied, dry, rich, fortified aperitif wines, best served slightly less chilled than the finos (54°F to 57°F).

Oloroso is a heavy, dry, brown sherry with walnut flavors.

Palo cortado is a fine and rare medium-dry aromatic sherry that started out as a fino (developed under minimal *flor*) with the flavor of an oloroso.

Cream sherry is made from the stronger olorosos and sweetened; it is usually dark in color.

------- **AROMATIZED WINES** -------

Aromatized wines are fortified wines infused with herbs and spices, such as vermouth, Punt e Mes, Dubonnet, and Lillet. Campari and Amer Picon are also considered aromatized wines but fall into the bitters category as well. For a description of these bitters, see page 226.

∾ **VERMOUTH**   A fortified wine–based drink, vermouth is named after the German word for wormwood, *wermut*, making it closely related to absinthe, although only the harmless flowers are used to make vermouth. This aperitif wine is typically flavored with various herbs, roots, berries, flowers, and seeds.

French (dry) vermouth generally has a delicate, slightly nutty flavor, with a color ranging from pale gold to colorless. Italian (sweet) vermouth has a darker color and a sweeter flavor.

There are three distinct styles of vermouth: Provençal is the most complex. Noilly Prat and Boissière are examples of premium-quality bone-dry Provençal vermouths that are just perfect for the classic dry Martini.

Savoie is more delicate. One example is Dolin Chambéry. The Bordeaux version is Lillet. Italian-style vermouths, such as Martini & Rossi and Cinzano, tend to be heavier and sweeter than the French style. They are created differently, using flavorings rather than maceration.

The term "French" is a classic cocktail term used when ordering a drink with dry vermouth, such as a "Gin and French." It harks back to a time when the French made dry vermouth and the Italians produced only sweet vermouth. These days both countries produce both varieties.

~ *BOISSIÈRE*   This bone-dry white vermouth, made in Italy, is sharp, dry, and fruity. It has been referred to as the perfect dry vermouth. It melds neutral, dry white wines with a mixture of 30 botanicals, lending hints of almond, oranges, and mint.

~ *NOILLY PRAT*   This bone-dry French vermouth is the quintessential Martini vermouth. It is colorless, with a slightly lemony nose and herbal notes. This was the first dry vermouth, produced in 1813. Until that time, only sweet vermouth had been produced, in Italy, which explains why dry vermouths are, to this day, referred to as French and sweet vermouths as Italian, although both varieties are made in various places. It is made from a blend of white wines, fruit eaux-de-vie, and botanicals, including chamomile, cloves, cilantro, bitter orange, and nutmeg. Once opened, it should be resealed and kept in the refrigerator for up to six months.

~ *CINZANO BIANCO*   A sweet white vermouth, which Stefano Cinzano, in 1757, began producing and selling in the area of Turin, Italy.

~ *CINZANO EXTRA DRY*   A colorless dry vermouth with a sweet, fragrant, herbal and floral nose. It is a blend of trebbiano wine fortified with neutral grape spirits and blended with 50 varieties of herbs and botanicals.

~ *MARTINI & ROSSI*   This internationally popular vermouth from Italy, first produced in 1863, is available in dry and sweet versions. Their extra-dry vermouth is made with light-bodied wines combined with herbal botanicals, including rhubarb and wormwood. It is colorless with faintly herbal and fruity tones.

Martini & Rossi Rosso is a sweeter style, a brandy-fortified wine mixed with botanicals. It is more similar in flavor to Lillet or Dubonnet (aperitifs) than to a dry vermouth.

 PUNT E MES   Also considered a bitter, this aperitif is partway between a vermouth and a bitter. It is frequently used as a variation in a Manhattan.

 CARPANO   Another bitters/vermouth hybrid, this deep-red vermouth is produced in Turin. It has a light bitterness balanced by fruit, oranges, and herbs.

 DUBONNET   A full-bodied, complex aromatic wine created in 1846 by French wine merchant Joseph Dubonnet, who perfected his product by blending red and white wines and aromatizing the blend with spices such as cinnamon, orange peel, chamomile, and green coffee beans, among other ingredients.

This aperitif wine is not a true vermouth but is frequently used in place of vermouth in many cocktails, including Martinis, to add a rich dimension to the drink. It is best served chilled or over ice, and once opened, the bottle should be stored (as is recommended with many aromatized wines) in the refrigerator. It is available in two types:

Dubonnet Rouge (or "red") is a garnet-hued red wine base flavored with quinine; it is full-bodied, rich, and sweet.

Dubonnet Blanc (or "blond") is drier than the red, making it a perfect substitute for dry vermouth in a Martini, and is a pale gold color, with flavors of honey, lemon, and herbs.

 LILLET   Made in the Bordeaux region of France, Lillet is an aperitif wine with delicate honey, citrusy orange and lime, and mint notes. Perfected around 1872 by Raymond and Paul Lillet, this blend of wine, brandy, and quinine was originally known as Kina-Lillet (as found listed in many older drink recipes), *kina* being the French abbreviation for quinine.

Two types of Lillet are produced; the only difference between the two is in the wine used.

Lillet Blanc is a blend of wines made from muscadelle, semillon, and sauvignon blanc grapes combined with orange and lemon brandies (including sweet and bitter oranges) and quinine, and aged a full year in oak casks. It is a dry aperitif that is pale straw in color, with citrus tones and an herbal and lilac nose.

Lillet Rouge blends wines from cabernet sauvignon and merlot grapes, lending a pink hue.

Like Dubonnet, Lillet is technically not a vermouth, but it is used as a delightful replacement in many Martinis, including the Vesper (see page 206), a favorite literary classic cocktail enjoyed by James Bond. It is best served well chilled (without ice) and must be refrigerated after opening.

FORTIFIED WINE DRINKS

Adonis   *A classic European-style aperitif, also called an Armour.*

2 ounces dry sherry
1 ounce sweet vermouth
2 dashes Peychaud's or orange bitters
Lemon twist

Stir the liquid ingredients in a mixing glass with ice. Strain into a chilled cocktail glass. Garnish with the lemon twist.

Amer Picon Cocktail

2 ounces Amer Picon
¼ ounce fresh lemon (or lime) juice
1 teaspoon grenadine
Orange twist

Shake the liquid ingredients vigorously with ice. Strain into a chilled cocktail glass. Twist the orange peel over the drink, and drop it in.

VARIATIONS: Serve over ice in an old-fashioned glass. Top with club soda.

For a Picon Cocktail, use 1 ounce each Amer Picon and sweet vermouth. Pour over ice in an old-fashioned glass.

Americano   *This classic cocktail, a precursor of the Negroni, was named in honor of Americans' fondness for the legally available Campari during Prohibition.*

1½ ounces Campari
1½ ounces sweet vermouth
2 to 3 ounces chilled club soda
Lemon twist
Orange twist

~ CONTINUED

Stir the Campari and vermouth in a mixing glass with ice. Strain into an ice-filled old-fashioned glass. Top with club soda and stir gently. Twist the lemon and orange peels over the drink, and drop them in.

VARIATION: **For a lighter version,** strain into an ice-filled highball glass and add more club soda.

Andalusia

1½ ounces dry sherry
½ ounce light rum
½ ounce brandy
2 dashes Angostura bitters

Stir the ingredients in a mixing glass with ice. Strain into a chilled cocktail glass.

Bamboo   *This classic aperitif cocktail, concocted in 1902 by bartender Charlie Mahoney of the Hoffman House in Manhattan, was purportedly named after a popular Bob Cole song, "Under the Bamboo Tree." Other versions call for sweet vermouth in place of the dry vermouth.*

2 ounces dry (fino) sherry
2 ounces dry vermouth
2 dashes orange bitters

Stir the ingredients in a mixing glass with ice. Strain into a chilled cocktail glass.

Brandied Madeira

1 ounce Madeira
1 ounce brandy
½ ounce dry vermouth
Lemon twist

Stir the liquid ingredients in a mixing glass with ice. Strain into a chilled cocktail glass. Run the lemon peel around the rim, twist it over the drink, and drop it in.

Brandied Port

1 ounce tawny port
1 ounce brandy
¼ ounce maraschino liqueur
½ ounce fresh lemon juice
Orange slice

Stir the liquid ingredients in a mixing glass with ice. Strain into an ice-filled wineglass. Garnish with the orange slice.

Campari and Soda

2 ounces Campari
2 to 3 ounces chilled club soda
Orange or lemon twist

Pour the Campari into an ice-filled old-fashioned glass. Top with club soda and stir gently. Run the orange or lemon peel around the rim, twist it over the drink, and drop it in.

VARIATION: **For a lighter drink,** pour into a chilled highball glass with ice, and add more club soda.

Campari Cooler

1½ ounces Campari
2 ounces fresh orange juice
¼ ounce raspberry syrup
3 to 4 ounces chilled club soda
Orange peel spiral

Shake the Campari, orange juice, and raspberry syrup vigorously with ice. Strain into an ice-filled highball glass. Top with club soda and stir gently. Garnish with the orange peel spiral.

Cynar Cola

1½ ounces Cynar
2 to 3 ounces chilled cola
Lemon wedge

Pour the Cynar into an ice-filled old-fashioned glass. Top with cola. Rub the rim with the lemon wedge, squeeze it over the drink, and drop it in.

Diplomat

1½ ounces dry vermouth
½ ounce sweet vermouth
½ teaspoon maraschino liqueur
2 dashes Angostura bitters
Lemon twist
Maraschino cherry

Stir the liquid ingredients in a mixing glass with ice. Strain into a chilled cocktail glass. Run the lemon peel around the rim, twist it over the drink, and drop it in. Garnish with the cherry.

Dubonnet Cocktail   *Some classic versions call for equal amounts of gin and Dubonnet.*

1 ounce Dubonnet Rouge
¾ ounce gin
Dash of orange bitters
Lemon twist

Stir the liquid ingredients in a mixing glass with ice. Strain into a chilled cocktail glass. Run the lemon peel around the rim, twist it over the drink, and drop it in.

VARIATION: **For a Diabola Cocktail,** add 2 dashes of orgeat syrup.

Ferrari

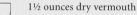

2 ounces dry vermouth
1 ounce amaretto
Lemon twist

Pour the liquid ingredients into an ice-filled old-fashioned glass. Stir well. Twist the lemon peel over the drink, and drop it in.

French Kiss

1½ ounces dry vermouth
1½ ounces sweet vermouth
Lemon twist

Pour the vermouths into an ice-filled old-fashioned glass. Stir well. Twist the lemon peel over the drink, and drop it in.

Indigo Jones

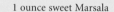

1 ounce sweet Marsala
1 ounce dry rosé wine
1 ounce Cognac
Dash of fresh orange juice
Dash of fresh lemon juice
Orange slice

Shake the liquid ingredients vigorously with ice. Strain into an ice-filled old-fashioned glass. Garnish with the orange slice.

Lillet and Soda   *Best enjoyed when the Lillet and club soda have been well chilled.*

4 ounces Lillet Blanc
1 to 2 ounces chilled club soda
Orange twist

Pour the Lillet over a few ice cubes in a chilled wineglass. Add the club soda and stir. Twist the orange peel over the drink, and drop it in.

Lillet Cocktail

1½ ounces Lillet Blanc
½ ounce gin
Orange twist

Shake the Lillet and gin vigorously with ice. Strain into a chilled cocktail glass. Twist the orange peel over the drink, and drop it in.

Lily

1 ounce Lillet
1 ounce gin
1 ounce crème de noyaux
Dash of fresh lemon juice
Lemon twist

Shake the liquid ingredients vigorously with ice. Strain into a chilled wineglass. Garnish with the lemon peel.

Little Princess

1½ ounces sweet vermouth
1½ ounces light rum

Stir the ingredients in a mixing glass with ice. Strain into a chilled cocktail glass.

Merry Widow *There are too many diverse versions of this drink to put them all in one book. From the one made with sherry and vermouth to one made with vodka to one that is completely out there, the liqueur-based cherry brandy cocktail on page 216. This is the refined aperitif version.*

1½ ounces dry vermouth
1½ ounces Dubonnet Rouge
Lemon twist

Stir the vermouth and Dubonnet in a mixing glass with ice. Strain into a chilled cocktail glass. Run the lemon peel around the rim, twist it over the drink, and drop it in.

Negroni *This classic of perfected alchemy began in Florence in 1919, when the Italian Count Negroni asked to have gin added to his Americano cocktail.*

¾ ounce sweet vermouth
¾ ounce Campari
¾ ounce gin
Orange twist

Stir the liquid ingredients in a mixing glass with ice. Strain into a chilled cocktail glass. Run the orange peel around the rim, twist it over the drink, and drop it in.

Parkeroo

2 ounces pale dry sherry
1 ounce tequila
Lemon peel spiral

Stir the sherry and tequila in a mixing glass with ice. Strain into a chilled wineglass filled with crushed ice. Garnish with the lemon peel spiral.

Picon Fizz

1½ ounces Amer Picon
½ ounce grenadine
3 to 5 ounces chilled club soda
½ ounce brandy

Pour the Amer Picon and grenadine into an ice-filled highball glass. Top with club soda and stir gently. Float the brandy on top of the drink.

Port Sangaree

4 ounces ruby port
1 ounce simple syrup
Freshly grated or ground nutmeg

Stir the port and simple syrup in a mixing glass with ice. Strain into an ice-filled wineglass. Sprinkle the nutmeg on top.

Sanctuary

1½ ounces Dubonnet Rouge
¾ ounce Amer Picon
¾ ounce Cointreau (or triple sec)
Lemon twist

Shake the liquid ingredients vigorously with ice. Strain into a chilled cocktail glass. Twist the lemon peel over the drink, and drop it in.

Sherry Sangaree

4 ounces dry sherry
¾ ounce Cointreau (or triple sec)
1 ounce simple syrup
Lemon twist

Stir the liquid ingredients in a mixing glass with ice. Strain into an ice-filled wineglass. Run the lemon peel around the rim, twist it over the drink, and drop it in.

Vermouth Cassis

2½ ounces dry vermouth
½ ounce crème de cassis
3 to 4 ounces club soda
Lemon twist

Pour the vermouth and cassis into an ice-filled highball glass. Top with club soda and stir gently. Twist the lemon peel over the drink, and drop it in.

Washington Cocktail

1½ ounces dry vermouth
½ ounce brandy
½ teaspoon powdered sugar
2 dashes Angostura bitters

Shake the ingredients vigorously with ice. Strain into a chilled cocktail glass.

Hot Drinks

THE MERE IDEA OF A STEAMY HOT MUG OF RICHNESS laced with a fiery, warm shot of spirit inspires an impulsive need for these soothing restorative drinks, which are warming to both body and soul.

Hot drinks have been an essential part of the social dynamic for centuries, from the wassail gatherings at harvesttime in thirteenth-century England to the toddies popularized by the British in the eighteenth century. By the nineteenth century, in many northern countries as well as the American colonies, pubs and taverns were still the prime meeting place, social hub, and village oasis to ward against chilly nights, serving up hot "flips" or rich Tom and Jerrys.

One drink that epitomizes the tavern's role in the hot drink genre is the original flip, a real throwback to a time when townsfolk gathered around the heat of the tavern's large fireplace to discuss public matters while sipping hot concoctions heated by a hot iron from the fire. Flips were named after a metal "flip iron" or "loggerhead" specifically used for heating beverages, usually made of rum, beer, spices, and sometimes egg. Flip irons were set in the fireplace to heat up until red-hot and then stuck into the large mug to "mull," or heat up, the beverage, then set back into the fire to prepare for the next one. This is no longer a viable practice, however, and flip irons will not be found in the bar equipment section. Most of the drinks here require just a saucepan or kettle and stove top, along with heat-proof mugs.

When preparing a hot drink, the alcohol is only to be heated, never brought to a boil; otherwise the alcohol in the spirit will boil away and the flavor will be compromised.

Although there are flaming drink recipes in this section, given alcohol's volatile nature when heated, extreme caution is required when attempting these drinks, or better yet, leave them up to the professionals. There is a description of flaming techniques on page 56.

Be sure to prewarm your mugs, especially the glass Irish coffee mug, which is otherwise prone to cracking, by filling them with hot tap water, to be discarded once the hot beverage is prepared. This also serves to keep the drink hot much longer. These hot beverages may come in many concoctionary styles, but after a blustery fall day kicking up leaves, or the end of a snowy winter day, they all have that relaxing, satisfying heat with which to warm yourself.

Aztec Eggnog *A South-of-the-Border concoction made with Ibarra cinnamon-flavored Mexican chocolate, available from most grocers.*

MAKES ENOUGH FOR 6 SERVINGS

4 cups eggnog

1 teaspoon ground nutmeg

½ teaspoon ground cloves

2 tablespoons unsweetened cocoa powder

½ cup grated Mexican chocolate

8 ounces (1 cup) reposado tequila

Mexican chocolate shavings

In a large saucepan, whisk together the eggnog, nutmeg, cloves, and cocoa powder until well combined. Heat the mixture over medium-low heat until simmering; do not boil. Slowly add the grated Mexican chocolate, whisking until the chocolate is melted. Remove from the heat, add the tequila, and stir. Serve in warmed 6-ounce punch cups or heat-proof mugs, garnishing each with a sprinkling of Mexican chocolate shavings.

VARIATION: Substitute your favorite bourbon, rum, or brandy for the tequila.

Bull's Milk

1½ ounces dark rum

¾ ounce Cognac

4 ounces hot milk

1 teaspoon maple syrup

Freshly grated or ground nutmeg

Pour the rum and Cognac into a warmed heat-resistant mug. Pour in the hot milk. Add the maple syrup and stir. Sprinkle the top with nutmeg.

Café Amaretto

1 ounce amaretto
½ ounce brandy
6 ounces hot coffee
Whipped cream

Pour the amaretto and brandy into a warmed heat-resistant mug. Add the hot coffee and stir. Top with whipped cream.

VARIATION: **For an Italian Coffee,** use ¾ ounce each brandy and amaretto, and substitute hot espresso in place of the coffee.

Café Diablo

1 ounce Cognac
½ ounce Cointreau
2 whole cloves
1 long strip of lemon peel
1 long strip of orange peel
6 ounces hot coffee

In a saucepan over medium heat, combine all ingredients except the coffee, stirring often. Pour the hot coffee into a heat-resistant mug, and set aside. As bubbles form around the edge of the pan, use a long-handled match to ignite the alcohol. Pour it flaming into the mug of hot coffee.

Café Royale

8 ounces (1 cup) hot coffee
1 sugar cube
½ ounce brandy
1 tablespoon heavy cream

Pour the hot coffee into a warmed heat-resistant mug. Soak the sugar cube with the brandy in a spoon. Place the spoon over the mug, resting it on the rim over the coffee. Ignite the brandy-soaked sugar cube. Once the flame has burned out, stir the brandied sugar into the coffee. Float the cream on top.

Hot Apple-Raspberry Rum Cider

8 ounces (1 cup) apple cider
1 ounce raspberry syrup
1 tablespoon grated orange zest
2 or 3 whole cloves
¼ teaspoon ground cinnamon
¼ teaspoon ground cardamom
1 ounce Haitian rum
Whipped cream
Ground cinnamon

In a small saucepan, combine the apple cider, raspberry syrup, orange zest, cloves, cinnamon, and cardamom. Heat the mixture until steam rises from the surface; do not boil. With a spoon, remove the cloves. Pour the hot mixture into a warmed heat-resistant mug. Add the rum and stir. Garnish with the whipped cream, and add a dusting of cinnamon on top.

Hot Buttered Rum   *A traditional favorite in the hot drink genre. Some prefer a richer variation, made with milk in place of the water.*

1 teaspoon brown sugar
4 ounces hot water
2 ounces dark rum
1 tablespoon butter
Freshly grated or ground nutmeg

In a warmed heat-resistant mug, combine the brown sugar and hot water, stirring until the sugar is dissolved. Add the rum, and float the butter on top. Sprinkle nutmeg over the top.

VARIATIONS: **For Hot Buttered Bourbon or Hot Buttered Comfort,** simply substitute bourbon or Southern Comfort for the rum.

Hot Chocolate Stinger

1 ounce dark crème de cacao
½ ounce peppermint schnapps
2 ounces prepared hot chocolate
3 ounces hot coffee
Whipped cream

Pour the crème de cacao and schnapps into a warmed heat-resistant mug. Add the hot chocolate and hot coffee, and stir. Top with a dollop of whipped cream.

Hot Jamaican

1 lime slice
3 whole cloves
½ ounce simple syrup
½ ounce fresh lime juice
2 ounces dark rum
4 ounces boiling water
1 cinnamon stick

Stud the lime slice with the cloves, and drop it into a warmed heat-resistant mug. Add the simple syrup, lime juice, and rum, and stir. Pour in the boiling water. Stir with the cinnamon stick.

Hot Marie

¾ ounce dark rum
¾ ounce brandy
¼ ounce Tia Maria
8 ounces (1 cup) hot coffee
Sugar to taste

Pour the rum, brandy, and Tia Maria into a warmed heat-resistant mug. Add the hot coffee and sugar to taste, and stir.

Irish Coffee *The popularity of this classic, created in the early 1940s, is ongoing, especially around Saint Patrick's Day, when it's served with a splash of green crème de menthe. First invented at the Shannon airport in Ireland by a Joe Sheridan, who was concocting it for arriving passengers, it was enjoyed by a traveler who happened to be American reporter Stanton Delaplane. Enamored, he brought this hot drink back to the States, to his local bar, the Buena Vista in San Francisco, and it's been a favorite there ever since.*

1½ ounces Irish whiskey
1 teaspoon brown sugar
5 to 6 ounces strong hot coffee
Heavy cream or whipped cream

Pour the Irish whiskey into a warmed Irish coffee glass, add the brown sugar, and stir until dissolved. Pour in the hot coffee, and slowly add the cream to float on top; do not stir.

Or top with a dollop of whipped cream.

Jamaican Coffee

1 ounce Jamaican rum
1 ounce Tia Maria
6 to 8 ounces hot coffee
Whipped cream
Pinch of ground allspice

Combine the rum, Tia Maria, and hot coffee in a warmed heat-resistant mug, and stir. Float the whipped cream on top. Sprinkle with the allspice.

Mexican Coffee

½ ounce gold tequila
¾ ounce Kahlúa or Tia Maria
1 teaspoon brown sugar
8 ounces (1 cup) hot coffee
Whipped cream

Combine the tequila, Kahlúa, and brown sugar in a warmed heat-resistant mug. Add the hot coffee and stir until the sugar dissolves. Top with a dollop of whipped cream.

Mulled Wine *Recipes for mulled wine go back centuries, with varying fruits and spices used. A cabernet sauvignon or Burgundy is best. For those who prefer a less alcoholic drink, boil all the ingredients together for at least 10 minutes to allow most of the alcohol to evaporate. Strain any leftover wine into a container, cap it tightly, and refrigerate.*

MAKES 10 TO 12 SERVINGS

Two 750-ml bottles dry red wine

½ cup brown sugar

12 whole cloves

4 cinnamon sticks

Zest of 1 orange, cut into strips

Zest of 1 lemon, cut into strips

16 ounces (2 cups) ruby port

16 ounces (2 cups) brandy

In a large, nonaluminum pot, combine all the ingredients but the port and brandy and bring to a simmer, stirring occasionally. Reduce the heat to low, and simmer for 10 minutes. Add the port and brandy, and heat briefly. Pour into a large heat-proof bowl, and ladle into mugs.

VARIATION: **For Mulled Cider**, substitute 10 cups apple cider for the wine, and omit the port.

Riki Tiki Toddy

1½ ounces spiced rum

½ ounce Drambuie

½ ounce Grand Marnier

1 tablespoon honey

1½ ounces coconut milk

Pinch of ground cloves

4 ounces boiling water

Whipped cream

1 lemon slice studded with 3 whole cloves

In a warmed heat-resistant mug, combine the rum, Drambuie, Grand Marnier, honey, coconut milk, and ground cloves. Add the boiling water and stir until the honey is dissolved. Top with a dollop of whipped cream. Garnish with the clove-studded lemon slice.

Sevilla Flip   *Although flips these days are shaken and served over ice, rather than being heated with a red-hot poker or "flip iron" as they were in the old days, this hot flip recipe is still a treat even when warmed by more conventional methods.*

1 ounce heavy cream
½ teaspoon sugar
1½ ounces light rum
1½ ounces ruby port
Freshly grated or ground nutmeg

In a small saucepan, combine the cream and sugar over low heat. Add the rum and port, and bring to a low simmer, stirring occasionally. Pour into a warmed heat-resistant mug, and sprinkle the top with nutmeg.

- -

Southern Chai   *A smooth combination of fragrant chai tea and aromatic liquors to warm the senses.*

Chai tea concentrate is available in most supermarkets. If it's unavailable, brew loose chai tea.

8 ounces chai tea concentrate
3 ounces milk
1 ounce bourbon
¼ ounce amaretto
¼ ounce Cointreau
Lemon wedge studded with 3 whole cloves

In a small saucepan, combine the chai concentrate and milk and bring to a simmer, stirring occasionally. Pour into a warmed heat-resistant mug. Add the bourbon, amaretto, and Cointreau, and stir briefly. Garnish with the lemon wedge.

Spiced Jamaican Java

½ ounce Captain Morgan Spiced Rum

1 ounce Cognac

1 teaspoon brown sugar

8 ounces hot, freshly brewed coffee
   (preferably Jamaican Blue Mountain)

Whipped cream

Freshly grated or ground nutmeg

Combine the rum, Cognac, and brown sugar in a warmed heat-resistant mug. Add the hot coffee, and stir to combine. Float the whipped cream on top, and dust with nutmeg.

Tom and Jerry   *This classic has been a winter weather favorite since its inception around the 1850s at the Planter's House Hotel in St. Louis, created by "Professor" Jerry Thomas, one of the founding fathers of cocktail mixology. The Tom and Jerry "batter" was traditionally made in large batches and ladled out into cups for chilled customers. Many enjoy this with bourbon in place of the brandy, and if the milk seems too rich, try half milk and half water. This recipe can be multiplied for a crowd.*

MAKES 2 SERVINGS

1 egg, separated

2 ounces dark Jamaican rum

2 ounces brandy

1 tablespoon sugar

Pinch of ground cinnamon

Pinch of ground cloves

Pinch of ground allspice

12 ounces hot milk (or 6 ounces hot milk and 6 ounces hot water)

Freshly grated or ground nutmeg

Whisk the egg yolk together with the rum and brandy in a small bowl. Beat the egg white with the sugar and spices until stiff, and fold into the yolk-liquor mixture. Divide the mixture evenly between 2 warmed heat-resistant mugs and top with the hot milk (or hot milk-water combination), stirring until foamy. Sprinkle the top with nutmeg.

Wassail   *This traditional drink is an old English salutary beverage typically made with hard apple cider and spiced ale or wine. Customarily the wassailer would toast to the health and well-being of his guests, and then commence in a celebratory passing around and partaking of the wassail bowl, with the wish Wass hael! or "Be healthy!" Wassail has been around since the 13th century, so it's not surprising that there are numerous variations, from different ales, such as amber ale, to the addition of sherry, brandy, and even roasted apples.*

MAKES 6 SERVINGS

1 teaspoon ground allspice

1 teaspoon freshly grated or ground nutmeg

½ teaspoon ground ginger

½ teaspoon ground cloves

½ cup brown sugar

Juice and spiral peel of 1 orange

Juice and spiral peel of 1 lemon

8 ounces (1 cup) hot water

32 ounces (4 cups) brown ale

12 ounces (1½ cups) hard cider

In a large, nonaluminum pot, combine the spices, brown sugar, and orange and lemon juice and spiral peels with the hot water. Cook over medium heat, stirring frequently, until hot. Add the ale and cider, and cook until steaming (not boiling). Ladle into warmed heat-resistant mugs.

Whiskey Hot Toddy   *The quintessentially soothing hot drink, usually made with bourbon, but a blended whiskey or rum is equally suitable.*

Lemon slice studded with 3 whole cloves

1 teaspoon granulated or brown sugar

Pinch of grated or ground nutmeg

1½ ounces bourbon

6 ounces boiling water

1 cinnamon stick

Drop the clove-studded lemon slice into a warmed heat-resistant mug. Add the sugar, nutmeg, and bourbon. Pour in the boiling water, and stir with the cinnamon stick.

Punches

PUNCHES ARE THE IDEAL LIBATION for relaxed entertaining, when larger groups require larger quantities of refreshment. Preserving a level of quality can, however, pose a daunting dilemma, as some punches tend to have an aura of weak, Hawaiian punch blandness surrounding them. With the right recipe, the freshest ingredients, and a few helpful tips, you can serve a sophisticated and festive bowlful of liquid excitement.

Here are a few key things to keep in mind to assist in the punch preparation:

Many recipes call for canned and frozen juice for convenience, but you should use fresh ingredients whenever possible; they will make all the difference between a just okay punch and a sublime one. Chill the ingredients before you start mixing, to help retain the chill factor once it is poured. Some punches can be conveniently mixed ahead of time and refrigerated.

Always add your sparkling ingredients last, to preserve the carbonation. That goes for the ice as well—the longer it sits in the punch, the more diluted the drink. As long as the liquid ingredients are adequately chilled, a block of ice can be the last element you add.

Ice cubes are best served in individual glasses, never in the punch; otherwise they will melt too fast and dilute your punch to a watery consistency. Big blocks of ice are better suited for punches; you can easily make these by filling a small metal pan, bowl, plastic container, or, more festively, your Bundt pan with filtered water and freezing it. Blocks and rings are a great opportunity to get creative, allowing for the addition of garnish ingredients frozen in the ice, from edible flowers to citrus slices and berries. Don't be afraid to tweak punches to your own taste, adding a favorite fruit, liqueur, or juice. Be adventurous and experiment.

Punches can be an elegant centerpiece to an occasion. Beautiful, large glass bowls, or even colorful glazed pottery bowls, are ideal for showing off the colorful liquid and floating fruit. For pitcher drinks, there is nothing more visually inviting than a glass pitcher filled with Sangria. Also consider replacing those cheap glass punch cups with more elegant glassware, such as small wine glasses. Your guests will more than likely be drinking two or more servings, at about 6 ounces each, so be sure to plan for the right amount, and have a backup pitcher and backup ice, if need be, to refill the bowl with.

Autumn Punch

MAKES 18 SIX-OUNCE SERVINGS
One 750-ml bottle dry red wine
Two 750-ml bottles dry white wine
3 ounces sweet vermouth
3 ounces dry vermouth
1 cup applejack
1 cup citrus vodka
1 cup cranberry juice
2 ounces simple syrup
1 block of ice
1 orange, sliced
1 lemon, sliced

Combine the liquid ingredients in a punch bowl, and stir well. Cover and refrigerate for at least 4 hours. When ready to serve, place the ice in the bowl. Float the orange and lemon slices on top of the punch. Ladle into punch cups.

Bombay Punch

MAKES 30 FIVE-OUNCE SERVINGS
2 cups sherry
2 cups brandy
3 ounces apricot liqueur (or brandy)
3 ounces Cointreau (or curaçao)
3 ounces maraschino liqueur
1 block of ice
One 750-ml bottle chilled champagne
1 liter chilled club soda
2 cups chilled ginger ale
1 lemon, sliced
1 orange, sliced
5 to 6 mint sprigs

Pour all liquid ingredients except the carbonated beverages into a punch bowl. Just before serving, add the ice, and pour in the champagne, club soda, and ginger ale. Float the lemon and orange slices and mint sprigs on top of the punch. Ladle into punch cups.

Caribbean Hurricane *A turbulent whirl of tropical juices is the base for this South Pacific punch.*

MAKES 8 SIX-OUNCE SERVINGS

2 cups light rum
2 cups spiced rum
1 cup passion fruit syrup
1 cup fresh grapefruit juice
1 cup fresh orange juice
1 cup pineapple juice
4 ounces fresh lime juice
4 trays lime-flavored ice cubes (made from limeade)
    or regular ice cubes
2 cups chilled club soda
8 pineapple wedges
Floating edible flowers (borage, nasturtium, or orange blossoms)

Chill 8 tall hurricane or highball glasses. In a large pitcher, combine the liquid ingredients and stir until well blended. Fill each glass with lime-flavored ice cubes, and pour the punch mixture over the ice. Top each with a splash of club soda. Garnish each drink with a pineapple wedge, and float a few flower petals on top.

Cardinal Punch

MAKES 20 SIX-OUNCE SERVINGS

4 ounces dark rum
4 ounces fresh lemon juice
3 ounces simple syrup
Two 750-ml bottles chilled dry red wine
One 750-ml bottle chilled champagne
8 ounces (1 cup) sweet vermouth
1 large block of ice
20 orange wheels

Shake together the rum, lemon juice, and simple syrup. Strain into a large punch bowl. Pour in the wine, champagne, and vermouth, and stir well. Chill for 30 minutes. Add the ice and ladle into punch cups. Garnish each with an orange wheel.

Champagne Punch

MAKES 20 FIVE-OUNCE SERVINGS

1 cup brandy

3 ounces triple sec

4 ounces Frangelico

One 750-ml bottle chilled white wine

4 ounces fresh lemon juice

4 ounces pineapple juice

3 ounces maraschino syrup

1 large block of ice

Three 750-ml bottles chilled champagne

Apple slices

Strawberry slices

Orange slices

Pour all liquid ingredients but the champagne into a punch bowl. Just before serving, add the block of ice, and pour in the champagne. Ladle into punch cups. Garnish each with fruit slices.

Citrus Sparkler Punch

MAKES 24 FIVE-OUNCE SERVINGS

3 cups gin

2 cups fresh orange juice

12 ounces frozen lemonade concentrate (thawed)

6 ounces pineapple juice

6 ounces fresh grapefruit juice

3 ounces fresh lime juice

1 large block of ice

2 liters chilled club soda

1 orange, sliced

1 lime, sliced

1 lemon, sliced

Pour all ingredients except the club soda into a punch bowl. Just before serving, add the ice, and pour in the club soda. Float the citrus slices on top of the punch. Ladle into punch cups.

Effervescent Apricot Punch

⅛ cup frozen orange juice concentrate

⅜ cup frozen lemon juice concentrate

5 cups chilled apricot nectar

2 cups pineapple juice

One 750-ml bottle chilled muscat white wine

One 750-ml bottle chilled light rum

1 large block of ice

2 liters chilled lemon-lime soda

1 orange, sliced

1 lemon, sliced

8 to 10 maraschino cherries

3 to 4 strawberries, hulled and sliced

Thaw the frozen juice. Combine all liquid ingredients but the lemon-lime soda in a punch bowl. Add the ice and soda just before serving. Garnish by adding fruit slices, cherries, and strawberries. Ladle into punch cups.

Fish House Punch   *A classic American punch, purportedly a favorite of George Washington's, dating back to Philadelphia in 1732.*

MAKES 30 FIVE-OUNCE SERVINGS

One 750-ml bottle chilled light rum

One 750-ml bottle chilled dark rum

One 750-ml bottle chilled brandy

8 ounces (1 cup) peach brandy

6 ounces simple syrup

24 ounces (3 cups) fresh lemon juice

1 large block of ice

2 liters chilled club soda

1 orange, sliced

1 lemon, sliced

4 to 6 mint sprigs

Pour all liquid ingredients but the club soda into a punch bowl. Just before serving, add a block of ice, and pour in the club soda. Float the citrus slices and mint sprigs on top of the punch. Ladle into punch cups.

Irish Eggnog *Substitute 5 cups of store-bought pasteurized eggnog for the eggs and milk if you are uncomfortable using raw eggs.*

MAKES 8 SIX-OUNCE SERVINGS

4 eggs
6 ounces Irish whiskey
2 ounces Irish Mist liqueur
1 teaspoon vanilla extract
½ teaspoon ground cinnamon
½ teaspoon ground allspice
4 cups (1 quart) milk
Freshly grated or ground nutmeg

In a large bowl, whisk the eggs, and add the whiskey, Irish Mist, vanilla extract, and spices. Slowly add the milk and whisk until well combined. Ladle into Irish coffee glasses and sprinkle each drink with nutmeg.

Red Velvet Punch

MAKES 20 SIX-OUNCE SERVINGS

8 cups cranberry juice
1 cup fresh cranberries
⅜ cup frozen orange juice concentrate
⅜ cup frozen pineapple juice concentrate
⅜ cup frozen lemon juice concentrate
16 ounces (2 cups) brandy
Two 750-ml bottles chilled champagne
20 orange slices

Freeze 2 cups of the cranberry juice into a block with the fresh cranberries. Thaw the frozen juices and combine with the remaining 6 cups cranberry juice and the brandy in a punch bowl. Just before serving, add the cranberry ice, and pour in the champagne. Ladle into punch cups, and garnish each with an orange slice.

Rum Punch

MAKES 12 FIVE-OUNCE SERVINGS

Juice and grated zest of 6 lemons (about 1 cup juice)

6 ounces simple syrup

2 teaspoons ground ginger

One 750-ml bottle gold rum

One 750-ml bottle brandy

8 ounces (1 cup) sherry

6 cups boiling water

Combine and muddle the lemon juice, zest, simple syrup, and ginger in a large, heat-proof glass bowl. Let stand for at least 1 hour. Add enough boiling water to cover. Stir thoroughly, and then add the rum, brandy, sherry, and the rest of the boiling water. Ladle into warmed heat-resistant mugs.

Sangria *This versatile wine-based drink is characteristically adaptable to various fruit and wine possibilities and can be prepared ahead of time. For the Classic Spanish Sangria, see page 380. These are all original recipes from* Sangria: Fun and Festive Recipes, *by Mittie Hellmich.*

LIMONADA ESPAÑA *A variation on a traditional favorite libation in Spain, the Limonada, with the addition of Spain's favorite liqueur, Licor 43—produced and blended according to an ancient recipe dating back to 200 B.C. This liqueur contains 43 fruits and herbal elements, imparting a dominant flavor of vanilla.*

MAKES ABOUT 6 FIVE-OUNCE SERVINGS

2 lemons, sliced

2 peaches, pitted and sliced

4 ounces fresh lemon juice

3 ounces Licor 43

¼ cup superfine sugar

One 750-ml bottle chilled dry red wine (preferably a Rioja)

One 12-ounce bottle chilled club soda

Combine the lemon and peach slices in a large glass pitcher. Add the lemon juice, Licor 43, and sugar, stirring to combine. Gently stir in the wine. Refrigerate for at least 2 hours. When ready to serve, add the club soda, stirring gently. Slowly pour into ice-filled wine goblets, allowing some of the fruit to fall into the glasses.

SANGRI-LA *A tropical twist on the classic Sangria, made with tropical fruit, champagne, and white wine.*

MAKES ABOUT 12 FIVE-OUNCE SERVINGS

3 cups cubed fresh or frozen pineapple

1 ripe banana, peeled and sliced

1 orange, sliced

1 lime, sliced

½ cup diced fresh coconut meat (or 2 ounces coconut milk)

3 ounces Grand Marnier

One 750-ml bottle chilled dry white wine

One 750-ml bottle chilled brut champagne

Combine the fruit and coconut in a large glass pitcher. Add the Grand Marnier, and stir to combine. Gently stir in the white wine. Refrigerate for at least 2 hours. When ready to serve, add the champagne, stirring gently with a long-handled wooden spoon. Pour into ice-filled wineglasses, allowing some of the fruit to fall into the glasses.

SPICED PEAR SANGRIA *A Sangria infused with fruit, spices, and Damiana liqueur, the herbal liqueur with citrus vanilla flavors and infamous aphrodisiac properties.*

MAKES ABOUT 10 FIVE-OUNCE SERVINGS

2 pears, cored and sliced

2 Granny Smith apples, cored and sliced

20 whole cloves

1 teaspoon ground nutmeg

3 ounces Damiana liqueur

One 750-ml bottle chilled dry white wine

One 750-ml bottle chilled champagne

Combine the pears, apples, cloves, and nutmeg in a large glass pitcher. Add the Damiana liqueur, stirring to combine. Gently stir in the wine. Refrigerate for at least 2 hours or as long as overnight to chill. When ready to serve, add the champagne, stirring gently with a long-handled wooden spoon to combine. Slowly pour into ice-filled wineglasses, allowing some of the fruit to fall into the glasses.

STRAWBERRY MINT SANGRIA

MAKES ABOUT 6 FIVE-OUNCE SERVINGS

2 cups sliced strawberries,

½ cup fresh mint leaves (approximately 20 leaves)

2 ounces brandy

One 750-ml bottle chilled dry white wine

One 12-ounce bottle chilled club soda

Combine the strawberries, mint, and brandy in a large glass pitcher. Gently stir in the wine. Refrigerate for at least 2 hours or as long as overnight to chill. When ready to serve, add the club soda, stirring gently with a long-handled wooden spoon to combine. Slowly pour into ice-filled wineglasses, allowing some of the fruit to fall into the glasses.

Times Square Cocktail

MAKES 6 EIGHT-OUNCE DRINKS

10 ounces (1¼ cups) Southern Comfort

2 ounces sweet vermouth

4 ounces grenadine

5 cups chilled champagne or other sparkling wine

6 orange wheels

Shake together the Southern Comfort, vermouth, and grenadine. Strain into a large pitcher. Add the champagne, and stir gently. Pour into ice-filled wineglasses. Garnish each with an orange wheel.

Shooters

THIS PARTICULAR GENRE OF DRINKS has quite the rowdy reputation as being a quick, cut-to-the-chase approach to cocktails. Some are streamlined and purposely expedient—potent shooters of liquid dynamite given names that are, shall we say, a bit lacking in refinement. Others have perfectly balanced ingredients and are more suitable for sipping (not that it is mandatory, however), such as the elegantly layered pousse-café-style shooters. Ironically, the evolution of the shooter has led to spirits suspended in gelatin. Perfectly compact and unspillable, these potent, brightly colored cubes have become the popular new wave in fun shooters. Whatever your preference, these drinks will give you an excuse to bring out all those kitschy shot glasses collected from places far and wide.

After 5

½ ounce Kahlúa
½ ounce Irish cream liqueur
½ ounce peppermint schnapps

Pour in the order given into a chilled shot glass. Drink in one gulp.

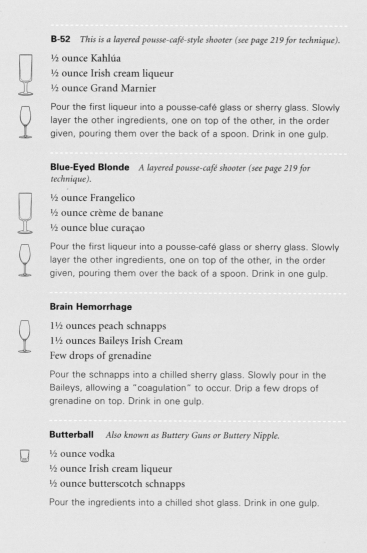

B-52 *This is a layered pousse-café-style shooter (see page 219 for technique).*

½ ounce Kahlúa
½ ounce Irish cream liqueur
½ ounce Grand Marnier

Pour the first liqueur into a pousse-café glass or sherry glass. Slowly layer the other ingredients, one on top of the other, in the order given, pouring them over the back of a spoon. Drink in one gulp.

Blue-Eyed Blonde *A layered pousse-café shooter (see page 219 for technique).*

½ ounce Frangelico
½ ounce crème de banane
½ ounce blue curaçao

Pour the first liqueur into a pousse-café glass or sherry glass. Slowly layer the other ingredients, one on top of the other, in the order given, pouring them over the back of a spoon. Drink in one gulp.

Brain Hemorrhage

1½ ounces peach schnapps
1½ ounces Baileys Irish Cream
Few drops of grenadine

Pour the schnapps into a chilled sherry glass. Slowly pour in the Baileys, allowing a "coagulation" to occur. Drip a few drops of grenadine on top. Drink in one gulp.

Butterball *Also known as Buttery Guns or Buttery Nipple.*

½ ounce vodka
½ ounce Irish cream liqueur
½ ounce butterscotch schnapps

Pour the ingredients into a chilled shot glass. Drink in one gulp.

Cement Mixer   *The key to this shooter is in the method—the standing time allows the lime juice to curdle the Irish cream.*

1 ounce Irish cream liqueur
1½ teaspoons fresh lime juice

Pour the ingredients into a chilled shot glass, and let stand for about 10 seconds. Drink in one gulp.

Chip Shot

¾ ounce Tuaca
¾ ounce Irish cream liqueur
1 ounce hot coffee

Pour the ingredients into a chilled shot glass in the order given. Drink in one gulp.

Chocolate-Covered Cherry   *A pousse-café layered shot.*

1 maraschino cherry
½ ounce grenadine
½ ounce Kahlúa
½ ounce Irish cream liqueur

Drop the cherry into a chilled shot glass. Slowly pour in the liquid ingredients, in the order given, over the back of a spoon. Do not stir.

Climax

½ ounce amaretto
½ ounce Cointreau
½ ounce crème de banane
½ ounce vodka
½ ounce crème de cacao
1 ounce heavy cream

Shake all ingredients vigorously with ice. Strain into a chilled cocktail glass.

Cordless Screwdriver

Orange wedge
Sugar
1 ounce freezer-chilled vodka

Coat the orange wedge with sugar. Pour the vodka into a chilled shot glass, gulp it down, and bite into the sugar-coated orange wedge.

French Kiss   *This pousse-café-style shooter is not to be confused with the classic vermouth cocktail of the same name.*

½ ounce amaretto
½ ounce crème de cacao
½ ounce Irish cream liqueur

Pour the amaretto into a pousse-café glass or sherry glass. Slowly layer the other ingredients, one on top of the other, in the order given, pouring them over the back of a spoon. Do not mix. Down in one gulp.

Girl Scout Cookie

¾ ounce peppermint schnapps
¾ ounce dark crème de cacao
½ ounce heavy cream

Shake the ingredients vigorously with ice. Strain into a chilled shot glass. Drink in one gulp

Green Lizard

¾ ounce green Chartreuse
¾ ounce 151-proof rum

Pour the Chartreuse into a chilled shot glass. Float the 151 on top. Drink in one gulp.

Harbor Lights

¾ ounce brandy
¾ ounce Galliano

Shake the ingredients vigorously with ice. Strain into a chilled shot glass. Drink in one gulp.

IRA

1 ounce Irish whiskey
1 ounce Irish cream liqueur

Shake the ingredients vigorously with ice. Strain into a chilled shot glass. Drink in one gulp.

Jelly Bean

1 ounce blackberry brandy
1 ounce anisette

Shake the ingredients vigorously with ice. Strain into a chilled shot glass. Drink in one gulp.

Kamikaze Shooter   *Although many insist on making this with Rose's lime juice, fresh lime juice greatly improves this classic shooter.*

¾ ounce chilled vodka
¾ ounce Cointreau (or triple sec)
¾ ounce fresh lime juice

Shake the ingredients vigorously with ice. Strain into a chilled shot glass. Drink in one gulp.

Key Lime Pie

½ ounce Licor 43
½ ounce Rose's lime juice (or fresh lime juice)
½ ounce half-and-half

Shake the ingredients vigorously with ice. Strain into a chilled shot glass. Drink in one gulp.

Lemon Drop Shooter

Lemon wedge
Sugar
2 ounces freezer-chilled citron vodka

Coat the lemon wedge with sugar. Pour the vodka into a chilled shot glass, gulp it down, and bite into the sugar-coated lemon wedge.

Liquid Cocaine　*Here are two of the many versions of this shooter.*

LIQUID COCAINE #1

½ ounce dark rum
½ ounce root beer schnapps
½ ounce Jägermeister
½ ounce Rumple Minze

Shake the ingredients vigorously with ice. Strain into a chilled shot glass. Drink in one gulp.

LIQUID COCAINE #2

½ ounce dark rum
½ ounce Rumple Minze
½ ounce Jägermeister
½ ounce Goldschläger

Shake the ingredients vigorously with ice. Strain into a chilled shot glass. Drink in one gulp.

Melon Ball Shooter

½ ounce vodka
½ ounce Midori liqueur
½ ounce pineapple juice

Shake the ingredients vigorously with ice. Strain into a chilled shot glass. Drink in one gulp.

Mind Eraser Shooter

¾ ounce Kahlúa
¾ ounce vodka
Splash of chilled club soda

Pour the Kahlúa and vodka into a chilled shot glass. Top with club soda. Drink in one gulp.

Oatmeal Cookie Shooter

½ ounce butterscotch schnapps
½ ounce Goldschläger
½ ounce Irish cream liqueur

Pour the schnapps into a chilled shot glass. Slowly layer the other ingredients, one on top of the other, in the order given. Drink in one gulp.

Orgasm

½ ounce amaretto
½ ounce Irish cream liqueur
½ ounce Kahlúa

Shake the ingredients vigorously with ice. Strain into a chilled shot glass. Drink in one gulp.

Peppermint Patty

¾ ounce crème de cacao
½ ounce peppermint schnapps

Pour the crème de cacao into a chilled shot glass. Slowly layer the peppermint schnapps on top. Drink in one gulp.

Piña-Salsa Shooter *A variation on the Sangrita.*

1 tablespoon salsa (medium to hot, according to taste)
½ ounce pineapple juice
1 ounce silver tequila
½ ounce fresh lime juice
Lime wedge

Pour the liquid ingredients, in the order given, into a chilled large shot glass. Drink in one gulp, and bite into the lime wedge.

Prairie Fire

2 to 4 dashes Tabasco sauce
1½ ounces tequila

Pour the Tabasco into a chilled shot glass, and add the tequila. Drink in one gulp.

Purple Hooter

¾ ounce vodka
¾ ounce Chambord
½ ounce cranberry juice

Shake the ingredients vigorously with ice. Strain into a chilled shot glass. Drink in one gulp.

VARIATION: Use ½ ounce each vodka, Chambord, triple sec, and fresh lime juice.

Red Snapper Shooter

¾ ounce blended Canadian whisky
¾ ounce cranberry juice
½ ounce amaretto

Shake the ingredients vigorously with ice. Strain into a chilled shot glass. Drink in one gulp.

Root Beer Shooter

½ ounce Galliano
½ ounce Kahlúa
¾ ounce chilled cola

Pour the ingredients into a chilled shot glass. Drink in one gulp.

Russian Quaalude

¾ ounce Frangelico
¾ ounce Irish cream liqueur
¾ ounce vodka

Shake the ingredients vigorously with ice. Strain into a chilled shot glass. Drink in one gulp.

VARIATION: **For a pousse-café,** reduce the ingredients to ½ ounce each, and layer.

Sangrita
This classic Mexican chaser, meaning "little blood," is the perfect hot, zesty mixological combination to follow a tequila shot. This makes enough for 6 shots, to be served as a chaser together with a shot of good-quality tequila. Chill the Sangrita mixture overnight for best results. It can be refrigerated for up to 5 days.

6 ounces tomato juice
6 ounces fresh orange juice
2 ounces fresh lime juice
¼ ounce grenadine
½ ounce green Tabasco (or other hot sauce), or to taste
1 teaspoon Worcestershire sauce
1½ ounces tequila per serving

Combine all ingredients except the tequila in a glass jar with a lid. Cover and chill for at least 2 hours. Pour 1½ ounces of the mixture into a chilled shot glass, and serve with a 1½-ounce shot of tequila. Toss back the tequila, and chase it with the Sangrita.

Savoy Hotel   *Another layered pousse-café-style shooter.*

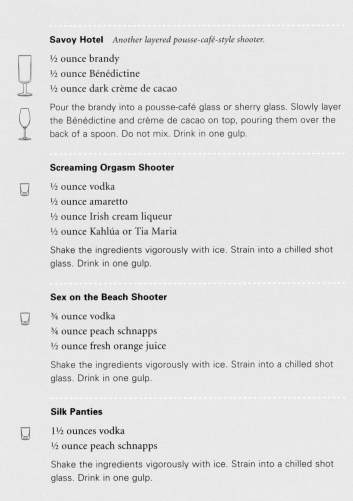

½ ounce brandy
½ ounce Bénédictine
½ ounce dark crème de cacao

Pour the brandy into a pousse-café glass or sherry glass. Slowly layer the Bénédictine and crème de cacao on top, pouring them over the back of a spoon. Do not mix. Drink in one gulp.

Screaming Orgasm Shooter

½ ounce vodka
½ ounce amaretto
½ ounce Irish cream liqueur
½ ounce Kahlúa or Tia Maria

Shake the ingredients vigorously with ice. Strain into a chilled shot glass. Drink in one gulp.

Sex on the Beach Shooter

¾ ounce vodka
¾ ounce peach schnapps
½ ounce fresh orange juice

Shake the ingredients vigorously with ice. Strain into a chilled shot glass. Drink in one gulp.

Silk Panties

1½ ounces vodka
½ ounce peach schnapps

Shake the ingredients vigorously with ice. Strain into a chilled shot glass. Drink in one gulp.

Surfer on Acid Shooter

¾ ounce Malibu rum
¾ ounce Jägermeister
½ ounce pineapple juice

Shake the ingredients vigorously with ice. Strain into a chilled shot glass. Drink in one gulp.

Terminator *This is a layered pousse-café shooter (see page 219 for technique).*

½ ounce Kahlúa (or Tia Maria)
½ ounce Irish cream liqueur
½ ounce sambuca
½ ounce Grand Marnier
½ ounce vodka

Pour the Kahlúa into a pousse-café glass or sherry glass. Slowly layer the other ingredients, one on top of the other, in the order given, pouring them over the back of a spoon. Do not mix. Drink in one gulp.

Tootsie Roll

½ ounce vodka
½ ounce crème de cacao
½ ounce fresh orange juice

Shake the ingredients vigorously with ice. Strain into a chilled shot glass. Drink in one gulp.

Volcanic Blast   *A layered pousse-café cocktail shooter (see page 219 for technique). For a description of flaming techniques, see page 56.*

¼ ounce Kahlúa
¼ ounce Cointreau
¼ ounce raspberry syrup
¼ ounce papaya juice
¼ ounce Captain Morgan Spiced Rum
½ teaspoon 151-proof rum

Pour the Kahlúa into a heat-proof 2-ounce shot glass or pousse-café glass. Continue to layer the ingredients by angling a spoon down into the glass and slowly pouring each liquid over the back of the spoon, in order and one at a time. Carefully ignite the 151 rum and let it burn for a few seconds. Blow out the flame, and let the glass cool a bit before sipping.

Woo Woo Shooter

¾ ounce vodka
¾ ounce peach schnapps
¾ ounce cranberry juice

Shake the ingredients vigorously with ice. Strain into a chilled shot glass. Drink in one gulp.

Gelatin Shots

IN THE ONGOING QUEST FOR THE QUICK and the potent, gelatin shooters have become a popular, jiggly answer to cocktail fun. These colorful fruity shooters can easily be made with a variety of gelatin flavors and various spirits. Once you get the basics down, you can transform just about any favorite cocktail into a gelatin shooter.

The basic formula is pretty straightforward. Simply substitute half of the water called for in the packaged gelatin directions with your liquor of choice. Dissolve the gelatin in the hot water, and add the alcohol only after the gelatin mixture is cool to the touch. The alcohol will evaporate if added too soon. Proportioned to one 3-ounce box of gelatin, these recipes make about 20 gelatin shots that will serve three to four people. They can easily be multiplied for a larger crowd.

There are quite a few ways to serve gelatin shooters. You can simply pour the mixture into a flat pan and cut it into 2-inch squares, or pour it into 2-ounce party cups, plastic cups, paper nut cups, or Dixie cups for the slider technique, or you can serve them elegantly in shot, cocktail, or cordial glasses. A fun option is to cut the gelatin into shapes with novelty cookie cutters, or pour it into ice cube trays to mold potent little sculptural shapes. These recipes are all original, from *Party Shots*, by Mittie Hellmich, a book of jigglicious fun.

Cognac Coco a-Go-Go *This is more like a dessert, made with Cognac, Godiva chocolate liqueur, Sparkling Mandarin gelatin, and Orangina, a sparkling orange beverage.*

MAKES 35 TO 40 SHOOTERS, SERVING 6 TO 8

14 ounces (1¾ cups) water
One 6-ounce box Sparkling Mandarin Orange gelatin
   (or orange gelatin)
6 ounces Cognac
4 ounces Godiva chocolate liqueur (or crème de cacao)
6 ounces Orangina (or other sparkling orange beverage)
¼ cup grated lime zest (optional)

In a small saucepan, bring the water to a boil. Pour the orange gelatin into a medium, heat-proof bowl and add the boiling water, stirring until the gelatin is dissolved. Let cool.

Add the Cognac, Godiva liqueur, and Orangina to the cooled mixture, stirring until well combined. Pour into forty 2-ounce paper or plastic cups, or 3 plastic ice cube trays, and refrigerate for 15 minutes, or until slightly set. Sprinkle a pinch of lime zest onto each cup. Chill until firm, 4 to 6 hours.

Cosmotique *A jiggly variation on the Cosmo, these can be made with cranberry-flavored vodka, for serious cranberry aficionados.*

MAKES ABOUT 20 SHOOTERS, SERVING 3 TO 4

8 ounces (1 cup) boiling water
One 3-ounce package cranberry gelatin
5 ounces vodka
1 ounce fresh lime juice
1 ounce triple sec (or other orange liqueur)
1 ounce limoncello liqueur

In a small saucepan, bring the water to a boil. Pour the cranberry gelatin into a medium, heat-proof bowl, and add the boiling water, stirring until the gelatin is dissolved. Let cool.

Add the vodka, lime juice, triple sec, and limoncello to the cooled mixture, stirring until well combined. Pour the mixture into twenty 2-ounce paper or plastic cups, and refrigerate. Chill until firm, 4 to 6 hours.

The Energizer   *There has to be at least one gelatin shooter apropos to the genre, and this one is it—pure liquid dynamite, fueled with Red Bull, the carbonated energy beverage, and rowdy peach-flavored Southern Comfort, for a party-sized batch of high-octane sliders.*

MAKES ABOUT 40 SHOOTERS, SERVING 6 TO 8

16 ounces (2 cups) water

One 3-ounce box cranberry gelatin

One 3-ounce box peach gelatin

8 ounces (1 cup)Southern Comfort

8 ounces (1 cup) Red Bull energy drink

In a small saucepan, bring the water to a boil. Pour the cranberry and peach gelatins into a medium, heat-proof bowl and add the boiling water, stirring until the gelatin is dissolved. Let cool. Add the Southern Comfort and Red Bull to the cooled mixture, stirring until well combined. Pour into forty 2-ounce paper or plastic cups, or 3 ice cube trays, and refrigerate. Chill until firm, 4 to 6 hours.

Piña Gelata   *All the decadence of a Piña Colada in one little shooter. Thai coconut milk can be found in the ethnic food section of your supermarket, or in Asian markets.*

MAKES 20 SHOOTERS, SERVING 4 TO 6

8 ounces (1 cup) water

One 3-ounce box pineapple gelatin

5 ounces rum

1½ ounces Thai coconut milk

1 ounce pineapple juice

1 ounce fresh lime juice

10 to 20 paper cocktail umbrellas

In a small saucepan, bring the water to a boil. Pour the pineapple gelatin into a medium, heat-proof bowl and add the boiling water, stirring until the gelatin is dissolved. Let cool.

Add the rum, coconut milk, pineapple juice, and lime juice to the cooled mixture, stirring until well combined. Pour into twenty 2-ounce paper or plastic cups, and refrigerate. Chill until firm, 4 to 6 hours. Garnish a few shots with the paper umbrellas.

The Nonalcoholic Zone

THESE SPIRIT-FREE LIBATIONS ARE FORMULATED for those who would rather abstain and catch their euphoric rush through a refreshing elixir of fresh fruit juices and nectars. A freshly shaken frosty mocktail poured into a chilled cocktail glass and accented with an alluring garnish can be as sophisticated and satisfying as one containing spirits. The key is in the presentation as well as the ingredients. Your guests will appreciate their drink served in the refined and appropriate cocktail glass, made with the same finesse as any other cocktail, and beautifully garnished to do it justice. In fact, the spirit-free drinks offered here are so perfectly balanced and mixed with care, you won't miss the jungle in the juice.

No longer are nondrinking guests faced with the dismal choice of soda pop or water, tea, or coffee; instead, they are offered an elegant and aromatic nonalcoholic cocktail as urbane and enjoyable as any other, by a thoughtful and discerning host. The new wave in creative mixology has not only influenced the spirit-based genre but also inspired a wide selection of alcohol-free elixirs made with fresh juices, exotic and familiar, infused with flavorful botanicals and inventive ingredients such as sorbets and syrups. Along with the classic spicy tomato drinks and rich chocolate concoctions, this selection offers everything from energizing frappés, shaken cocktails, and refreshing coolers to creamy smoothies and minty highballs, all guaranteed to have even those imbibing the high-octane drinks requesting one of these fabulous libations instead.

Apricot Mocktail

2 ounces apricot nectar
¾ ounce fresh lemon juice
¾ ounce fresh orange juice
Lemon twist

Shake the liquid ingredients vigorously with ice. Strain into a chilled cocktail glass. Twist the lemon peel over the drink, and drop it in.

Banana Mocha Frappé

½ ripe banana, sliced
¼ cup softened coffee ice cream
3 ounces fresh orange juice
1 ounce chocolate syrup
1 teaspoon vanilla extract
Pinch of ground cinnamon
Pinch of ground cardamom
6 ounces chilled club soda
Orange slice

Combine all ingredients but the garnish in a blender with 1 cup crushed ice. Blend until smooth. Pour the mixture into a highball glass, garnish with the orange slice, and serve with a straw.

VARIATION: For a malted version, add 2 tablespoons malt powder.

Beach Breeze

4 ounces pineapple juice
2 ounces fresh lime juice
2 ounces cranberry juice
Lime wedge

Pour the liquid ingredients into an ice-filled highball glass, and stir. Squeeze the lime wedge over the drink, and drop it in.

Bergamot-Berry Iced Tea   *The perfect nonalcoholic punch for a crowd, this crimson-hued libation is made with aromatic Earl Grey tea and black-currant nectar. You can find black-currant nectar at many supermarkets and natural food stores, but either red grape juice or raspberry juice is a fine substitute. This recipe can be made a day in advance if need be. It will make a pitcherful.*

MAKES 4 TO 6 SERVINGS

6 cups water

4 Earl Grey tea bags

¼ cup grated orange zest or four 2½-inch-long strips of orange peel

½ cup fresh mint leaves

½ cup honey

2 cups black-currant nectar

Mint sprigs

Bring the water to a boil in a large saucepan. Add the tea bags, orange zest, and mint leaves. Remove from the heat and add the honey, stirring to dissolve. Cover and steep for 15 to 20 minutes. Strain into a large glass pitcher. Add the black-currant nectar and stir. Place in the refrigerator to chill. Pour the mixture into ice-filled highball glasses. Garnish each drink with a mint sprig.

Cilantro Limeade Cooler

6 to 8 fresh cilantro leaves

1 ounce simple syrup (or 1 tablespoon superfine sugar)

3 ounces fresh lime juice

3 to 5 ounces chilled lemon-lime soda

Lime wedge

Muddle together the cilantro, syrup, and lime juice in the bottom of a highball glass. Fill the glass with ice and add the lemon-lime soda, stirring gently. Squeeze the lime wedge over the drink, and drop it in.

VARIATION: **For a Mock Mojito,** substitute mint leaves for the cilantro.

Chocolate Citrus Cocktail   *A virgin variation on a chocolate-orange Martini.*

4 ounces fresh tangerine juice
1 tablespoon chocolate syrup
¼ teaspoon vanilla extract
Mint sprig

Shake the tangerine juice, chocolate syrup, and vanilla vigorously with ice. Strain into a chilled cocktail glass. Garnish with the mint sprig.

VARIATION: **For a Chocolate Citrus Cooler,** strain the shaken mixture into an ice-filled highball glass, and top with a sparkling orange beverage.

Coconut Fizz   *If coconut sorbet is unavailable, substitute 2 ounces well-chilled Thai coconut milk.*

½ cup softened coconut sorbet or coconut gelato
2 ounces fresh lime juice
1 ounce raspberry syrup
3 to 4 ounces chilled Jamaican ginger beer or ginger ale
Lime wedge
2 to 3 raspberries

Shake the coconut sorbet, lime juice, and raspberry syrup vigorously with ice. Strain into an ice-filled highball glass. Top with the ginger beer, and stir gently. Squeeze the lime wedge over the drink, and drop it in. Garnish with the raspberries on a skewer.

Cucumber Lemonade

4 to 5 cucumber slices (thinly sliced, preferably English cucumbers)
3 ounces fresh lemon juice
1 ounce simple syrup
6 to 8 ounces chilled filtered water
Lemon peel spiral

Muddle together the cucumber, lemon juice, and simple syrup in the bottom of a highball glass. Fill the glass with ice and add the chilled water, stirring gently. Garnish with the lemon peel spiral.

VARIATION: **For a fizzy cooler,** substitute chilled club soda or lemon-lime soda for the water.

Fuzzless Navel   *A virgin version of the Fuzzy Navel.*

2 ounces peach nectar
5 to 6 ounces fresh orange juice
Lime twist

Pour the liquid ingredients into an ice-filled highball glass and stir well.
Twist the lime peel over the drink, and drop it in.

Ginger and Fred

2 ounces fresh grapefruit juice
2 ounces fresh orange juice
1 ounce cranberry juice
3 to 4 ounces chilled ginger beer or ginger ale
Orange slice

Shake the juices vigorously with ice. Strain into an ice-filled highball glass.
Top with ginger beer and stir gently. Garnish with the orange slice.

Ginger Citrus Cocktail

1 ounce fresh lemon juice
1 ounce fresh lime juice
2 ounces fresh orange juice
3 slices fresh ginger
Candied ginger slice

Shake the liquid ingredients and fresh ginger vigorously with ice.
Strain into a chilled cocktail glass. Garnish with the candied ginger.

VARIATION: Strain the shaken mixture into an ice-filled highball glass.
Top with ginger beer.

Ginger Julep

6 to 8 fresh mint leaves
½ ounce fresh lime juice
1 teaspoon sugar
¼ ounce grenadine
4 to 6 ounces chilled ginger ale
Mint sprig

Muddle together the mint leaves, lime juice, sugar, and grenadine in the bottom of a chilled collins glass. Fill with ice and top with ginger ale. Garnish with the mint sprig.

Hibiscus-Lemongrass Iced Tea Cooler *This zesty iced tea is made with vibrant-hued hibiscus and sweet lemongrass syrup (see page 73).*

MAKES 4 SERVINGS
6 cups boiling water
6 hibiscus tea bags (Red Zinger tea)
1 cinnamon stick, broken into pieces
Grated zest of 1 orange
½ cup lemongrass syrup (page 73)
4 lemongrass stalks

Bring the water to a boil in a large saucepan. Remove from the heat and add the tea bags, cinnamon, orange zest, and lemongrass syrup. Cover and let steep until cool. Strain into ice-filled highball glasses. Garnish each glass with a stalk of lemongrass to stir.

NOTE: Lemongrass syrup is great to have on hand; it makes a light summer thirst-quencher when a few tablespoons are added to a glass of ice and sparkling mineral water.

Iced Mocha Java *When the heat of the afternoon hits, this cool and creamy jolt of java is just the ticket, with all the attributes of a good cappuccino.*

2 tablespoons chocolate syrup
3 ounces half-and-half
Pinch of ground cinnamon
Tiny pinch of ground cloves
3 ounces cooled coffee or espresso

2 ounces cold milk
Mint sprig
Cinnamon stick

In a chilled collins glass, stir together the chocolate syrup, half-and-half, cinnamon, and cloves until well combined. Fill the glass with ice and pour in the coffee, stirring gently. Froth the cold milk with an espresso-machine steamer (or in a blender on high speed). Top the drink with the frothed milk, and garnish with the mint sprig and cinnamon stick.

Jill-in-the-Box

2 ounces apple juice
1 ounce pineapple juice
1 ounce fresh lemon juice
2 to 4 dashes Angostura bitters (optional)

Shake the ingredients vigorously with ice. Strain into a chilled cocktail glass or over ice in an old-fashioned glass. Note: Bitters are alcohol-based and can be omitted if preferred.

Lemonade

2 ounces fresh lemon juice
1 tablespoon simple syrup
6 to 8 ounces chilled filtered water
Lemon slice

Pour the liquid ingredients into an ice-filled collins glass, and stir gently. Garnish with the lemon slice.

VARIATION: **For Limeade,** substitute fresh lime juice for the lemon juice.

Lemon Berry Ambrosia *Raspberries meld together with the pure lemon essence of lemon sorbet and a sparkling orange beverage such as San Pellegrino Aranciata.*

½ cup softened lemon sorbet
½ cup fresh or frozen raspberries, rinsed
2 ounces cranberry juice
4 to 6 ounces chilled sparkling orange beverage
Lemon wedge

~ CONTINUED

In a blender, combine the lemon sorbet, raspberries, and cranberry juice. Blend until smooth. Add the sparkling orange beverage, and blend for a few more seconds. Pour the mixture into an ice-filled highball glass. Garnish with the lemon wedge.

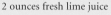

Mango Tango *A great fruit drink for Sunday brunch. Some even enjoy the addition of a little banana syrup to complete the tropical vibe. You can find ginger syrup in some supermarkets, but freshly made is best (see page 73).*

2 ounces fresh lime juice
1 ounce ginger syrup (see page 73)
½ cup cubed fresh mango
½ cup cubed fresh pineapple
3 to 4 ounces chilled club soda
Mango slice
Pineapple wedge

Combine the lime juice, ginger syrup, mango, and pineapple in a blender with 1 cup ice. Blend until well combined and smooth. Pour into a chilled highball glass. Top with club soda and stir well. Garnish with the mango slice and pineapple wedge.

Mexicocoa Eggnog *A South-of-the-Border concoction made with Ibarra cinnamon-flavored Mexican chocolate, available from most grocers. For the spirited version, see page 399.*

MAKES 4 SERVINGS

4 cups eggnog
1 teaspoon ground nutmeg
½ teaspoon ground cloves
2 tablespoons unsweetened cocoa powder
½ cup grated Mexican chocolate
Mexican chocolate shavings

In a large saucepan, whisk together the eggnog, nutmeg, cloves, and cocoa powder until well combined. Heat the eggnog mixture over low to medium-low heat until simmering; do not boil. Slowly add the grated Mexican chocolate to the simmering mixture, whisking together until the chocolate is melted. Remove from the heat, and pour into warmed 6-ounce punch cups or heat-resistant mugs. Garnish each drink with a sprinkling of Mexican chocolate shavings.

Orangeade

4 ounces fresh orange juice
¼ ounce grenadine
2 ounces chilled club soda
Lemon slice

Pour the liquid ingredients into an ice-filled collins glass, and stir gently. Garnish with the lemon slice.

Papaya Banana Restorative   *The papaya is a rich source of vitamins and minerals—and it's great for the digestive system as well as being widely believed to prevent many ailments, including colds. What better way to take on the day than with a tall, frosty glass of healthy papaya, orange sorbet, and fresh fruit juices?*

½ ripe papaya, peeled, seeded, and cubed
½ ripe banana, peeled and sliced
¼ cup softened orange sorbet
1 ounce fresh lemon juice
1 ounce apple juice
1 ounce fresh grapefruit juice
Splash of chilled club soda

In a blender, combine the ingredients and blend together until smooth. Pour into a large highball glass.

Paradise Cooler

2 ounces guava nectar
2 ounces fresh lime juice
1 ounce pineapple juice
1 ounce fresh orange juice
½ ounce grenadine
½ ounce orgeat syrup
2 to 3 ounces chilled club soda
Lime wedge

Shake all liquid ingredients except the club soda vigorously with ice. Strain into an ice-filled wineglass. Top with club soda and stir gently. Squeeze the lime wedge over the drink, and drop it in.

Piña Un-Colada

3 ounces pineapple juice

2 ounces Thai coconut milk

1 ounce fresh lime juice

¼ cup crushed pineapple

½ ripe banana, peeled and sliced

Pineapple wedge

Combine all ingredients except the garnish in a blender with 1 cup crushed ice. Blend until smooth. Pour into a chilled wineglass. Garnish with the pineapple wedge.

Pink Grapefruit

6 ounces fresh grapefruit juice

1 ounce grenadine

2 dashes Peychaud's bitters
(optional, as bitters have traces of alcohol)

Lemon slice

Pour the liquid ingredients into an ice-filled collins glass, and stir gently. Garnish with the lemon slice.

Plum Mango Lassi   *A refined smoothie with a pan-Pacific edge.*

½ cup vanilla yogurt

2 ounces mango nectar

½ mango, peeled, pitted, and cubed

1 small plum, fresh or frozen, peeled and pitted

¼ teaspoon almond syrup or orgeat syrup

Pinch of ground cardamom

Pinch of ground cloves

Mango slice

Combine all ingredients but the mango slice in a blender with 1 cup ice. Blend until well combined and smooth. Pour into a chilled wineglass. Garnish with the mango slice.

Raspberry Pamplemousse Cocktail   *For a lighter version, substitute club soda for the Orangina.*

4 ounces fresh grapefruit juice
1 ounce raspberry syrup
3 to 4 ounces chilled Orangina (or other sparkling orange beverage)
Mint sprig
2 raspberries

Shake the grapefruit juice and syrup vigorously with ice. Strain into an ice-filled highball glass. Top with Orangina and briefly stir. Garnish with a mint sprig skewered between 2 raspberries.

Roy Rogers   *This cowboy classic nonalcoholic cocktail is still refreshing.*

2 ounces fresh orange juice
½ ounce grenadine
6 ounces chilled ginger ale
Orange slice
Maraschino cherry

Pour the orange juice and grenadine into an ice-filled highball glass. Top with ginger ale and stir gently. Garnish with the orange slice and cherry.

Shirley Temple   *This classic was named after the famous 1930s child actor, who later became a U.S. diplomat.*

6 to 8 ounces chilled ginger ale
¼ ounce grenadine
Orange slice
Maraschino cherry

Pour the ginger ale and grenadine into an ice-filled highball glass, and stir gently. Garnish with the orange slice and cherry.

Springtime Smoothie

½ cup peeled, pitted, cubed mango
½ pear, peeled, cored, and cubed
2 large strawberries, hulled and sliced
4 ounces chilled cranberry juice
1 ounce fresh lemon juice
Strawberry
Mint sprig

In a blender, combine the mango, pear, strawberries, cranberry juice, and lemon juice and blend until smooth. Pour the mixture into an ice-filled highball glass. Garnish with the strawberry and mint sprig.

Summer Cooler

1½ ounces fresh orange juice
Dash of Angostura bitters
    (optional, as the bitters have traces of alcohol)
4 to 6 ounces chilled 7-Up
Orange slice

Pour the ingredients into an ice-filled collins glass, and stir gently. Garnish with the orange slice.

Virgin Bite of the Iguana *For those who enjoy a spicy Bloody Mary but want to skip the spirits, this zippy cocktail, made with hot and spicy habanero pepper sauce and sweet Mexican orange cherry tomatoes, is more like a nip than a bite. For the spirited version, see page 315.*

Lime wedge
Kosher salt
1½ ounces fresh lime juice
1 ounce fresh lemon juice
1 ounce fresh orange juice
1 ounce tomato juice
½ cup washed, stemmed, and halved orange cherry tomatoes
1 clove garlic, finely minced
1 scallion, chopped

3 to 4 sprigs cilantro

1 teaspoon white horseradish

2 to 3 dashes Worcestershire sauce

½ teaspoon Golden Habanero pepper sauce

Lime wedge

Rub the rim of a chilled collins glass with the lime wedge and rim with salt. In a blender, combine all ingredients except the garnish with ½ cup ice. Blend until smooth. Pour the blended mixture into the pre-pared glass. Squeeze the lime wedge over the drink, and drop it in.

- -

Virgin Mary *Also called Contrary Mary, this is the low-octane spicy version of the classic Bloody Mary.*

4 ounces chilled tomato or V8 juice

½ ounce fresh lemon juice

2 to 3 dashes Worcestershire sauce

2 to 3 dashes Tabasco sauce

½ teaspoon horseradish

Pinch of celery salt

Pinch of ground black pepper

Salt to taste

Lime wedge

Celery stalk

Shake all ingredients but the garnish vigorously with ice. Strain into an ice-filled highball glass. Squeeze the lime wedge over the drink, and drop it in. Garnish with the celery stalk to stir.

Hangover Remedies

IF THE HEADACHE WOULD ONLY PRECEDE THE INTOXICATION, ALCOHOLISM WOULD BE A VIRTUE. —SAMUEL BUTLER, English author

YOU'VE HAD TOO MUCH OF A GOOD TIME with too much of a good thing, and now you're searching for that elusive, mythological tonic called the hangover cure. It is best to begin with a good dose of skepticism regarding the traditional "hair of the dog" myth, in which a spirit-based remedy is actually a helpful reviver the morning after to combat the effects of too much drinking. The idea that a "pick-me-up" concocted of more liquor is going to make you feel better is archaic. In reality, these so-called remedies simply revive what made you hung over in the first place. Those classic "corpse reviver" cocktails are good only for perpetuating inebriation. The theory is somewhat logical, given that a hangover is a state of post-inebriation, and the remedy is simply reinebriation. Which brings me to myth number two—that drinking coffee will sober you up and set you right. In actuality, coffee does more harm through dehydration than any sobering effects it may bring, which are minimal.

The classic hangover "cures" usually involved Pernod or absinthe, or a carbonated concoction made with champagne and bitters, ginger ale, or beer, but everyone has their own favorite remedy that they swear by. Some people may take aspirin and a large glass of water, whereas others will drink a sports-type drink full of electrolytes before retiring for the evening. Sound advice indeed, as alcohol dehydrates your body and drains it of its supply of nutrients and vitamins (as well as being a depressant), so when you are feeling the effects of a hangover, your body is suffering from malnutrition and dehydration.

FROM PREPARE TO REPAIR

The best way to avoid an acute hangover, besides the obvious wisdom of drinking in moderation and pacing yourself, is through preventative side steps and practical guidelines.

Here are some helpful tips, along with a few classic and quaint remedies.

Fortify with B complex, vitamin C, and antioxidants to help detoxify the liver. Drinking depletes vitamin B, and a strong B complex (100 milligrams of each major B) and vitamin B-12, taken before drinking, before bedtime, and again the next day can have restorative effects.

It is imperative that you eat before and during the consumption of alcohol. This will slow the absorption of the alcohol, particularly if the foods contain high amounts of sugar.

A glass of milk taken before you go out drinking is another way to slow down the effects of alcohol in your system.

ALWAYS PREHYDRATE

It is very helpful to hydrate while imbibing by drinking lots of water in between cocktails. A good rule of thumb is to drink one glass of water for every alcoholic drink consumed. Alcohol is a diuretic, and the more you replenish, the better you will feel.

Preventative cocktails are another strategy. Choosing cream-based drinks, such as a White Russian, Cognac and Cream, or other low-alcohol cocktails, is a great way to keep the drinking at a moderate level.

SELECTIVE COCKTAILS

This may sound like splitting hairs, but some spirits are better than others for avoiding a hangover. Most spirits produced by a continuous still that removes toxins and impurities, such as vodka or silver tequila, are less likely to give you a whopper of a hangover than the darker spirits produced by pot stills, such as Cognac or scotch, which contain more elements of congeners. As a rule, drinking clear liquors such as white wine, light-colored beers, or gin, instead of whiskies, red wine, or dark beers, may actually help avoid an ugly hangover the next morning.

ALWAYS REHYDRATE

Drink lots of water and rejuvenate with food the next day, to replenish some of the nutrients you lost. Start out slow, drinking room-temperature or hot water, and then move into more substantial nourishment as the day progresses. Once your stomach is ready, proceed with soda crackers or Alka-Seltzer. You may then want to get your stomach juices going with a good aperitif of seltzer with bitters, Pernod, or Tabasco, along with an easily digestible raw egg or cucumbers, all of which rehydrate the system. Honey on soda crackers and herbal mint tea is another soothing pairing to help calm your queasy stomach.

The best nourishment for a hangover includes fruits and vegetables (especially bananas or tomatoes, which are high in potassium), light foods high in carbohydrates such as oatmeal (a great detoxer), and a good chicken or bean soup. Bread, fruits, and fruit juices are all good sources of fructose, which helps to burn off alcohol. Dairy products and, of course, junk food are to be avoided.

SLEEP IT OFF

Sleep is one of the best hangover cures, so get plenty of rest, and try to avoid any major stimulation.

DRINK RECIPES

Although good wisdom suggests that you lean in the direction of the healthy liquids and non- to low-alcoholic remedies, this selection of hangover cures and pick-me-ups offers everything from milder herbal tea soothers to the fizzy classics and the traditionally potent hangover remedies.

------- MODERN TONICS FOR DETOXING -------

From sipping green tea to freshly juiced fruits and vegetable combinations, a natural approach to hangover cures is a lot less jarring to the system than the traditional "corpse revivers." If you have a juicer, this is a good opportunity to put it to good use. Try healthy combinations of juiced fresh fennel root or ginger and basil, known to quell nausea. Or rehydrate with fresh carrot juice, cucumber, or juiced red pepper, carrot, and fresh orange juice. Echinacea and ginseng are great restorative herbal additions to the juice as well.

The Japanese swear by the pickled umeboshi plum together with purple perilla (a minty herb) as a surefire hangover remedy. The combination is found in jars, available at Asian markets and natural food stores. The key is in its salty pickled character, which helps the body reverse the effects of the alcohol. It is most effective when you keep both the plum and perilla in your mouth until they dissolve (about a quarter of a plum along with a strip of perilla). Continue to suck on the pit for about an hour after the plum and perilla have dissolved.

Iced Green Tea with Orange Juice and Ginger *Green tea is a natural antioxidant. When combined with fresh ginger to settle the stomach and a splash of vitamin C–rich orange juice, it makes for a soothing tonic.*

1½ cups water
1 green tea bag
2 to 3 thin slices fresh ginger
2 ounces fresh orange juice
2 to 3 ounces chilled club soda (optional)

In a small saucepan, bring the water to a boil. Remove from the heat and add the teabag and the ginger. Cover the pan and steep for 5 minutes. Let the liquid cool before refrigerating or using. Strain the steeped tea mixture into an ice-filled highball glass. Add the orange juice, top with club soda, if desired, and stir.

Peppermint Tea *Peppermint tea is an herbal remedy that helps normalize the digestive system and eases headaches. It can be sipped warm or chilled for iced tea. Some claim that fresh rosemary also has a soothing effect, and you can add a teaspoon of it to this tea, if desired.*

1½ cups water
2 teaspoons fresh peppermint leaves
    (or 1 teaspoon dried peppermint)

In a small saucepan, bring the water to a boil. Remove from the heat and add the peppermint leaves. Cover the pan and steep for 5 minutes. Strain the tea into a warmed heat-resistant mug.

THE CLASSIC HANGOVER REMEDIES

------- **THE SIMPLE APPROACH** -------

The essential restoratives are carbonated to settle the stomach and refresh, from ginger ale, cola, or club soda with a few dashes of bitters to a glass of light beer or a flute of effervescent champagne.

Barbatoge

3 to 5 ounces chilled champagne
¼ ounce brandy
Dash of Cointreau

Slowly pour the champagne into a chilled champagne flute. Add the brandy and Cointreau.

Bitters and Soda   *You can use either Peychaud's, Underberg, or Angostura bitters. Some prefer this without ice.*

4 to 6 ounces chilled club soda
2 to 3 dashes Angostura or other bitters

Pour the club soda into an ice-filled collins glass. Add a few dashes of bitters, and stir briefly.

Campari and Orange Juice   *A refreshing combination of Campari bitters with a hit of vitamin C from the orange juice and a good dose of carbonation to settle the stomach.*

1 ounce Campari
2 ounces fresh orange juice
5 to 6 ounces chilled club soda

Pour the Campari and orange juice into an ice-filled old-fashioned glass. Top with club soda and stir.

------ **THE TRADITIONAL "HAIR OF THE DOG" APPROACH** ------

Black Velvet *Made with equal parts stout and champagne, this fizzy "cure" was created in 1861 to commemorate Prince Albert.*

6 ounces chilled Guinness

6 ounces chilled brut champagne

Slowly pour the stout and champagne into a chilled beer mug or champagne flute. Don't stir.

Bloody Mary *Tomato juice is a natural choice. Packed with vitamin C and potassium, it easily segues into this classic remedy. Of course, a Virgin Mary, without the vodka, is an even better cure.*

1½ ounces vodka

4 ounces tomato juice

½ ounce fresh lemon juice

¼ teaspoon horseradish

2 to 3 dashes Tabasco sauce

2 to 3 dashes Worcestershire sauce

Lemon wedge

Celery stick

Shake all ingredients except the garnishes vigorously with ice. Strain into an ice-filled highball glass. Rim the glass with the lemon wedge, squeeze it over the drink, and drop it in. Garnish with the celery stick.

Bull Shot *This variation on the Bloody Bull, which is made without tomato juice, has long been regarded as a hangover cure in the "hair of the dog" tradition. It can also be made with gin in place of the vodka.*

2 ounces vodka (or gin)

4 ounces cold beef broth or bouillon

¼ ounce fresh lemon juice

2 to 3 dashes Worcestershire sauce

1 to 2 dashes Tabasco sauce

Lemon wedge

Shake the liquid ingredients vigorously with ice. Strain into an ice-filled highball glass. Squeeze the lemon wedge over the drink, and drop it in.

- - - - - - - - - -

Fernet Branca Cocktail   *Considered one of the best "morning after" cocktails, this hangover remedy uses Fernet Branca, a dark, aromatic bitter that is purportedly a great headache cure.*

1 ounce gin

½ ounce Fernet Branca

½ ounce sweet vermouth

Shake the ingredients vigorously with ice. Strain into a chilled cocktail glass.

- - - - - - - - - -

Horse's Neck

2 dashes Angostura bitters

Lemon peel spiral

2 ounces bourbon

1 ounce Bénédictine

3 to 5 ounces chilled ginger ale

Coat a chilled highball glass with bitters. Fill the glass with ice, and insert the lemon peel spiral. Pour in the bourbon and Bénédictine. Top with ginger ale, stirring gently.

- - - - - - - - - -

Pink Gin   *A classic cocktail remedy from the early days of the British Empire's time in India. Popular with the British officers for its purported medicinal properties to soothe the stomach. The classic method is prepared in a sherry glass and is usually served with a glass of water on the side.*

4 to 5 dashes Angostura or Peychaud's bitters

2½ ounces chilled gin

Lemon twist

Pour the bitters into a chilled sherry or cocktail glass, and swirl to coat the glass. Discard the excess. Pour in the gin. Garnish with the lemon twist.

Corpse Revivers

THESE DRINKS WERE ORIGINALLY CONCOCTED as "pick-me-up" hangover remedies, a highly dubious claim, but given the potent and powerful flavor combinations I could certainly see them living up to their name. Technically, all drinks that are made with equal parts of three different liquors are considered Corpse Revivers.

Corpse Reviver #1

¾ ounce brandy
¾ ounce applejack
¾ ounce sweet vermouth

Stir the liquid ingredients in a mixing glass with ice. Strain into a chilled cocktail glass.

Corpse Reviver # 2

¾ ounce brandy
¾ ounce Fernet Branca
¾ ounce white crème de menthe

Stir the liquid ingredients in a mixing glass with ice. Strain into a chilled cocktail glass.

Corpse Reviver #3

¾ ounce gin
¾ ounce Swedish punsch
¾ ounce Cointreau
¾ ounce fresh lemon juice
2 dashes Pernod (or other anise-flavored liqueur)

Stir the liquid ingredients in a mixing glass with ice. Strain into a chilled cocktail glass.

Sea Captain's Special   *In the tradition of the hair of the dog approach, this really packs a wallop.*

1 sugar cube (or ½ teaspoon sugar)
3 to 4 dashes Angostura bitters
2½ ounces bourbon or rye
3 to 4 ounces chilled brut champagne
2 dashes absinthe (or Pernod)

Soak the sugar cube with the bitters in the bottom of an old-fashioned glass. Crush the sugar and add an ice cube. Pour in the bourbon and then slowly top with champagne. Add the absinthe, floating it on top.

Sufferin' Bastard   *This 1940s classic was originally called the Suffering Bar Steward, after the inventor who concocted it, Joe Scialom, bartender for Shepheard's Hotel in Cairo. This potent "cure" is somewhat redeemed with the addition of ginger ale, bitters, and mint.*

1 ounce bourbon
1 ounce gin
¼ ounce fresh lime juice
Dash of Angostura bitters
3 to 4 ounces chilled ginger ale
Mint sprig

Shake the bourbon, gin, lime juice, and bitters vigorously with ice. Strain into an ice-filled collins glass. Top with ginger ale. Garnish with the mint sprig.

Third Rail   *A corpse reviver–style drink made with dark rum.*

1 ounce dark rum
1 ounce applejack
1 ounce brandy
Dash of Pernod

Stir the ingredients in a mixing glass with ice. Strain into a chilled cocktail glass.

Egg was a traditional ingredient used in many hangover cures, as it expediently adds an easily digested element of nourishment. Again, use raw eggs at your own discretion.

Eye-Opener

2 ounces Rhum Barbancourt
Dash of orange curaçao
Dash of apricot brandy
1 teaspoon grenadine
1 egg yolk

Shake the ingredients vigorously with ice. Strain into a chilled cocktail glass.

Morning After

2 ounces Pernod
1 teaspoon sambuca
1 egg white
1 to 2 ounces chilled club soda

Shake all ingredients except the club soda vigorously with ice. Strain into an ice-filled old-fashioned glass. Top with club soda and stir gently.

Prairie Oyster   *This has got to be one of the least appealing concoctions of the classic hangover remedy genre. I can only assume that it was invented under the premise that if it sounds repellent it must be good for what ails you. Some variations include the addition of 1½ ounces of brandy, a dash of cayenne pepper, and a pinch of celery salt.*

1 egg
1 teaspoon Worcestershire sauce
Pinch of salt
Pinch of ground black pepper
2 to 3 dashes Tabasco sauce

Crack the egg into a chilled old-fashioned glass (yolk unbroken). Add the Worcestershire sauce, salt, pepper, and Tabasco. Drink down in one gulp.

457

467

469

470

471

W

------- **BIBLIOGRAPHY** -------

Broom, Dave. *Spirits and Cocktails*. London: Carlton Books, 1988.

Craddock, Harry. *The Savoy Cocktail Book*. London: Constable and Company, 1930.

Crockett, Albert Stevens. *The Old Waldorf Astoria Bar Book*. New York: New Day Publishing, 2003. First published in 1935 by Dodd, Mead, and Co.

Editors at *Esquire Magazine*. *Esquire's Handbook for Hosts*. New York: Grosset and Dunlap, 1945.

Foulkes, Christopher (general editor). *Larousse Encyclopedia of Wine*. New York: Larousse, 1994.

Hellmich, Mittie. *Paradise on Ice*. San Francisco: Chronicle Books, 2002.

Hellmich, Mittie. *Party Shots*. San Francisco: Chronicle Books, 2003.

Hellmich, Mittie. *Sangria: Fun and Festive Recipes*. San Francisco: Chronicle Books, 2004.

Jeffers, H. Paul. *High Spirits*. New York: Lyons and Burford, 1997.

Johnson, Hugh, and Jancis Robinson. *The World Atlas of Wine*. Great Britain: Mitchell Beazley, Octopus Publishing Group, 2001.

Lanza, Joseph. *The Cocktail: The Influence on the American Psyche*. New York: St. Martin's Press, 1995.

Regan, Gary, and Mardee Haidin. *The Martini Companion: A Connoisseur's Guide*. New York: Running Press, 1997.

Walton, Stuart. *The Complete Guide to Spirits and Liqueurs*. London: Hermes House, 1998.

------- **ACKNOWLEDGMENTS** -------

A book of this scope could only be created by a culmination of premium-quality assistance in perfected proportions as finely balanced as the perfect Martini: shaken and stirred with equal parts expert advice, knowledge and guidance, research and assistance, and cultural experiences from many talented and cocktail-savvy people.

First and foremost, to my editors at Chronicle Books: a huge thanks to Bill LeBlond, editor extraordinaire, for bringing this brilliant book idea to me, and for giving me great encouragement, wisdom, and guidance while writing this monster; the enthusiastic and supportive, sharp and savvy associate editor Amy Treadwell; and the wonderfully meticulous and thoughtful copy editor Rebecca Pepper, who brought a polished clarity to the text. Thanks also to the rest of the Chronicle Books team; and to designer Robyn Warmbo and illustrator Arthur Mount for their fabulous illustrations and book design.

Besides the extensive and endless list of very helpful and instructional professional bartenders, Web sites, articles, and stacks of books, which are too numerous to list them all, I was very fortunate to be surrounded by many dedicated individuals willing to offer their expert assistance, great advice, and cocktail insights.

Many heartfelt thanks to friends, colleagues, and family who generously contributed their time, guidance, brilliant suggestions and opinions, enthusiasm and support to this project.

A special thanks to Nicholas Pierce for his meticulous data-gathering and research skills, and to Nicole Hudson Pierce-Rhoads for her discerning editorial assistance in wading through a huge database of drinks. To Geoff Rhoads, and Bryan and Shannon Rhoads, for contributing their editorial guidance and excellent insights. Dirk and Lisa Pierce, Donna Peterson, Taylor Pierce and Masha Turchinsky, Janet Keating and Steven Corson, Bobbie Rhoads and John Magee, Karen Von Klezie and Scott Bartley, Mark Miller, Alison and Mark Nightingale, and Amanda Rhoads for their willingness to share their worldly experiences, opinions, and to fearlessly lend their discerning palates to the cause. To Eduardo Gustamante, who taught me the fine art of mixology those many years ago, and is still a dependable divining rod to the best-made cocktails in town (always with premium spirits). And to bartenders and master mixologists Lara Turchinsky, Felicia Sledge, and Rebecca Steele, who along the way lent their drinkological expertise and liquid masterpieces to enrich this book.